AN ANNUAL GROWTH MODEL OF THE U.S. ECONOMY

CONTRIBUTIONS TO ECONOMIC ANALYSIS

100

Honorary Editor

J. TINBERGEN

Editors

D. W. JORGENSON

J. WAELBROECK

NORTH-HOLLAND PUBLISHING COMPANY
AMSTERDAM · NEW YORK · OXFORD

AN ANNUAL GROWTH
MODEL OF
THE U.S. ECONOMY

BERT G. HICKMAN

Stanford University

ROBERT M. COEN

Northwestern University

1976

NORTH-HOLLAND PUBLISHING COMPANY
AMSTERDAM · NEW YORK · OXFORD

3-1303 - 0060-8027

ISBN North-Holland for this series: 0 7204 3100 X
ISBN North-Holland for this volume: 0 7204 0372 3
ISBN American Elsevier for this volume: 0 444 11013 5

Publishers:

NORTH-HOLLAND PUBLISHING COMPANY
AMSTERDAM · NEW YORK · OXFORD

Sole distributors for the U.S.A. and Canada:

AMERICAN ELSEVIER PUBLISHING COMPANY, INC.
52 VANDERBILT AVENUE
NEW YORK, N.Y. 10017

Library of Congress Cataloging in Publication Data

Hickman, Bert G   1924-
  An annual growth model of the U. S. economy.

  (Contributions to economic analysis ; 100)
  Bibliography: p. 277
  1. United States--Economic conditions--Math-
ematical models. I. Coen, Robert M., joint author.
II. Title. III. Series.
HC106.H53   330.9'73   75-31586
ISBN 0-444-11013-5 (American Elsevier)

PRINTED IN THE NETHERLANDS

Introduction to Volume 100

In 1952 I consulted with the then Director of North-Holland, Mr. M. D. Frank, about the possibility of publishing a manuscript too large for an article and too small for an individual book. He suggested a Series of publications under the general title of "Contributions to Economic Analysis", to be edited by three Dutch economists: P. J. Verdoorn, H. J. Witteveen and myself. In the "Introduction to the Series", still printed in each volume, we expressed the hope that "the publication of these studies will help to stimulate the exchange of scientific information and to reinforce international co-operation in the field of economics".

Looking back over the Series today, I think we may state that our hopes, and Mr. Frank's initiative, as so many of his initiatives, were successfully realised. The editors are no longer only Dutch, the scope and contributors are quite international. The results of scientific work by many successful authors are to be found among the 100 volumes, some of whom have even given birth to new Series. The "Contributions" have included many highly original texts–on aggregation, forecasting, and planning (Kornai, Theil), production functions (Griliches, Ringstad, Johansen), income inequality (Taubman), utility functions (van Praag) to mention but a few.

The Series has not only grown healthily–it has had its "offspring" as well, both in the form of new Series and as larger books by authors who got their start–or inspiration–in scientific life from this Series.

JAN TINBERGEN

To Edythe and Margery

Preface

The Hickman–Coen Model is the result of a collaborative effort extending over six years and involving many people besides the principal authors. Wherever possible, specific contributions are identified by footnotes to the text, but a general acknowledgement is in order at this point.

Among our faculty colleagues, Michael D. Hurd and John L. Scadding collaborated closely in the study. The wage equation was developed and estimated by Hurd but his contributions over the past three years extend more widely to include advice on specification and estimation of equations in other sectors, as well as on systems programming and interpretation of model results. The model of the monetary sector was built by John Scadding, who also gave generously of his time in interpreting the complete model results involving interactions between the monetary and other sectors. He was ably assisted in his work on the monetary sector by Jae-ik Kim, who also independently developed the equation for the rate of interest on time deposits.

Several "generations" of graduate students have been associated with the project as research assistants over the past six years and have made important contributions to the various stages of data gathering, model building, and operation of the complete system. In order of time of association, they are: Joseph Bisignano, Charles Blitzer, Jay Siegel, Edward Ray, Richard Freeman, Margaret Sims, Warren Sanderson, Robert Willig, Margaret Oyaas, John Gemello, Dana Stevens, Jay Chambers, John Taylor, David Waterman, Peter Klein, Sang Suh, Warren B. Cornell, Carl Van Duyne, Abbott Lipsky, Andrea Kusko, and Anthony Lima. Finally, Mary Hinz served as a research assistant for two years and contributed importantly to the housing sector of the model with her work on development of the time series in Appendices E and F.

The basic databank and model simulation programs were written by George R. Green of the Bureau of Economic Analysis, Department of Commerce. Improvements and extensions of these programs are the work of John Taylor, Carl Van Duyne, Michael D. Hurd and Robert M. Coen. Our program for data processing and estimation–MODAM–was adapted from the original DAM program of Rudolf R. Rhomberg, Lorrette Boissonneault and Leonard Harris of the International Monetary Fund. The authors of MODAM are Charles Blitzer, Jay Siegel, Bridger Mitchell, and Robert M. Coen.

The index was prepared by Margery Coen. The successive drafts of major portions of the manuscript were efficiently typed by Nell Neil, whose forebearance and good cheer in the face of frequent textual alterations is greatly appreciated. Molly Fabian also provided valuable typing assistance.

We also wish to thank Lawrence R. Klein, who somehow found time to read the manuscript and offer numerous constructive criticisms and suggestions despite his crowded schedule.

This volume would not have been possible without the financial assistance of the National Science Foundation. We wish to express our gratitude to the Foundation for its support of the research under NSF Grants No. GS1686, GS2581, and GS41684.

Stanford, California   BERT G. HICKMAN
Evanston, Illinois   ROBERT M. COEN

Contents

List of Tables

CHAPTER 1

Overview of the Model

1. Introduction

In this book we present a new macro-econometric model for studying the medium-term growth path of the U.S. economy. The model is designed to predict the annual time paths of the major aggregative variables–actual and potential GNP; labor force, employment and unemployment; wages and prices–over a 5- to 10-year horizon. It therefore incorporates those variables and processes which are most important for determining the movement of the economy over the medium-term, rather than emphasizing the minor (inventory-cycle) characteristics which primarily affect short-term stability.

The model structure includes elements of both the Keynesian and neo-classical approaches to the determination of aggregate economic activity. The neo-classical strands are most evident in the derivation of the factor demand equations from marginal productivity conditions incorporating relative factor prices, in the use of an explicit production function for potential output, and in the introduction of the real wage as a determinant of the long-run labor supply. Keynesian elements are prominent in an income–expenditure framework, which excludes real balance effects, for the determination of effective demand in real terms and in a linkage of real and monetary sectors through interest rates as well as other variables. Money wages are proximately determined by changes in labor demand, expected wages, and unemployment, whereas prices depend directly on long-run average cost and a markup which varies with the degree of capacity utilization.

Since the model structure is not recursive, both direct and indirect interactions condition the responses of endogenous variables to changes in policy instruments or other exogenous variables. Thus, while the behavioral relationships among endogenous variables, such as those noted above, provide a basis for understanding these interactions, they should not be construed as one-way causal relationships. The properties of the complete system are best described in terms of the short- and long-term influences of policy changes on the endogenous variables, and these will depend not only on structural ingredients but also on the parameter estimates and the strength of various interactions. Because our system is not only non-recursive, but also non-linear with a high proportion of logarithmic behavioral functions, simulation methods are required to establish its properties.

The model contains about 50 stochastic equations and 170 endogenous variables. It is fitted to annual observations for the sample period 1924–40 and 1949–66. Our reason for terminating the sample in 1966 was to preserve a set of recent observations for use in evaluating the post-sample predictive performance of the model. Where significant structural change has occurred, separate functions are estimated for the pre- and post-war periods. However, our decision to truncate the post-war sample in 1966 removed opportunities in the estimation process to test for likely structural shifts in the late 1960's and early 1970's.

The principal novelties of the model include the introduction of interrelated demand functions for labor and capital; discrimination among concepts of potential, full-employment and capacity output; an integrated cost, production, and pricing framework; a long-run housing model featuring economic–demographic interactions in a disequilibrium framework; a new model of the money supply mechanism; and an approach to wage determination utilizing elements of the search theory of unemployment rather than the Phillips curve approach commonly found in macro-economic models.

These innovations, together with the annual time unit and long sample period, distinguish the model from existing econometric models of the U.S. and other nations. The model thus provides a new, and hopefully more adequate vehicle for understanding the sources of growth and instability in the U.S. economy over the past half century, as well as for exploring interactions among major macro-economic variables which have either been neglected or treated unsystematically in previous research. In the following pages, we shall document the current form and parameter estimates of the model and examine some of its interesting contributions to those topics. We shall not, however, present projections of the path of the economy over the years ahead, because notable changes in the economic environment in recent years seem to us to limit severely use of the model in its current form for this purpose. The sample period to which the present equations are fitted covers a rich and varied history, but ending as it does in 1966, it omits observations reflecting the persistent inflation, including the sharp, exogenous rise in energy prices, which subsequently occurred.

Although the theoretical specification of the model pays heed to the role of expectations in wage–price behavior, our statistical estimates of post-war expectation parameters are based on a period of relatively stable prices. Hence, the empirical form of the model will display properties characteristic of inelastic inflationary expectations, a situation that does not appear in accord with recent experience. The dramatic changes in energy supply conditions since 1973 raise more fundamental problems regarding the theoretical specification of the model. Not forseeing these events, we ignored the role of energy inputs in the production process, and the impact of energy prices on costs. Some possible approaches to remedying these deficiencies are noted in the concluding chapter, but we have not yet attempted to implement them.

Thus, the present model does not incorporate some recent structural changes of major significance. Nonetheless, we believe that it does offer fresh insights in important areas of model specification and analysis, as well as in evaluation of the performance of the U.S. economy.

2. Bloc Structure and Principal Features of the Model

An overview of the model is presented in table 1.1, which lists the equation blocs and principal endogenous variables. Three basic markets are distinguished: those for goods (blocs 1–8 and 12), labor (9–11) and money (13). The market for goods is more highly disaggregated in demand than supply, since most of the components of *GNP*

TABLE 1.1
Bloc structure of the Hickman–Coen model.

Bloc	Principal endogenous variables
(1) CONS (Consumption)	(1) Expenditures on automobiles; other durable goods; non-durable goods; services.
(2) INV (Business investment)	(2) Gross business fixed investment; stock of fixed business capital; inventory investment; inventory stock.
(3) HOUS (Housing and residential construction)	(3) Rent; non-farm households; stock of non-farm dwelling units; occupancy ratio; non-farm housing starts; value per non-farm housing start; residential construction expenditure.
(4) GOVT (Government purchases of goods and services	(4) State and local government purchases of goods and services.
(5) FORT (Foreign trade)	(5) Imports; exports.
(6) OUT (Output)	(6) *GNP* in current and constant prices; gross private non-residential product in current and constant prices.
(7) INC (Incomes)	(7) Gross corporate profits; dividends; capital consumption allowances; labor income; national income; personal income; disposable personal income.
(8) TXTR (Taxes and transfers)	(8) Unemployment compensation; unemployment contributions; contributions to social insurance; federal personal taxes; federal corporate taxes; indirect business taxes; investment tax credit.
(9) LBIN (Labor-input)	(9) Private man-hours.
(10) EMLF (Employment and labor force)	(10) Labor force participation rate; average hours; labor force; employment; unemployment.
(11) WAGE (Money wages)	(11) Change in aggregate wage rate.
(12) PRIC (Product prices)	(12) Implicit price deflators for: *GNP*; gross private non-residential product; 12 final demand sectors.
(13) MONY (Money stock and interest rates)	(13) Currency; demand deposits; time deposits; commercial paper rate; average Moody's corporate bond rate.
(14) UTIL (Resource utilization)	(14) Levels and rates of utilization of capacity output; full-employment output; potential output. Full-employment labor force; average hours at full employment; man-hours at full employment.

are treated as if they were perfect substitutes in production and there is only one aggregate production function in the model. The principal exceptions are housing services and income originating in general government employment, which are subtracted from *GNP* to derive the basic output variable of the model, gross private non-residential product (*XNR*).[1] The corresponding implicit deflator (*PXNR*) is the basic price variable for goods. Similarly, labor is viewed as a homogenous input in the aggregate production function and measured in private man-hours. The private wage rate is endogenous, but both the number of government employees and their wage are treated as exogenous control variables for government policy. Finally, the basic quantity variable in the money market is *M2*, the money stock defined to include time deposits as well as currency and demand deposits, and the corresponding price is the short-term interest rate.

The first five blocs comprise the system of final demand equations. Consumption expenditure is disaggregated into four components. Separate equations determine business fixed investment and the rate of inventory change. Residential construction is explained in a sub-model of the housing sector. State and local purchases of goods and services are endogenous, as are aggregate imports and exports in real terms. Nominal exports and federal purchases of goods and services are among the principal exogenous variables in the model.

For the most part, the behavioral equations in these five blocs are demand functions. This is true of the consumption, business invest-ment and import functions. Although most of these functions incor-porate relative price variables, the prices are determined elsewhere in the model, as explained below. However, the housing bloc is an exception to these generalizations, since it contains a complete sub-model of the housing sector and residential construction indus-try. A demand and supply model of the housing market determines the rental rate and occupancy ratio for existing dwelling units. These variables in turn affect builders' production decisions and help to determine the volume of new residential construction via a supply equation for new starts.

---

[1] Housing services are produced by the housing stock without labor input, and government capital is not measured in the model. Hence the private non-residential capital and labor inputs of the model are related to *XNR* in the production function rather than to real *GNP*.

Apart from prices and interest rates, the principal arguments in the expenditure functions for goods and services are real gross private non-residential product, which affects business investment and imports; personal income, which appears in the state and local equation; and disposable personal income which enters the consumption functions and several of the housing equations. The primary purpose of the output, income and tax and transfer blocs is to close this part of the model by completing the income–expenditure loop for given prices.

The output bloc is composed entirely of definitional identities. Real *GNP* is determined as the sum of its real expenditure components, and *XNR* is obtained from *GNP* by subtracting income originating in housing rentals and government employment. The constant-dollar estimates are then converted to current prices through multiplication by the appropriate implicit price deflators.

The income bloc includes equations for dividends, gross corporate profits, and capital consumption allowances, whereas the tax and transfer bloc provides endogenous explanations of unemployment contributions and benefits, contributions to social insurance, federal personal income and corporate profits tax receipts, and federal indirect business taxes. These items when combined with several exogenous income leakages, provide the links between *GNP*, personal income, and disposable personal income. Together with the expenditure blocs, they form a complete system of national income determination, given exogenous interest rates, wages and prices. Thus the first eight blocs may be viewed as comprising a rather sophisticated and disaggregated version of the textbook multiplier–accelerator model. In itself this truncated system is inadequate for growth analysis, since it neglects supply constraints except in the housing sector.

The remainder of the model incorporates such constraints as they affect the growth of labor force, capital stock, potential output, and money supply. Real and monetary ceilings are not treated as impenetrable, however, but rather as supply factors that interact with demand to determine the evolution of prices, production and employment.

Manpower constraints are modeled in the employment and labor force bloc, which contains equations for labor force participation and hours of work as functions of real wages, employment and population. The labor-input bloc consists entirely of a demand function for man-hours, with output and factor prices as principal arguments. With real wages and the rental rate of capital given exogenously, these two blocs determine the labor force, employment, unemployment, and hours of work as functions primarily of output and population. Together with the income–expenditure blocs, they form a complete model of the real sector explaining *GNP* and the unemployment rate along with important detail on expenditures, income and labor market variables. The labor force and hours equations also provide the basic ingredients for estimating output under full-employment conditions as will be discussed below when we come to the utilization bloc.

The wage bloc completes the labor sector. It explains changes in money wages by an excess-demand hypothesis incorporating changes in labor demand, expected wage rates, and unemployment, and it forms part of the wage–price sub-system of the model.

Prices are obtained by a markup or price-setting equation reflecting both cost and demand factors and allowing for market imperfections instead of assuming competitive pricing. More specifically, the price bloc contains a master markup equation for the aggregate price level and a dozen auxiliary equations relating the sector deflators to the aggregate deflator and to cyclical and trend variables as proxies for systematic forces affecting the relative price structure.

Since wage rates affect production costs and hence product prices, and since the latter in turn affect labor demands, there is an internal feedback loop between the wage and price blocs in addition to those connecting the wage–price system and the income–expenditure–employment system.

The money bloc contains a supply and demand model of the commercial banking sector to determine the money stock and Treasury bill rate as well as a term–structure model to relate short- and long-term interest rates. Interest rates enter the housing starts and consumer durables equations and provide the channels for monetary policy to affect production and income directly and employment and prices indirectly. There is also a reverse feedback to the money bloc via the transactions demand for money balances.

Finally, the utilization bloc provides several measures of aggregate resource utilization. We distinguish between capacity output, full-employment output, and potential output and provide estimates of all three magnitudes and the associated utilization ratios. Capacity is a cost-based concept referring to the output that would be produced if the existing capital stock were operated with the optimal input of labor under existing techniques and relative factor prices. It is inferred from the investment demand function. Full-employment output is also related to costs and is defined as that output which would have to be demanded in order to induce entrepreneurs to hire the full-employment labor supply at existing relative factor prices. It is calculated from the labor demand function and information on the full-employment supply of man-hours. Potential is defined as that output which could be produced with existing technology if the full-employment labor supply were combined with the existing capital stock irrespective of cost considerations and hence it is estimated from the production function. Finally, the "full-employment" supply of man-hours needed for the estimation of full-employment output and potential output is derived from the labor force participation and average hours equations on the conventional assumption that full-employment occurs when four percent of the labor force is unemployed.

Thus far the model has been described primarily in terms of its market structure and the interdependencies within and between blocs. With this background, some of its special features may now be discussed.

In line with the long-run orientation of the model, special care has been taken with the supply or production side. The demand functions for labor and capital have been estimated so as to be consistent with each other and also with the long-run production function. That is to say, the key production function parameters—the elasticities of output with respect to capital and labor and the rate of technical progress—are identical in the two-factor demand equations. This ensures consistency between the long-run properties of the factor demand equations, so that the growth rates of the factor inputs will not diverge from the appropriate values to maintain a viable production relationship as output grows.

The factor demand equations also reflect two other basic principles in the construction of the model. First, factor substitution can and does occur in response to changes in relative factor prices. It is especially important in a long-term model not to neglect this feature of the economy, and hence the relative price of labor and capital services appears as an argument in the factor demand functions. This is not uncommon in investment functions, but short-term models usually exclude prices from the labor equation, which is treated as an inverted short-run production function rather than as a market demand function. Comparable care has been taken to include price variables wherever appropriate elsewhere in the model.

Second, the factor demand equations have been estimated as disequilibrium relations that account for lagged adjustments of inputs to output or price changes. Long-run models often abstract from short-run variations by data smoothing or other assumptions. Not only may these practices yield biased estimates of the underlying long-run parameters, but they effectively prevent an analysis of the time paths or trajectories of the economy as it moves from unemployment to full employment or adjusts to changes in growth rates. Since the analysis of time paths is one of our basic goals we have consistently specified behavioral relationships to ensure both a viable long-run equilibrium and provision for short-term disequilibrium.

The model also incorporates an unusual approach to labor force participation, combining the hypotheses of long-run labor supply determination by the real wage rate and short-run labor market adjustment governed by the state of job opportunities.

As a further extension of the idea of an integrated cost and production framework for the model, the production function has been used in the derivation of long-run average cost, which is one of the two principal arguments in the price markup equation, the other being the capacity utilization index. Thus the explicit Cobb–Douglas production function is combined with the money wage and the rental price of capital to measure the long-run average cost of current output in the price equation.

The housing sector is another example of specification for long-run analysis in the model. Most recent econometric work on the sector has concentrated on the short-term fluctuations of residential construction in the post-war economy, and there is a general concensus that the contracyclical pattern of home construction is due to variations in credit conditions. This factor finds a place in our housing model, but in a subordinate role. We are more concerned with the factors governing the long-run trends of the housing stock and new construction. The current demand for dwelling space is a function of population and its age distribution, the ratio of housing rent to the consumer price index, and real income. The short-run supply depends on the standing stock of dwelling units and the same price ratio. Together demand and supply determine the occupancy rate and rental level, with due allowance for market disequilibrium. These variables in turn affect the flow of new housing starts, along with external determinants. Current starts augment the stock of dwelling units in the next period, which in turn affects occupancies and rents, and so on. Thus, in the long-run the housing stock depends on population and income growth, but the stock-adjustment process is complicated and subject to lengthy lags.

A final observation concerning general principles is in order. The model has been structured for policy analysis, and among other things this means that care has been taken to incorporate the main policy instruments in the appropriate markets and behavioral functions. The monetary instruments include the quantity of unborrowed reserves, required reserve ratios, and the discount rate. (The money supply itself is an endogenous variable.) The fiscal instruments include federal purchases of goods and services, tax rates on personal, corporate and indirect business taxes and on contributions for social insurance, the investment tax credit, and the parameters for depreciation tax policy.

Further discussion of some of the foregoing features of the model–especially the housing, labor force participation and wage sectors–is best deferred to the later chapters on structural specification. The detailed survey of the various blocs offered in those chapters, however, may obscure some of the important interrelations in the model, by failing to highlight the unified view of firms' decision processes which connects the investment, employment, production and price equations. It will therefore be useful to discuss the theoretical specification of these decision processes before turning to the detailed examination of estimated structural equations in Chapters 2–6.

3. The Production and Factor Demand Functions

Our approach stresses the interdependence of firms' decisions on capital and labor inputs. Imperfect competition is assumed in product markets, with product price set as a markup on average cost. For given product prices, output is demand-determined in the short run. Firms base their employment and investment decisions on expected output and expected factor prices in order to minimize production costs. The algebraic framework is as follows.

The production function is viewed as a planning relation between expected long-run output, X^*, desired labor input measured in man-hours, M^*, and desired capital stock, K^*. We assume that technological progress occurs smoothly over time at the rate γ and that the production function is of the Cobb–Douglas form. Thus,

$$X_t^* = A \, e^{\gamma t} (K_t^*)^\alpha (M_t^*)^\beta, \qquad A, \alpha, \beta, \gamma > 0. \tag{1.1}$$

Desired inputs of labor and capital are presumed to be chosen so as to minimize the cost of producing expected output in long-run equilibrium. If there is no monopsony in factor markets, then cost minimization requires that the ratio of marginal products of labor and capital be equated to the ratio of their expected prices. Making use of this assumption, and denoting the expected ratio of the price of capital (an implicit rental rate) to the wage rate $(Q/W)^*$, we derive the following desired or long-run input relations:

$$M_t^* = [(\alpha/\beta)^{-\alpha} A^{-1}]^{1/(\alpha+\beta)} [(Q/W)_t^*]^{\alpha/(\alpha+\beta)} (X_t^*)^{1/(\alpha+\beta)} \, e^{-[\gamma/(\alpha+\beta)]t}, \tag{1.2}$$

and

$$K_t^* = [(\alpha/\beta)^{\beta} A^{-1}]^{1/(\alpha+\beta)} [(Q/W)_t^*]^{-\beta/(\alpha+\beta)} (X_t^*)^{1/(\alpha+\beta)} \, e^{-[\gamma/(\alpha+\beta)]t}. \tag{1.3}$$

Firms may not adjust immediately to variations in desired inputs, however, owing to the adjustment costs involved in changing input levels.[2] These adjustment costs are not explicitly modeled in our

---

[2] Examples of these costs for labor are search, hiring, training and layoff costs. In the case of capital, adjustment costs may stem from purchase costs which are external to the firm or from internal installation costs.

system, but instead are represented indirectly by the conventional partial-adjustment hypothesis. Thus the observed or measured inputs are assumed to be partially adjusted toward these desired levels at constant (geometric) rates per period,

$$M_t/M_{t-1} = (M_t^*/M_{t-1})^{\lambda_1}, \qquad 0 < \lambda_1 \leq 1, \tag{1.4}$$

and

$$K_t/K_{t-1} = (K_t^*/K_{t-1})^{\lambda_2}, \qquad 0 < \lambda_2 \leq 1. \tag{1.5}$$

Hence, our short-run demand functions are obtained by combining equations (1.2) and (1.4) and equations (1.3) and (1.5) to yield

$$M_t = \{[(\alpha/\beta)^{-\alpha}A^{-1}]^{1/(\alpha+\beta)}[(Q/W)_t^*]^{\alpha/(\alpha+\beta)}$$
$$\times (X_t^*)^{1/(\alpha+\beta)} e^{-[\gamma/(\alpha+\beta)]t}\}^{\lambda_1}(M_{t-1})^{1-\lambda_1}, \tag{1.6}$$

and

$$K_t = \{[(\alpha/\beta)^{\beta}A^{-1}]^{1/(\alpha+\beta)}[(Q/W)_t^*]^{-\beta/(\alpha+\beta)}$$
$$\times (X_t^*)^{1/(\alpha+\beta)} e^{-[\gamma/(\alpha+\beta)]t}\}^{\lambda_2}(K_{t-1})^{1-\lambda_2}. \tag{1.7}$$

Finally, expected factor prices and expected output are specified as weighted geometric averages of current and past levels of those variables, with weights determined by the data.

4. Effective Inputs and Production in the Short Run

In the derivation of the desired input functions, the production function was viewed as a planning relation between equilibrium input and output levels, as in equation (1.1). The corresponding short-run or disequilibrium production function is

$$X_t = A \ e^{\gamma t}(k_t K_{t-1})^{\alpha}(m_t M_t)^{\beta}, \tag{1.8}$$

where k_t and m_t are indexes of the *intensity* of use respectively of the observed or measured inputs K_{t-1} and M_t and where output is measured at its actual current level instead of its expected long-term level. Under stationary conditions,[3] actual and expected output would

---

[3] The qualification is necessary because the normal intensity indexes consistent with growth equilibrium may exceed unity, as explained below.

be equal and the measured inputs would be fully adjusted to the optimum levels K_t^* and M_t^*, and hence $k_t = k^* = 1$ and $m_t = m^* = 1$, where k^* and m^* are the *normal* utilization intensities. In the short run, however, expectations lags and adjustment costs may cause k_t and m_t to diverge from normal, in which case the *effective* capital and labor inputs are $k_t K_{t-1}$ and $m_t M_t$. Of course, the effective inputs are not directly observable, but we propose to infer them from observed investment and employment behavior.

The basic idea is that a given quantity of measured input, such as a man-hour, may represent a greater or lesser amount of labor services or effective labor input when a man-hour is used more or less intensively. Just how this will be accomplished in a particular situation will depend on the nature of production techniques and the incentive system. Perhaps the most obvious example of an increase in intensity of use of measured labor input is a situation where people work the same number of hours but at a faster pace, so that more output is produced with a given bundle of man-hours.[4] Similarly, the capital stock may be used more intensively by operating equipment at a faster rate or by increasing the number of machine-hours per day or week. This last possibility is an additional degree of freedom as compared with labor input, since we are using capital stock rather than machine-hours as an argument in the production function. Even if a machine-hour were our unit of measured capital input, however, the intensity of use of capital input could still be increased by operating the machinery at a faster rate.

Variations in the intensity of factor utilization occur in the process of adjusting measured inputs to changes in the desired equilibrium quantities. The desired quantities would minimize production costs for the new expected output. The adjustment is not instantaneous, however, for two reasons. First, expected output may lag changes in actual output so that even if the measured inputs were adjusted immediately to the new optimum levels, they would be over- or under-utilized in current production. Second, immediate movements of inputs to desired levels may be uneconomical because of adjust-

---

[4] They might also take fewer or briefer coffee breaks, take greater care to avoid errors, do less day-dreaming, and so forth. The payment of piece rates is one method for inducing an increase in labor intensity per man-hour by encouraging people to work faster.

ment costs. As noted in the previous section, these costs are represented indirectly in our system by the partial-adjustment hypotheses of equations (1.4) and (1.5).

While there may be an infinite number of technologically feasible combinations of k_t and m_t that could satisfy (1.8), our premise is that intensities of factor use are revealed by firms' investment and employment actions as they adjust toward equilibrium. Let us abstract temporarily from the first source of disequilibrium by assuming that $X_t = X_t^*$. The existing disequilibria in the measured inputs are then the only source of deviations of factor utilization from the normal or equilibrium intensities, and we may make the model operational by assuming that the intensity of use of each factor is exactly proportional to the degree of disequilibrium in each. We therefore specify

$$k_t = K_t^*/K_{t-1},\qquad(1.9)$$

and

$$m_t = M_t^*/M_t.\qquad(1.10)$$

By hypotheses (1.4) and (1.5), however, the observed changes in measured inputs are proportional to the desired changes, so that (1.9) and (1.10) may be rewritten in terms of observable variables as

$$k_t = (K_t/K_{t-1})^{1/\lambda_2},\qquad(1.11)$$

and[5]

$$m_t = (M_t/M_{t-1})^{(1-\lambda_1)/\lambda_1}.\qquad(1.12)$$

These expressions are the operational statement of our verbal hypothesis that factor intensities are revealed by investment and employment behavior.

The intensity indexes are defined in terms of input quantities in (1.11) and (1.12). Factor utilization is frequently measured in output units, however, as in many commonly used indexes of capacity

---

[5] The difference in the exponents in (1.11) and (1.12) comes from the convention in (1.8) of dating the available capital stock as of the end of the previous period, whereas the available labor input is the flow during the current period.

utilization. Output-denominated utilization measures are also available in our model, and the next task is to derive them and show how they are related to the input-based intensity indexes.

We follow the tenets of neo-classical theory in defining capacity as the output that would be produced if the existing capital stock were operated with the optimal input of labor for existing techniques and factor prices. In order to produce any given output at minimum total cost, the capital–labor ratio must satisfy the expansion path equation

$$\beta Q_t^* K_t^* - \alpha W_t^* M_t^* = 0. \tag{1.13}$$

Using (1.13) to eliminate M_t^* from (1.1) leads to

$$X_t^c = A(\beta/\alpha)^\beta \, e^{\gamma t} [(Q/W)_t^*]^\beta (K_{t-1})^{\alpha+\beta}, \tag{1.14}$$

when actual capital K_{t-1} is regarded as the equilibrium stock. Expression (1.14) may also be obtained by substituting actual for desired stock in (1.3) and solving for output.[6] It can be shown that X_t^c is the abscissa of the point on the long-run average cost curve for a firm with capital stock of size K_{t-1}.

We define an index of capacity utilization as the ratio $(X/X^c)_t$. Under our present simplifying assumption that desired and actual output are equal, the investment function (1.7) may be solved for X_t to obtain

$$X_t = A(\beta/\alpha)^\beta \, e^{\gamma t} [(Q/W)_t^*]^\beta K_t^{(\alpha+\beta)/\lambda_2} (K_{t-1})^{-(1-\lambda_2)(\alpha+\beta)/\lambda_2}. \tag{1.15}$$

Division of (1.15) by (1.14) results in a simple expression for the capacity utilization ratio,

$$(X/X^c)_t = (K_t/K_{t-1})^{(\alpha+\beta)/\lambda_2}. \tag{1.16}$$

An analogous index for labor utilization may be derived by regarding labor as the limiting factor and inverting equation (1.2) to obtain the expression for "labor-optimizing output",

$$X_t^m = A(\beta/\alpha)^{-\alpha} \, e^{\gamma t} [(Q/W)_t^*]^{-\alpha} M_t^{\alpha+\beta}. \tag{1.17}$$

---

[6] This was the approach used earlier in Hickman (1964, 1965).

Solving the labor demand function (1.6) for output and dividing the resulting expression by (1.17) yields the utilization ratio for labor,

$$(X/X^m)_t = (M_t/M_{t-1})^{(1-\lambda_1)(\alpha+\beta)/\lambda_1}. \tag{1.18}$$

This completes the derivation of the expressions for capacity and labor utilization in the Cobb–Douglas framework. To show how they are related to k_t and m_t, we combine expressions (1.11) and (1.12) with (1.16) and (1.18) to obtain

$$k_t = (K_t/K_{t-1})^{1/\lambda_2} = (X/X^c)_t^{1/(\alpha+\beta)}, \tag{1.19}$$

and

$$m_t = (M_t/M_{t-1})^{(1-\lambda_1)/\lambda_1} = (X/X^m)_t^{1/(\alpha+\beta)}. \tag{1.20}$$

Hence either the factor intensity indexes (1.11) and (1.12) or the factor utilization ratios (1.16) and (1.18) may be used in the short-run production function (1.8) to convert the measured inputs into effective inputs.

Expressions (1.11) and (1.12), and their equivalents (1.19) and (1.20), were derived on the assumption of equality between current and expected output and must be modified if that assumption is dropped. No fundamental conceptual change is necessary, however, provided that X_t^* is proportional to X_t. Thus, suppose that $X_t = l_t X_t^*$. Since the Cobb–Douglas function is homogenous, it may then be written as

$$\begin{aligned}
X_t &= A\ e^{\gamma t} (l_t^{1/(\alpha+\beta)} K_t^*)^\alpha (l_t^{1/(\alpha+\beta)} M_t^*)^\beta \\
&= A\ e^{\gamma t} (l_t^{1/(\alpha+\beta)} k_t K_{t-1})^\alpha (l_t^{1/(\alpha+\beta)} m_t M_t)^\beta \\
&= A\ e^{\gamma t} (k_t' K_{t-1})^\alpha (m_t' M_t)^\beta,
\end{aligned} \tag{1.21}$$

where use is made of (1.1) and (1.8) and the new definitions,

$$k_t' = l_t^{1/(\alpha+\beta)} k_t,$$

and

$$m_t' = l_t^{1/(\alpha+\beta)} m_t.$$

When $l_t \neq 1$, the expected and actual outputs differ, so that even if the measured inputs were immediately adjusted to the equilibrium levels for the expected output, they would temporarily be used at abnormally high or low intensities in the production of current output. Thus expectations lags as well as adjustment costs may cause short-term variations in utilization intensities, and they can be incorporated into the model by appropriate specfication of l_t. In the empirical work our maintained hypothesis was that $X_t^* = X_t^w X_{t-1}^{1-w}$, which implies $l_t = (X_t/X_{t-1})^{1-w}$. The best estimates of the aggregate factor demand functions (1.6) and (1.7) were obtained for $w = 1$, however, so that $l_t = 1$ and the unmodified expressions for the intensity and utilization indexes hold for our aggregative measures.

5. Potential and Full-employment Output

We distinguish between two measures of output at full employment of the labor force. Potential is defined as that output which could be produced with existing technology if the full-employment supply of man-hours were combined with the existing capital stock irrespective of cost considerations, and hence it is estimated from the production function. In contrast, full-employment output is related to production costs and is defined as the output which would have to be demanded in order to induce entrepreneurs to hire the full-employment labor supply at existing factor prices. The distinction is important because an economy may produce at the potential level without enjoying full employment of the labor force if capital, labor, or both are overutilized relative to their normal intensities. For either concept, the "full-employment" supply of man-hours is calculated from equations for average hours and labor force participation on the conventional assumption that full employment occurs when four percent of the labor force is unemployed (see Chapter 4, sections 2 and 3).

The equation for full-employment output is obtained by solving the labor demand function (1.6) for output and substituting full-employment man-hours (M^f) for actual man-hours,

$$X_t^f = A(\beta/\alpha)^{-\alpha}[(Q/W)_t^*]^{-\alpha} e^{\gamma t}(M_t^f)^{(\alpha+\beta)/\lambda_1}(M_{t-1})^{-(1-\lambda_1)(\alpha+\beta)/\lambda_1}.$$

$$(1.22)$$

Expression (1.22) holds only for the case where $X_t^* = X_t$. If X_t^* in equation (1.6) depended on lagged as well as current output, the lagged output term would appear on the right-hand side of (1.22).

A simple expression for the rate of utilization of full-employment output is also available for the case of equality of actual and expected output,

$$(X/X^f)_t = (M/M^f)_t^{(\alpha+\beta)/\lambda_1}. \tag{1.23}$$

Equation (1.23) is obtained by solving the labor demand function (1.6) for output and dividing the resulting expression by (1.2). It is clear from (1.23) that the rate of utilization of full-employment output is independent of the current utilization of physical capital.

Potential output is determined from the production function (1.8) by inserting full-employment man-hours and measuring the effective labor and capital inputs at their normal utilization rates,

$$X_t^P = A \, e^{\gamma t} (n_c^{1/(\alpha+\beta)} K_{t-1})^\alpha (n_m^{1/(\alpha+\beta)} M_t^f)^\beta, \tag{1.24}$$

where n_c is the normal capacity utilization ratio and n_m the normal labor utilization ratio. We base the estimate of potential output on the normal rates of capacity and labor utilization so that it changes over time only when available factor supplies and technology change, rather than varying from year to year as factors are used more or less intensively.

To implement equation (1.24) empirically, we must estimate the normal capacity and labor utilization ratios. One might suppose that these normal rates would be unity (or one-hundred percent), but this is likely to be true only under stationary conditions. The basic point that must be kept in mind is that firms adjust measured inputs to their desired levels with some lag. Hence, if the economy is experiencing steady growth, we would expect to observe firms using factor inputs which are below desired levels, provided that they do not make a practice of "building ahead of demand". Put another way, we expect to observe factor intensity indexes for capital and labor, and the corresponding capacity and labor utilization rates, that exceed unity. The amounts by which they would exceed unity will depend, among other things, on how rapidly firms adjust their inputs. The higher the growth rate of output and the slower the adjustment speeds, the higher will be the normal utilization rates.

The calculation of the normal or long-run utilization rate of capacity output is straightforward. The capacity utilization rate will remain constant if capacity grows as fast as output. Given the secular growth rate of output and relative factor prices, equation (1.14) may be used to calculate the growth rate of capital stock required for capacity output to increase at the same rate as actual output. Finally, the required growth rate of capital stock is inserted in equation (1.16) to compute the normal rate of capacity utilization, n_c. The normal labor utilization rate is derived in the same manner, using equations (1.17) and (1.18). We should expect n_c to exceed n_m, since the speed of adjustment of capital stock is much slower than that of man-hours.

To derive a convenient expression for the rate of utilization of potential output, we rewrite equation (1.8) in terms of the capacity and labor utilization indexes (1.19) and (1.20), and divide the resulting short-term production function by (1.24) to obtain

$$(X/X^P)_t = [(X/X^c)_t/n_c]^{\alpha/(\alpha+\beta)}[(X/X^m)_t/n_m]^{\beta/(\alpha+\beta)}(M/M^f)_t^\beta.$$

$$(1.25)$$

Since (1.23) provides a relationship between $(M/M^f)_t$ and $(X/X^f)_t$, we can also write (1.25) as

$$(X/X^P)_t = [(X/X^c)_t/n_c]^{\alpha/(\alpha+\beta)}[(X/X^m)_t/n_m]^{\beta/(\alpha+\beta)}(X/X^f)_t^{\beta\lambda_1/(\alpha+\beta)}.$$

$$(1.26)$$

Equation (1.26) integrates the four utilization concepts and shows that the utilization rate of potential varies directly with the utilization rates of capacity, labor-optimizing, and full-employment output.

6. Costs and Prices

We employ a variant of the markup hypothesis of price setting. Firms are assumed to base price on an estimate of normal or long-run average total cost but may vary the markup according to current demand pressures as measured by the rate of capacity utilization.

Average cost is derived explicitly from the production function and factor prices by use of the following identity:

$$AC_t = A_0(Q_t)^{\alpha/(\alpha+\beta)}(W_t)^{\beta/(\alpha+\beta)}(X_t)^{[1-(\alpha+\beta)]/(\alpha+\beta)} e^{-\gamma/(\alpha+\beta)t}. \tag{1.27}$$

The markup ratio (the ratio of desired price to average cost) is

$$\mu_t = \mu_0(X/X^c)_t^\delta. \tag{1.28}$$

Combining equations (1.27) and (1.28) and assuming partial adjustment of actual to desired price at the goemetric rate ϵ, yields the price equation

$$P_t = \mu_0^\epsilon(X/X^c)_t^{\delta\epsilon}(AC)_t^\epsilon(P_{t-1})^{1-\epsilon}. \tag{1.29}$$

Equation (1.29) is used to predict the implicit price deflator for aggregate output in the model. Sectoral deflators for the various components of *GNP* are then linked to the aggregate deflator in auxiliary equations which also include capacity utilization and trend variables as proxies for systematic forces affecting relative prices. Notice that average cost is independent of output in equation (1.27) when constant returns ($\alpha + \beta = 1$) prevails.

7. Plan of the Book

Chapters 2–6 provide a detailed account of the specification and estimation of the model equations. In Chapter 7 we investigate the predictive accuracy of the model in the sample and post-sample periods. Chapter 8 reports on an extensive series of policy simulations and compares the effects of expansionary monetary and fiscal policies on key economic variables. Certain dynamic properties of the model are investigated in Chapter 9. The first part of the chapter examines the dynamic multipliers of federal expenditure on *GNP* and its components as major equation blocs are successively endogenized to augment the scope for interaction in the model. The second section compares pre-war and post-war multipliers in order to assess the importance of structural change for post-war stability. In Chapter 10 we compare model solution errors and dynamic multipliers in the post-war period under alternative assumptions of constant and increasing returns to scale of production. Finally, Chapter 11 describes some significant by-products of the research, summarizes our findings on policy simulations and dynamic properties, and discusses potential applications and improvements of the model in future research.

A description of variables in the model is included as an appendix to this chapter. Six data appendixes follow Chapter 11 to round out the volume.

Appendix to Chapter 1

Description of Variables (= exogenous variable)*

*ABUC$	Average weekly benefit for unemployment compensation, dollars per beneficiary.
*ADJUC$	Adjustment factor for federal emergency unemployment benefits during 1958–62, billions of dollars.
AH	Average hours, private sector, thousands per person per year.
AH1	Average hours, entire economy, thousands per person per year.
AH7	Average hours at full employment, private sector, thousands per person per year.
CA	Personal consumption expenditures, autos, billions of 1958 dollars.
CAK	Stock of autos, billions of 1958 dollars.
CC$	Capital consumption allowances, billions of dollars.
CCC$	Capital consumption allowances, corporate, billions of dollars.
*CCCR	Capital consumption rate, corporate, decimal fraction.

CCNC$	Capital consumption allowances, non-corporate, billions of dollars.
*CCNCR	Capital consumption rate, non-corporate, decimal fraction.
CE	Personal consumption expenditures, billions of 1958 dollars.
CE$	Personal consumption expenditures, billions of dollars.
CND	Personal consumption expenditures, non-durables, billions of 1958 dollars.
COD	Personal consumption expenditures, other durables, billions of 1958 dollars.
CODK	Stock of other consumer durables, billions of 1958 dollars.
CS	Personal consumption expenditures, services, billions of 1958 dollars.
*D31	Equals 1 for 1931–40 and zero otherwise.
*D34	Equals 1 for 1934 and zero otherwise.
*D3637	Equals 1 for 1936–37 and zero otherwise.
*D5153	Equals 1 for 1951–53 and zero otherwise.
*D65	Equals 1 for 1965-date and zero otherwise.
*DCDD	Credit terms, consumer durables dummy ($0 =$ normal, $-1 =$ tight, $+1 =$ easy).
*DHOUS	Dummy for regulation X, equals 1 for 1950, -1 for 1951 and zero otherwise. (Credit terms for new housing mortgages were tightened late in 1950 under this regulation and subsequently eased in 1951.)
*DMOAS	Dummy variable measuring proportion of military wages and salaries entering OASDHI tax base.
*DODGO$	Gross obligations, Department of Defense, billions of dollars.
*DRLRG	Equals zero for 1930–40 and 1 otherwise.
*DSEOAS	Dummy variable measuring proportion of proprietors' income (adjusted for relation between

	labor income in proprietorships and total proprietors' income) entering OASDHI tax base.
*DUMAC	Dummy for pre-accord years (= 1.0 in 1949–52; = 0 other years).
*DUMMY1	Equals 0 for 1922–48 and 1 for 1949-date.
*DYD$	Adjustment factor for dividends, 1936–38, reflecting effect of tax on undistributed corporate profits, billions of dollars.
*DYLOAS	Dummy variable measuring proportion of private labor income entering OASDHI tax base.
E	Total civilian employment, millions of persons.
ECB$	Federal corporate tax base, billions of dollars.
*EGFNW	Federal government civilian employment, excluding work relief, millions of persons.
*EGFWR	Federal government civilian employment, work relief, millions of persons.
*EGSNW	State and local government employment, excluding work relief, millions of persons.
*EGSWR	State and local government employment, work relief, millions of persons.
EP	Private employment, millions of persons
EP7	Private employment at full employment, millions of persons.
*ERR$	Statistical discrepancy, billions of dollars.
F	Net exports, billions of 1958 dollars.
F$	Net exports, billions of dollars.
FEX	Exports, billions of 1958 dollars.
*FEX$	Exports, billions of dollars.
FIM	Imports, billions of 1958 dollars.
FIM$	Imports, billions of dollars.
G	Government expenditures on goods and services, billions of 1958 dollars.
*GAID$	Federal grants in aid to state and local governments, billions of dollars.

GBSF$	Federal government budget surplus, NIPA,[7] billions of dollars.
GBSSL$	State and local government budget surplus, NIPA, billions of dollars.
GEXPF$	Federal government expenditures, NIPA, billions of dollars.
GEXPSL$	State and local government expenditures, NIPA, billions of dollars.
*GF	Federal government purchases, billions of 1958 dollars.
*GGF	Federal government expenditures on goods and services, excluding wages and salaries of government workers, billions of 1958 dollars.
GGF$	Federal government expenditures on goods and services, excluding wages and salaries of government workers, billions of dollars.
GRECF$	Federal government receipts, NIPA, billions of dollars.
*GRECSL$	State and local government receipts, NIPA, billions of dollars.
GRM1	Growth rate of money supply, *M1* definition, percent per annum.
GRM2S	Growth rate of money supply, *M2S* definition, percent per annum.
GROUT	Growth rate of output (real *GNP*), percent per annum.
GRPROD	Growth rate of productivity (XNR/MH), percent per annum.
GRX7	Growth rate of full-employment output, increasing returns, percent per annum.
GRX7C	Growth rate of full-employment output, constant returns, percent per annum.
GRX8	Growth rate of potential output, increasing returns, percent per annum.

---

[7] I.e., as measured in the National Income and Product Accounts.

GRX8C	Growth rate of potential output, constant returns, percent per annum.
GRX9	Growth rate of capacity output, increasing returns, percent per annum.
GRX9C	Growth rate of capacity output, constant returns, percent per annum.
GSL	State and local government purchases, billions of 1958 dollars.
GSLN	State and local government purchases, billions of 1958 dollars per capita.
*HA	Housing net additions, non-farm (excluding starts), millions.
HCCA	Value per non-farm private housing start, thousands of 1958 dollars.
*HGAA	Gross expenditures, non-farm additions and alterations, billions of 1958 dollars.
*HGBC	Brokers' commissions, sales of residential structures, billions of 1958 dollars.
*HGIF	Gross investment, farm residences, billions of 1958 dollars.
HGIN	Gross investment, non-farm residences, billions of 1958 dollars.
HGIND	Gross investment, non-farm dwelling units, billions of 1958 dollars.
*HGNH	Gross investment, non-housekeeping units, billions of 1958 dollars.
*HGP	Public residential construction, billions of 1958 dollars.
*HGUS	Net purchases of used residential structures, billions of 1958 dollars.
HH	Number of non-farm households, millions.
*HHS	Number of standardized non-farm households, based on headship rates in 1940, millions.
HKN	Net stock, non-farm residential structures, billions of 1958 dollars.

HO	Housing occupancy ratio ($= HH/HU_{-1}$), decimal fraction.
HSPR	Non-farm private housing starts, millions.
*HSPU	Non-farm public housing starts, millions.
HU	Stock of non-farm dwelling units, millions.
IGB	Gross business fixed investment, billions of 1958 dollars.
IGPD	Gross private domestic investment, billions of 1958 dollars.
*IIF	Inventory investment, farm, billions of 1958 dollars.
IINF	Inventory investment, non-farm, billions of 1958 dollars.
INFL	Inflation rate, implicit *GNP* deflator, percent per annum.
INFLC	Inflation rate, implicit consumer expenditures price deflator, percent per annum.
ITC$	Investment tax credit, corporate, billions of dollars.
*ITCD	Proportion of investment tax credit that must be deducted from depreciable base of asset, decimal fraction.
*ITCR	Investment tax credit rate, decimal fraction.
*ITCRAT	Investment tax credit ratio (*ITC$/IGB$*), decimal fraction.
*IVA$	Inventory valuation adjustment, billions of dollars.
*IVAC$	Inventory valuation adjustment, corporate, billions of dollars.
*KG$	Net capital gains on federal income tax returns, billions of dollars.
*KGBLIF	Useful life for tax purposes of business equipment and structures, years.
KINF	Stock of inventories, non-farm, billions of 1958 dollars.
KLRA	Capital–labor ratio (*KNB/MH*).

KNB	Net business fixed capital stock, billions of 1958 dollars.
KYRA	Capital–output ratio ($KNB/XGNP$).
*LA	Armed forces, millions of persons.
LC1	Civilian labor force, millions of persons.
LC17	Civilian labor force at full employment, millions of persons.
LPC	Labor force participation rate, decimal fraction.
M1	Money 1 = demand deposits + currency, billions of dollars.
M2S	Money 2 = Money 1 + time deposits excluding large certificates of deposit, billions of dollars.
MC	Currency held by public, billions of dollars.
*MCR	Ratio of currency to money stock ($MC/M2S$), decimal fraction.
MDD	Demand deposits, billions of dollars.
MH	Total man-hours, private sector, billions of hours.
MH7	Total man-hours at full employment, private sector, billions of hours.
MMR	Money multiplier [$= M2S/(RESU + RB)$ pre-war and $M2S/RESU$ post-war].
*MTCD	Large certificates of deposit, billions of dollars.
MTD	Time deposits, billions of dollars.
MTDR	Ratio of time deposits net of large certificates of deposit to money supply ($MTDS/M2S$), decimal fraction.
MTDS	Time deposits less large certificates of deposit ($MTD - MTCD$), billions of dollars.
*MTOAS$	Maximum annual wages and salaries subject to OASDHI tax, dollars.
MV1	Income velocity ($M1/XGNP\$$).
MV2S	Income velocity ($M2S/XGNP\$$).
*N	Population, total, millions of persons.
NBUC	Number of beneficiaries receiving unemployment compensation (state), millions of persons.

*NF	Population, non-farm, millions of persons.
*NIT	Population, ages 5–18, millions of persons.
*NNI	Total non-institutional population, millions of persons.
OASB$	Tax base for contributions to OASDHI programs, billions of dollars.
*OASR	Tax rate for contributions to OASDHI programs, percent.
PCA	Deflator for consumer expenditures on automobiles, 1958 = 1.000.
PCE	Deflator for consumer expenditures, 1958 = 1.000.
PCND	Deflator for consumer non-durable goods, 1958 = 1.000.
PCOD	Deflator for other consumer durables, 1958 = 1.000.
PCS	Deflator for consumer services, 1958 = 1.000.
PFEX	Deflator for exports, 1958 = 1.000.
*PFIM	Deflator for imports, 1958 = 1.000.
PGF	Deflator for federal purchases, 1958 = 1.000.
PGGF	Deflator for federal expenditures on goods and services, excluding wages and salaries of government workers, 1958 = 1.000.
PGGSL	Deflator for state and local expenditures on goods and services, excluding wages and salaries of government workers, 1958 = 1.000.
PGSL	Deflator for state and local goods and services, 1958 = 1.000.
PHGIN	Deflator for non-farm residential structures investment, 1958 = 1.000.
PIGB	Deflator for business fixed investment, 1958 = 1.000.
PIGPD	Deflator for gross private domestic investment, 1958 = 1.000.
PROD	Man-hour productivity (XNR/MH).

PXGNP	Deflator for *GNP*, 1958 = 1.000.
PXGNP1	Unconstrained estimate of deflator for gross national product, 1958 = 1.000.
PXGNPR	Index of permanent price level, 1958 = 1.000.
*PXGNPRT	Index of permanent price level, trend value, 1958 = 1.000.
PXNR	Deflator for gross private non-residential product, 1958 = 1.000.
PXNR1	Unconstrained estimate of deflator for gross private non-residential product, 1958 = 1.000.
PXNRNT	Deflator for gross private non-residential product, net of indirect business taxes, 1958 = 1.000.
PXNRNT1	Unconstrained regression estimate of deflator for gross private non-residential product, net of indirect business taxes, 1958 = 1.000.
PXP	Deflator for private *GNP*, 1958 = 1.000.
*PYFNW	Deflator for income originating in federal civilian employment, excluding work relief, 1958 = 1.000.
PYHR	Deflator for housing rent, 1958 = 1.000.
*PYLA	Deflator for income originating in military employment, 1958 = 1.000.
PYSLNW	Deflator for income originating in state and local government, excluding work relief, 1958 = 1.000.
Q4	Implicit rental price of capital goods, decimal fraction.
QWRAT	Ratio of rental price of capital to money wage ($Q4/W$).
RB	Member bank borrowing from Federal Reserve Banks, billions of dollars.
*RD	Federal Reserve Bank discount rate, decimal fraction.
*RDISC	Discount rate in rental price of capital, decimal fraction.
RESF	Member bank free reserves, billions of dollars.

RESRD	Member bank required reserves for demand deposits, billions of dollars.
RESRT	Member bank required reserves for time deposits, billions of dollars.
*RESU	Member bank unborrowed reserves, billions of dollars.
RESX	Member bank excess reserves, billions of dollars.
*RFNDL$	Federal personal tax refunds in succeeding year from NIPA, billions of dollars.
RL	Long-term interest rate, private, Moody's corporate average, decimal fraction.
RLM1	Durand one-year commercial bond rate, decimal faction.
RLM1X1	One-year bond rate expected next year, decimal fraction.
RLM1X2	One-year bond rate expected two years hence, decimal fraction.
RLM1X3	One-year bond rate expected three years hence, decimal fraction.
RLM1X4	One-year bond rate expected four years hence, decimal fraction.
RLM1X4A	Geometric average of expected one-year bond rates over next four years, decimal fraction.
RLM5	Durand five-year commercial bond rate, decimal fraction.
RLP1	Term premium on one-year bond relative to commercial paper, decimal fraction.
RLP4	Term premium on five-year bond relative to a one-year bond, decimal fraction.
*RQ	Maximum rate of interest payable on time deposits under regulation *Q*, decimal fraction.
*RRDB	Effective reserve ratio on member bank demand deposits, decimal fraction.
*RRT	Member bank required reserve ratio on time deposits, decimal fraction.

RS	Short-term interest rate, private, commercial paper, 4–6 months, decimal fraction.
RSGB	Interest rate on three-month Treasury bills, decimal fraction.
RSX1	Expected interest rate on commercial paper six months hence, decimal fraction.
SAVRATE	Personal saving ratio (*SP$/YPD$*), percent.
SHLAB	Share of labor income in national income, percent.
SHOTH	Share of income other than labor and corporate profits in national income, percent.
SHPRO	Share of corporate profits in national income, percent.
SP$	Personal saving, billions of dollars.
*SRD	Ratio of total demand deposits to member bank demand deposits subject to reserve requirement, decimal fraction.
*SRT	Ratio of total time deposits (less large certificates of deposit) to member bank time deposits (less large certificates of deposit) subject to reserve requirement, decimal fraction.
*SUB$	Subsidies less current surplus of government enterprises, billions of dollars.
*SUBF$	Subsidies less current surplus of federal government enterprises, billions of dollars.
*SUBSL$	Subsidies less current surplus of state and local government enterprises, billions of dollars.
*SW$	Wage accruals less disbursements, billions of dollars.
*TIME2	Linear trend, 1924–on, 1924 = 1.0.
*TIME3	Linear trend, 1924–40, 1924 = 1.0.
*TIME5	Linear trend, 1949–on, 1949 = 26.0.
*TPB$	Transfer payments from business, billions of dollars.
TPG$	Transfer payments from government, billions of dollars.

*TPGFF$	Federal government transfer payments to foreigners (net), billions of dollars.
*TPGFO$	Federal transfer payments to persons, other than unemployment compensation, billions of dollars.
*TPGO$	Transfer payments from government excluding unemployment compensation, billions of dollars.
*TPPF$	Transfer payments to foreigners, billions of dollars.
*TPSLG$	Transfer payments from state and local governments, billions of dollars.
TPUC$	Transfer payments for unemployment compensation, billions of dollars.
*TXBR	Tax rate on business income.
TXC$	Total corporate taxes, billions of dollars.
TXCF$	Federal corporate taxes, billions of dollars.
TXCFI$	Federal corporate taxes plus investment tax credits, billions of dollars.
*TXCQE$	Equivalent federal corporate tax exemption, i.e., exemption which makes application of top-bracket rate to income minus exemption equivalent to application of progressive rate structure to total income, billions of dollars.
*TXCR	Federal corporate tax rate (statutory top-bracket rate), decimal fraction.
*TXCSL$	State and local corporate taxes, billions of dollars.
*TXEPF$	Federal personal income tax exemption per capita (statutory exemptions weighted by relative proportions of appropriate groups in total population), dollars.
TXI$	Indirect business taxes, billions of dollars.
TXIF$	Federal indirect business taxes, billions of dollars.
*TXISL$	State and local indirect business taxes, billions of dollars.
TXOAS$	Employer and employee contributions to OASDHI programs, billions of dollars.

TXOASE$	Employee contributions to OASDHI programs, billions of dollars.
TXP$	Total personal taxes, billions of dollars.
TXPF$	Federal personal taxes, billions of dollars.
TXPFR$	Federal personal taxes plus current year refunds less succeeding year refunds, billions of dollars.
TXPSL$	State and local personal taxes, billions of dollars.
TXR50	Effective federal personal tax rate, $50,000 bracket, percent.
TXRD	Statutory tax rate on dividends for income of $50,000, decimal fraction.
TXRPF	Average federal personal income tax rate for $2,000–$4,000 bracket, percent.
TXRW	Tax rate on personal income, decimal fraction.
TXS$	Total contributions to social insurance programs, billions of dollars.
TXSFO$	Contributions to federal social insurance (other than OASDHI and unemployment), billions of dollars.
TXSSL$	Contributions to social insurance, state and local, billions of dollars.
TXUN$	Contributions to unemployment insurance programs, billions of dollars.
U1	Unemployment as percent of civilian labor force.
U7	Full-employment unemployment rate, set equal to 4 percent in current work.
UN1	Number of unemployed in civilian labor force, millions of persons.
UNCR	Tax rate for contributions to unemployment insurance programs, percent.
UTMH	Utilization rate of full-employment private man-hours, decimal fraction.
UTXNR7	Utilization rate of full-employment output, increasing returns, decimal fraction.

UTXNR7C	Utilization rate of full-employment output, constant returns, decimal fraction.
UTXNR8	Utilization rate of potential output, increasing returns, decimal fraction.
UTXNR8C	Utilization rate of potential output, constant returns, decimal fraction.
UTXNR9	Utilization rate of capacity output, increasing returns, decimal fraction.
UTXNR9C	Utilization rate of capacity output, constant returns, decimal fraction.
W	Money wage rate, private sector, before tax, dollars per hour.
W1	After-tax money wage rate, entire economy, dollars per hour.
W3	After-tax money wage rate, private sector, dollars per hour.
W17	After-tax money wage rate at full employment, total economy, dollars per hour.
*WHT1	Ratio of private employment to total civilian employment at full employment (derived from a regression of the ratio of actual private employment to actual total civilian employment on the unemployment rate and a time trend).
*WHTACAM	Weight for accelerated amortization in rental price of capital identity, decimal fraction.
*WHTDB	Weight for declining-balance depreciation in rental price of capital identity, decimal fraction.
*WHTSL	Weight for straight-line depreciation in rental price of capital identity, decimal fraction.
*WHTSYD	Weight for sum-of-years-digits depreciation in rental price of capital identity, decimal fraction.
*WT	Share of gross investment in non-farm dwelling units from current year housing starts, decimal fraction.
*XF	Gross farm product, billions of 1958 dollars.
XGNP	Gross national product, billions of 1958 dollars.

XGNP$	Gross national product, billions of dollars.
XN$	Net national product, billions of dollars.
XNPR	Permanent income per capita, billions of 1958 dollars per person.
*XNPRT	Permanent income per capita, trend value, billions of 1958 dollars per person.
XNR	Gross private non-residential product, billions of 1958 dollars.
XNR$	Gross private non-residential product, billions of dollars.
XNR7	Full-employment gross private non-residential output, increasing returns, billions of 1958 dollars.
XNR7C	Full-employment gross private non-residential output, constant returns, billions of 1958 dollars.
XNR8	Potential gross private non-residential output, increasing returns, billions of 1958 dollars.
XNR8C	Potential gross private non-residential output, constant returns, billions of 1958 dollars.
XNR9	Capacity gross private non-residential output, increasing returns, billions of 1958 dollars.
XNR9C	Capacity gross private non-residential output, constant returns, billions of 1958 dollars.
XP	Private gross national product, billions of 1958 dollars.
XP$	Private gross national product, billions of dollars.
YC$	Corporate profits plus *IVA* (*YCB$* + *IVAC$*), billions of dollars.
YCB$	Corporate profits (before *IVA* and taxes), billions of dollars.
YCBT$	Corporate profits (before *IVA* and after tax), billions of dollars.
YCFC$	Corporate cash flow, billions of dollars.
YCFCG$	Corporate profits before tax (including *IVA*) plus corporate capital consumption allowances, billions of dollars.

YD$	Dividends, billions of dollars.
*YFGWR$	Income originating in federal government work relief, billions of dollars.
*YFWR	Income originating in federal government work relief, billions of 1958 dollars.
*YGF	Income originating in federal government, billions of 1958 dollars.
*YGF$	Income originating in federal government, billions of dollars.
*YGSL	Income originating in state and local government, billions of 1958 dollars.
YGSL$	Income originating in state and local government, billions of dollars.
*YHR	Housing rent (income originating), billions of 1958 dollars.
*YIC$	Net interest paid by consumers, billions of dollars.
*YIG$	Net interest paid by government, billions of dollars.
*YIGF$	Net interest paid by federal government, billions of dollars.
*YIGSL$	Net interest paid by state and local governments, billions of dollars.
YL$	Private labor income (compensation of private employees + imputed labor income of proprietors), billions of dollars.
*YLA	Military wages and salaries, billions of 1958 dollars.
YN$	National income, billions of dollars.
YPD	Disposable personal income, billions of 1958 dollars.
YPD$	Disposable personal income, billions of dollars.
YPE$	Personal income, billions of dollars.
YSLWR	Income originating in state and local government work relief, billions of 1958 dollars.
YSLWR$	Income originating in state and local government work relief, billions of dollars.

CHAPTER 2

Aggregate Demand

1. Introduction

All components of aggregate demand are endogenous except for
nominal exports and federal expenditures. The major sectors distinguished in the model are consumer goods and services, business
investment, residential construction, government spending, and
foreign trade. For each sector we discuss general principles and
specification before presenting the estimated equations as a group at
the end of the section.

The following statistics are presented for the estimated equations
in this and later chapters: ($\bar{R}^2$) coefficient of multiple determination
adjusted for degrees of freedom; ($\bar{S}_e$) standard error of estimate
corrected for degrees of freedom; (DW) Durbin–Watson statistic.
The t-ratios for the estimated regression coefficients are given in
parentheses under the coefficients. When an equation is estimated on
the hypothesis of autocorrelated disturbances, the equation includes
a term for the estimated lagged disturbance $\hat{u}_{-1}$ with the associated
estimate of ρ, the autocorrelation parameter. Neither DW nor $\bar{R}^2$
statistics are shown for these equations. Equations estimated by
two-stage least-squares are denoted 2SLS.

Estimated coefficients are carried to five or six decimal places in
order to reduce round-off error in model calculations. In many cases
they may actually be significant (in the numerical sense) only to two
or three places and should not be taken to imply any greater accuracy.

It should also be stressed that the equations of the model are the
final outcome of considerable experimentation with respect to functional form, lag distribution, included variables, alternative proxies,
and so forth. The choice of the final equations was frequently a

compromise between goodness-of-fit and judgmental criteria involving prior constraints on coefficients suggested by economic theory. Although *t*-statistics are shown for the estimated coefficients, they should be interpreted with caution owing to the large amount of statistical experimentation which was undertaken.

2. Consumer Goods and Services [1]

Consumer purchases are dissaggregated into four categories: non-durables, services, automobiles, and other durable goods. Absence of money illusion is assumed in all cases.

The equations for non-durables and services include real disposable income and lagged expenditure as explanatory variables. As is well known, this specification is consistent with either a habit persistence [Brown (1952)] or permanent income [Friedman (1957)] hypothesis. Because the Chow test led us to reject the hypothesis of equivalent pre-war and post-war structures, we adopted separate functions for the two samples. The pre-war equations are corrected for autocorrelation in the residuals.

Our estimated marginal propensities to consume differ rather markedly between the pre-war and post-war eras, especially in the case of services. For both non-durables and services, current income exerts a stronger influence on pre-war than on post-war expenditures, while lagged consumption received greater weight in the post-war than in the pre-war period. The unusually sharp and prolonged reductions in income growth during the 1930's must largely account for these differences. Consumers may be able to substantially maintain past spending levels when they experience moderate, temporary declines in income growth, as in the post-war period. But if reductions in income are large and persistent, past consumption habits may have to be sacrificed, and expenditures will be more closely attuned to current income.

Acquisitions of automobiles and other consumer durable goods are treated as personal investment decisions. The desired stock of automobiles is assumed to depend on real income, relative prices and

---

[1] Margaret Oyaas participated extensively in the work on this sector.

employment,

$$CAK^* = a_0[(YPD\$ - TPG\$)/PCE]^{a_1}$$
$$\times [PCA(0.25 + RL)/PCE]^{a_2}(U1)^{a_3}. \tag{2.1}$$

(In this and subsequent equations we have omitted the time subscript for convenience, so that unsubscripted variables always refer to the current period.) Transfer payments are subtracted from disposable income on the hypothesis that transfers are not used for automobile purchases. The price of automobile services follows a rental price formulation analogous to that discussed more fully below in relation to business fixed investment. Thus, instead of the price of a new automobile (PCA) entering independently, it is multiplied by the sum of the depreciation rate, set at 0.25 per year,[2] and the long-term interest rate, RL. The unemployment rate is included as a proxy for job uncertainty, on the hypothesis that employed persons with maintained incomes may nonetheless decide to postpone purchases of durables when unemployment is high.

When combined with the stock adjustment hypothesis,

$$CAK/CAK_{-1} = (CAK^*/CAK_{-1})^{a_3}, \tag{2.2}$$

equation (2.1) leads to a logarithmic estimating form which is linear in the parameters. A dummy variable ($DCDD$) was added to allow for credit restrictions during the Korean War and the shift to lengthened installment contracts thereafter. The equation was fitted to the entire sample but allowance was made for a shift in the intercept term after World War II ($DUMMY1$).

The specification of the equation for other consumer durables is basically the same as for automobiles. The principal difference is that the price of new durables ($PCOD$), instead of the rental price on the

---

[2] This rate also appears in identity (2.10). A depreciation rate of 0.25 on a declining balance basis is consistent with an eight-year useful life. The corresponding depreciation rate for other durable goods [identity (2.12)] is 0.1667. It is twice the weighted-average straight-line depreciation rate for eight categories of consumer goods as calculated from data in Goldsmith (1955). The stock series CAK and $CODK$ were calculated for this study by applying equations (2.10) and (2.12) to annual estimates of gross expenditures since 1896.

services of durable goods, enters the relative price variable. This means that purchases of other durables (primarily furniture and household equipment) are estimated to be unaffected by changes in interest rates, unlike automobile purchases.

The consumption sector is completed with some stock-flow identities and definitional relationships.

2.1. Estimated Equations: Personal Consumption Expenditures (CONS)

(1) *Consumer Non-durables*
     1924–40

$$CND = 32.9210 + 0.29477\,(YPD\$/PCE) + 0.11751\,CND_{-1}$$
$$\quad\;\;(2.6934)\quad(8.2870)\qquad\qquad\qquad(1.0725)$$
$$\quad\;\; + 0.95048\,\hat{u}_{-1};\tag{2.3}$$
$$\bar{S}_e = 1.254.$$

1949–66

$$CND = 15.081 + 0.20988\,(YPD\$/PCE) + 0.42683\,CND_{-1};\quad(2.4)$$
$$\quad\;\;(4.78)\quad\;\;(7.38)\qquad\qquad\qquad(4.84)$$
$$R^2 = 0.998,\qquad \bar{S}_e = 0.865,\qquad DW = 2.16.$$

(2) *Consumer Services*
     1924–40

$$CS = 18.5964 + 0.15656\,(YPD\$/PCE) + 0.19346\,CS_{-1}$$
$$\quad\;\;(2.85)\quad\;\;(7.09)\qquad\qquad\qquad(4.63)$$
$$\quad\;\; + 0.52274\,\hat{u}_{-1};\tag{2.5}$$
$$\bar{S}_e = 0.803.$$

1949–66

$$CS = -3.9402 + 0.067161\,(YPD\$/PCE) + 0.8769\,CS_{-1};\quad(2.6)$$
$$\quad\;\;(4.47)\quad\;\;(3.41)\qquad\qquad\qquad(16.15)$$
$$\bar{R}^2 = 0.999,\qquad \bar{S}_e = 0.578,\qquad DW = 1.92.$$

(3) *Investment in Automobiles*
     1924–40, 1949–66

$$\ln CAK - \ln CAK_{-1} = -1.2646 + 0.44822$$
$$\qquad\qquad (6.1322)\ (7.2577)$$
$$\qquad\qquad \times \ln [(YPD\$ - TPG\$)/PCE]$$
$$\qquad\qquad -0.31995 \ln [PCA(0.25 + RL)/PCE]$$
$$\qquad\qquad (2.9238)$$
$$\qquad\qquad +0.10941\ DUMMY1 + 0.05416\ DCDD$$
$$\qquad\qquad (2.9138) \qquad\qquad (3.8569)$$
$$\qquad\qquad -0.04784 \ln U1 - 0.4162 \ln CAK_{-1}; \quad (2.7)$$
$$\qquad\qquad (4.0832) \qquad\qquad (12.2117)$$

$\bar{R}^2 = 0.9201, \qquad \bar{S}_e = 0.02395, \qquad DW = 1.76.$

(4) *Investment, Other Consumer Durables*
     1924–40, 1949–66

$$\ln CODK - \ln CODK_{-1} = -0.3444 - 0.01613 \ln U1$$
$$\qquad\qquad (7.7843)\ (5.0276)$$
$$\qquad\qquad -0.00344\ DCDD$$
$$\qquad\qquad (0.9263)$$
$$\qquad\qquad +0.24195 \ln (YPD\$/PCE)$$
$$\qquad\qquad (15.2926)$$
$$\qquad\qquad -0.08150 \ln (PCOD/PCE)$$
$$\qquad\qquad (1.6726)$$
$$\qquad\qquad -0.20736 \ln CODK_{-1}; \qquad\qquad (2.8)$$
$$\qquad\qquad (14.0509)$$

$\bar{R}^2 = 0.9446, \qquad \bar{S}_e = 0.0068, \qquad DW = 1.18.$

(5) *Consumption Identities*

$$CAK = \exp (\ln CAK), \qquad\qquad\qquad\qquad (2.9)$$

$$CA = CAK - 0.75\ CAK_{-1}, \qquad\qquad\qquad (2.10)$$

$$CODK = \exp (\ln CODK), \qquad\qquad\qquad\quad (2.11)$$

$$COD = CODK - 0.8333\ CODK_{-1}, \qquad\qquad (2.12)$$

$$CE = CA + COD + CS + CND. \qquad\qquad\quad (2.13)$$

3. Business Investment

3.1. Business Fixed Investment

The basic approach to our analysis of fixed investment demand was discussed in Chapter 1. It will be recalled that the labor and investment demand functions (1.6) and (1.7) share common parameters from the production function (1.1). This triplet of equations was estimated jointly by a sequential procedure. The labor demand function was fitted by ordinary least squares (OLS) and the estimated values of the underlying production parameters ($\hat{\alpha}$, $\hat{\beta}$ and $\hat{\gamma}$) were inferred from the estimated coefficients of the labor function. These estimated production parameters were then imposed on the investment regression, and the latter was used to determine the expectations and adjustment parameters.

The procedure may be clarified by reference to equation (1.7), repeated here for convenience and using full variable names as coded in the model,

$$KNB = \{[(\alpha/\beta)^{\beta} A^{-1}]^{1/(\alpha+\beta)} [(Q4/W)^*]^{-\beta/(\alpha+\beta)}$$
$$\times (XNR^*)^{1/(\alpha+\beta)} e^{-[\gamma/(\alpha+\beta)]\eta}\}^{\lambda_2} (KNB_{-1})^{1-\lambda_2}.$$

The expression for desired capital stock in the first term of the function depends on the production parameters and on the parameters entering the expressions for expected output and relative factor prices. Expected output and factor prices were assumed to be weighted geometric averages of current and past outputs and prices, respectively. The investment function was converted to log-linear form and a screening procedure was employed to determine that combination of expectations weights and adjustment parameter (λ_2) which minimized the sum of squared residuals under the constraints of the given parameters.

The factor demand system was estimated both with and without the constraint of constant returns to scale of production. The constant-returns version performs better in complete model simulations (see Chapter 10) and is chosen as the basic specification of the model. The estimated constant-returns investment function (2.15) implies that expected output equals current output and expected price equals lagged price. The estimated adjustment speed for net capital stock is

0.175. This may appear low, but it should be remembered that it refers only to net investment. Replacement needs are assumed to be equal to current depreciation and to be met without lag. Replacement represents the bulk of gross investment expenditure and hence the combined speed of adjustment is much greater than for net investment alone. The alternative investment function involving increasing returns is included for comparison as equation (2.15a).

The estimated values of the Cobb–Douglas production parameters, as inferred from the labor demand function and imposed on the investment function, are discussed in Chapter 3, section 2.

The factor demand system comprising equations (1.6) and (1.7) involves nonlinear restrictions across the parameters of the two functions. Our two-stage procedure for estimation of the investment function is an inexpensive and flexible method for honoring these constraints while preserving linearity in the estimating forms. As shown in our previous paper [Coen and Hickman (1970)], the sequential estimates for an earlier version of the system were virtually indistinguishable from direct estimates of the joint nonlinear system using full-information maximum-likelihood procedures. Since the present system differs from the earlier one only in the use of different time series for the capital stock and the rental price variables, it is likely that the same observation would hold for it.

Our neo-classical derivation of the investment function is a modification of the approach pioneered by Jorgenson (1963). As compared with his formulation, ours is similar in assuming a Cobb–Douglas production function, but it differs in several other respects. We assume that firms minimize production costs in their input decisions, which is less restrictive than Jorgenson's assumption of profit maximization in perfectly competitive product markets. (Operationally this means that our relative price variable is the ratio of the rental price of capital to the money wage rate instead of to the product price.) Our formulation of investment dynamics also differs from his. Finally, and most important, is our recognition of the interdependent nature of input decisions and the need for constrained joint estimation of the labor and investment functions.[3]

---

[3] Interdependence of inputs was also recognized independently by Nadiri and Rosen (1969), but they did not impose the constraint when estimating their system.

The model for fixed investment is completed by the identity relating gross investment expenditure and capital stock,

$$IGB = KNB - (1 - \delta)KNB_{-1}, \tag{2.14}$$

where δ is the depreciation rate. This equation is not a regression but rather the identity used to generate the capital stock series itself by the perpetual inventory method. A straight-line depreciation rate was first computed as a weighted average of the annual depreciation rates implicit in the Department of Commerce data on depreciation and gross capital stock. In accord with the usual practice, this straight-line rate was then doubled to yield the declining balance rate δ to be applied in equation (2.14). Because of a shift in the composition of investment toward shorter-lived units after World War II, separate depreciation rates of 0.1071 and 0.1390 were calculated for 1924–40 and 1949–66, respectively.

In equation (2.14) capital stock is measured net of depreciation. We view the measurement of capital net of depreciation as a method of vintage weighting to allow for embodied technical progress. That is to say, if δ includes an allowance for obsolescence as well as deterioration as ours does, then measuring capital in depreciated units is equivalent to measuring it in Solow-type (1959) productivity units, except that a trend term for the rate of embodied technical progress must be included in the production and factor demand functions in the former case, as explained in Hickman (1965, pp. 39–41). Accordingly, separate trend terms for the pre-war and post-war periods are included in the demand functions for labor and capital, since the value of δ differs in the two periods.

3.2. Inventory Investment[4]

Non-farm inventory investment is an endogenous variable in the model, whereas farm inventory investment is not. Inventory investment is notoriously difficult to predict even in a quarterly model, and

---

[4] Jay Chambers and Edward J. Ray participated in the specification and estimation of the inventory investment function.

the difficulties are compounded in an annual model because of the crudeness of the time unit. The best equations that we have been able to devise are standard stock-adjustment formulations. In addition to final sales, the post-war equation includes the real value of gross obligations of the Department of Defense as an important explanatory variable. This variable is a proxy for new orders of defense goods. As is well known, defense goods must often be ordered far in advance of their final delivery to the government, and the gradual accumulation of value-added in the lengthy production process is reflected in private inventory investment during the gestation period. The orders variable accounts in part at least for that portion of inventory change related to defense production in anticipation of final delivery and hence not yet reflected in the final sales variable.

3.3. Estimated Equations: Business Investment (INV)

(1) Net Business Fixed Investment Demand
     (constant returns production function constraint)
     1925–40, 1950–66

$$\ln KNB - \ln KNB_{-1} = -0.18523 + 0.6201 \, DUMMY1 + 0.17585$$
$$(8.1196) \quad (3.2878) (9.8842)$$
$$\times [-0.06136 \, DUMMY1 + \ln XNR$$
$$-0.68366 \ln (Q4/W)_{-1} - 0.01550 \, TIME3$$
$$-0.01959 \, TIME5 - \ln KNB_{-1}]$$
$$+0.84185 \, \hat{u}_{-1}; (2.15)$$

$\bar{S}_e = 0.0085.$

(1a) Net Business Fixed Investment Demand
      (increasing returns production function)
      1925–40, 1950–66

$$\ln KNB - \ln KNB_{-1} = 0.05884 \, DUMMY1 + 0.19824 \, [-0.17064$$
$$(4.3153) (9.1583)$$
$$+0.79364 \ln XNR - 0.77565 \ln (Q4/W)_{-1}$$
$$-0.01626 \, TIME3 - 0.01547 \, TIME5$$
$$-\ln KNB_{-1}] + 0.83894 \, \hat{u}_{-1}; (2.15a)$$

$\bar{S}_e = 0.0090.$

(2) *Inventory Investment*
     1924–40

$IINF = 5.1577 + 0.16569 \,(XNR - XF - IINF) - 0.19006 \,TIME2$
     (1.1892) (7.9042)   (2.2088)
     $- 0.52399 \,KINF_{-1};$ (2.16)
     (5.9185)
$\bar{R}^2 = 0.8092, \qquad \bar{S}_e = 1.4254, \qquad DW = 1.63.$

1950–66

$IINF = 9.1806 + 0.28703 \,(XNR - XF - IINF)$
     (2.7358) (9.9925)
     $+ 0.12592 \,(DODGO\$/PXNR)$
     (3.8058)
     $- 0.72099 \,TIME2 - 0.88024 \,KINF_{-1};$ (2.17)
     (7.7009)   (3.8058)
$\bar{R}^2 = 0.8966, \qquad \bar{S}_e = 1.3563, \qquad DW = 1.52.$

(3) *Investment Identities*

$KNB = \exp\,(\ln KNB),$ (2.18)

$IGB = KNB - 0.8929\,(KNB)_{-1}, \qquad (1924\text{–}40)$ (2.19)

$IGB = KNB - 0.8610\,(KNB)_{-1}, \qquad (1949\text{–}66)$ (2.20)

$KINF = KINF_{-1} + IINF,$ (2.21)

$IGPD = IGB + HGIN + HGIF + IINF + IIF.$ (2.22)

4. Residential Construction[5]

Unlike the preceding equation blocs for consumer expenditure and
business investment, which were systems of demand equations,
residential construction is a function of explicit supply and demand

---

[5] This section is based on Hickman, Hinz and Willig (1973). The housing model was
used in a simulation study of the building cycle in the 1920's and 1930's in Hickman
(1974).

factors in our model. Housing starts and construction expenditures are predicted as part of a self-contained model of the housing market and construction industry.

The model contains four behavioral equations. The first pair relate to the demand and supply for the total stock of dwelling units–the housing market–and together determine the level of housing rent and the number of households or occupied dwelling units. Owner-occupied units are treated as if they are rented by their owners from themselves at an implicit price which is equal to the market-determined rent index. The second pair is concerned with the construction of new dwellings. One equation explains builders' decisions to start construction of new units, and the other predicts the average value of a new start in constant prices. Several identities relate the number and value of new housing starts to residential construction expenditure (value put in place) and to the stock of dwelling units and its constant-dollar value.

4.1. The Rent and Household Equations

The structural demand function for dwelling units to rent is assumed to be of constant elasticity form,

$$HH^D = a_0(PYHR/PCE)^{-a_1}[YPD\$/(HHS)(PCE)]^{a_2}(HHS)(v),$$
(2.23)

where HH is the number of non-farm households (occupied dwelling units); $PYHR$ and PCE are, respectively, indexes of housing rent and consumer prices; $YPD\$$ is disposable personal income in current dollars; HHS is the number of standardized non-farm households; v is a disturbance term; and the superscript D signifies that this is the demand function for dwelling units to occupy.

The standardized household variable HHS is designed to isolate the influence of population change on the demand for dwelling units. It is a weighted sum of the number of persons in each age group in the given year, with the weights given by the "headship rates" (i.e., the ratio of household heads to total population in an age class) of the year 1940.[6] Thus *HHS* takes account of changes in the age composition as well as the size of the population.

If headship rates had remained constant at the 1940 values, the number of actual households in any other year would be equal to *HHS*, assuming that *HHS* < *HU*, where *HU* is the number of housing units in existence. Marked changes in headship rates can and do occur, however, so that the actual number of households in any year may be quite different from the standardized number reflecting demographic influences alone. It is our hypothesis, expressed in equation (2.23), that changes in the propensity to form households, and hence in the ratio of HH^D to *HHS*, are a function of economic determinants. Increases in real disposable income per standardized household are postulated to increase the desire for household formation, whereas increases in the real rental rate on dwelling units are assumed to depress it.

The supply function for dwelling units to rent takes the form

$$HH^S = b_0(PYHR/PCE)^{b_1}(HU)_{-1}(w),\tag{2.24}$$

where *HU* is the number of dwelling units in existence; *w* is a disturbance term; the superscript *S* stands for supply; and the other variables are as defined above. Since rental units may be withheld from the market, the number supplied depends positively on the real rental rate, as well as on the standing stock of dwelling units.

In static equilibrium, the level of rent and the number of households would be jointly determined by the demand and supply of dwelling units and the market clearing condition $HH^D = HH^S$. Thus equations (2.23) and (2.24) could be solved for the equilibrium values of *PYHR* and *HH* as functions only of predetermined variables exogenous to the housing market. Because rents are sticky, however, owing to market imperfections and leases, it will not do to assume equilibrium in the housing market.

It is assumed instead that rent adjusts toward its equilibrium value each period by a constant proportion of the relative discrepancy between the actual level in the previous period and the current

---

[6] Details are given in Appendix F. Our variable is similar to the concept developed by Campbell (1961, 1963).

equilibrium level,[7]

$$PYHR/PYHR_{-1} = (PYHR^e/PYHR_{-1})^{\lambda_4}. \tag{2.25}$$

The expression for the equilibrium value of rent is obtained from the solution of the static supply and demand system (2.23) and (2.24),

$$PYHR^e = (PCE)\{(a_0/b_0)[YPD\$/(HHS)(PCE)]^{a_2} \\ \times (HHS/HU_{-1})(v/w)\}^{1/(a_1+b_1)}. \tag{2.26}$$

Combining (2.25) and (2.26) and converting to logarithms yields the reduced-form estimating equation for rent,

$$\ln PYHR - \ln PYHR_{-1} = c_0 + c_1 \ln [YPD\$/(HHS)(PCE)] \\ + c_2 \ln (HHS/HU_{-1}) \qquad (2.27) \\ + c_3 \ln (PCE/PYHR_{-1}) + c_4 \ln (v/w),$$

with reduced-form coefficients which are mixtures of the structural parameters from (2.25) and (2.26).

On the side of quantity adjustment, we first assume that landlords are price setters and tenants are price takers. Again because of adjustment lags, however, tenants are not necessarily on the demand curve at all times. Accordingly, it is assumed that the actual number of households adjusts partially each period toward the desired quantity as determined by the structural demand function and the current rent established by landlords. That is to say, we assume

$$HH/HH_{-1} = (\overline{HH}^D/HH_{-1})^{\lambda_5}, \tag{2.28}$$

where $\overline{HH}^D$ is the point on the demand curve (2.23) corresponding to the rent level, $\overline{PYHR}$, as set by landlords,

$$\overline{HH}^D = a_0(\overline{PYHR}/PCE)^{-a_1}[YPD\$/(HHS)(PCE)]^{a_2}(HHS)(v). \tag{2.29}$$

---

[7] An alternative specification leading to the same estimation form is based on the assumption that rent changes each period by a constant fraction of the excess demand measured at the current rent level. The alternative specification results in the same estimated structural parameters for equations (2.23) and (2.24), but a different value for the "adjustment" parameter in the reduced-form rent equation (2.27).

Combining (2.28) and (2.29) and converting to logarithms, we obtain the estimating equation

$$\ln HH - \ln HH_{-1} = d_0 - d_1 \ln (\overline{PYHR/PCE})$$
$$+ d_2\{a_2 \ln [YPD\$/(HHS)(PCE)]$$
$$+ \ln (HHS/HH_{-1})\} + d_3 \ln v. \qquad (2.30)$$

4.2. The Residential Construction Equations

The equation for housing starts is a supply function in our model. The typical builder is assumed to be a small entrepreneur who is a price taker in factor markets and who produces dwelling units on speculation rather than to order. The number of new starts depends on the expected profitability of building and selling new units and on the builders' ability to secure production loans.

The builders' production decision may be formalized as follows. Assume a Cobb–Douglas production function for the ith firm,

$$HSPR_i = AK_i^{(1-\alpha)}V_i^\alpha, \qquad i = 1, \ldots, n. \qquad (2.31)$$

$HSPR$ is the number of private housing starts of the ith firm, K is its capital stock, V refers to its variable inputs, and n is the number of firms in the industry. The factor inputs may differ from firm to firm, but all are equally efficient and share the same technology.

Assuming short-run profit maximization, the quantity of starts will be determined by the usual marginal productivity condition,

$$\partial HSPR_i/\partial V_i = \alpha(HSPR_i/V_i) = PHGIN/PNHU^*, \qquad (2.32)$$

where $PHGIN$ is an index of construction costs and $PNHU^*$ is the (average) expected sales price of a new housing unit as viewed by builders.

Taken together, (2.31) and (2.32) imply

$$HSPR_i = AK_i^{(1-\alpha)}[\alpha HSPR_i(PHNU^*/PHGIN)]^\alpha$$
$$= (\alpha^\alpha A)^{1/(1-\alpha)}K_i(PHNU^*/PHGIN)^{\alpha/(1-\alpha)}. \qquad (2.33)$$

Aggregating over the n firms yields

$$HSPR = A_0 K (PHNU^*/PHGIN)^{\alpha/(1-\alpha)}, \qquad (2.34)$$

where

$$A_0 = (\alpha^\alpha A)^{1/(1-\alpha)}.$$

Instead of measuring capital stock directly, we reason as follows. Homebuilding is a labor-intensive process, and the amount of physical capital needed to operate a firm is small, thus making for free and rapid entry into the industry if working capital is available. Hence the aggregate capital stock in the industry in any given year is primarily a function of the number of firms which can secure production loans. If we represent credit availability to builders by the proxy variable (RL/RS), the ratio of the long-term and short-term private interest rates, we may write

$$K = B(RL/RS)^{\beta}_{-k}, \qquad (2.35)$$

where k is a time lag constant. The amount of capital employed in the industry, and hence the number of starts, varies positively with (RL/RS), since the ratio falls as credit tightens and builders are prevented from obtaining construction loans.

The model is completed by adding an expression for the expected sales price,

$$PNIIU^* = C(PYHR/RL)(HH/HU)^{\gamma_1}(YPD\$/HH)^{\gamma_2}. \qquad (2.36)$$

Thus in forming their basic price expectations, builders are assumed to capitalize current market rents on existing dwellings by the long-term interest rate. They will adjust their initial estimates up or down, however, according to the probability of quick sales of finished units to avoid the necessity of price reduction or, equivalently, to avoid the losses of carrying vacant units while awaiting willing buyers. The probability of quick turnover is assumed to depend positively on the lagged occupancy ratio for existing dwelling units and on the level of disposable personal income per household.

Upon substituting (2.35) and (2.36) into (2.34), converting to logs, and adding a disturbance term, we obtain the estimating equation for aggregate housing starts,

$$\ln HSPR = e_0 + e_1 \ln (RL/RS)_{-k} + e_2 \ln [PYHR/(RL)(PHGIN)]$$
$$+ e_3 \ln (HH/HU)_{-1} + e_4 \ln (YPD\$/HH) + w.$$

(2.37)

The rent and occupancy variables appearing in the starts equation provide the links between the housing market and the building industry. The reverse feedback is from housing starts to the stock of dwelling units, as given by identity (2.49). In this relationship, it is assumed that one-half the private units started each year are completed in the following year. Public housing starts (*HSPU*) are given exogenously and are assumed to be completed with a lag of one year, since they are predominantly multi-family units with longer construction times. Allowance is also made for net additions (*HA*) to the housing stock from other sources than new starts. Net additions are given exogenously and may be either positive or negative according to the balance of conversions and demolitions.

Equations (2.27), (2.30), (2.37) and (2.49) form a closed sub-system to determine the time paths of *PYHR, HH, HSPR* and *HU*, for given values of the other variables. The sub-system is useful for some purposes, but it must be augmented with an equation to determine the average value of new housing starts in constant dollars (*HCCA*) if the housing sector is to be incorporated in a macro-economic model. In this way the constant dollar value of new residential construction can be determined endogenously and used as an input to the aggregate demand sector of the macroeconomic model, which in turn allows for feedback to the housing sector via the income and price variables in the housing and construction equations.

The average value of a new start in constant prices is made a function of real disposable income per household [$YPD\$/(PCE)(HH)$], the short-term interest rate (*RS*), the average size of non-farm households (*NF/HH*), where *NF* is the non-farm population, and the value of a unit of the existing housing stock (*HKN/HU*), where *HKN* is the value of the housing stock in constant dollars,

$$\ln HCCA = g_0 + g_1 \ln [YPD\$/(PCE)(HH)] - g_2 \ln RS$$
$$+ g_3 \ln (NF/HH) + g_4 \ln (HKN/HU)_{-1} + w,$$

(2.38)

where w is a disturbance term. This equation contains two underlying demand factors in real income per household and average household size. In accordance with the philosophy of the model, these variables are assumed to reflect the builders' views of the potential real values per dwelling unit that will be demanded by consumers. The short-term interest rate reflects the cost and availability of credit to builders and influences their decision about the quality of construction to undertake. Finally, the value per new dwelling unit is assumed positively related to that of the existing housing stock, reflecting the long-run trend of real capital per dwelling unit.

Three identities complete the constant-dollar stocks and flows of the housing model. The first, equation (2.50), shows that the real value of the housing stock is augmented by gross private investment in new non-farm housing units ($HGIND$), gross public investment in new residential structures (HGP), and gross expenditures for additions and alterations on non-farm housing units ($HGAA$), and is diminished by depreciation on the existing stock at the annual rate of two percent.

Since residential construction is measured by value put in place in the national income accounts, equation (2.43) is necessary to convert value of starts into value in place, with the latter a weighted average of the value of starts in the same and the previous year to reflect construction lags. Finally, identity (2.44) defines real investment in non-farm residential structures ($HGIN$) to be the sum of construction of new non-farm dwelling units ($HGIND$), expenditures for additions and alterations ($HGAA$), construction of non-housekeeping units ($HGNH$), brokers' commissions on sale of structures ($HGBC$), and net purchases of used structures ($HGUS$). In the present model only $HGIND$ is explained endogenously, but it accounts for the bulk of fixed investment in residential structures as measured in the GNP accounts.

The rent and household equations were estimated sequentially. Equation (2.39) was estimated by OLS, and the predicted value of rent from the equation was then used as the regressor $\widehat{PYHR}$ in the household equation. If the original series on $PYHR$ had been used as a regressor, it would have been correlated with the disturbance term in equation (2.30), as can be seen from the stochastic specification of equation (2.27).[8] Note also that a_2, the income elasticity for dwelling

---

[8] Simultaneous equation bias is not a serious problem for the rent equation itself, since the right-hand variables are exogenous to the housing bloc or predetermined.

units in equation (2.23), is a parameter in the reduced-form equations for rent (2.27) and households (2.30). To achieve consistency in the latter equations, the estimated value of a_2 implicit in (2.27) was imposed on the bracketed term in (2.30). Since credit rationing was presumably an unimportant factor in the 1930's owing to the excess liquidity of the banking system, the (RL/RS) term in equation (2.41) is multiplied by a dummy variable $(DRLRG)$ which is zero during 1930–40 and one otherwise. The $DHOUS$ dummy allows for the influence of regulation X on housing starts during 1950–51. Finally, because of evidence of serial correlation in the original estimates, all four equations were re-estimated on the assumption of first-order autocorrelation of the disturbances.

4.3. Estimated Equations: Housing and Residential Construction (HOUS)

(1) *Rent*
1925–40, 1950–66

$$\ln PYHR - \ln PYHR_{-1} = -0.1114 + 0.1336$$
$$(1.1048)\ (2.4708)$$
$$\times \ln\,[YPD\$/(HHS)(PCE)]$$
$$+0.7381 \ln\,(HHS/HU_{-1})$$
$$(3.0950)$$
$$+0.2673 \ln\,(PCE/PYHR_{-1})$$
$$(5.2475)$$
$$+0.8025\ \hat{u}_{-1}; \qquad (2.39)$$

$$\bar{S}_e = 0.0138.$$

(2) *Non-farm Households*
1925–40, 1950–66

$$\ln HH - \ln HH_{-1} = -0.0781 - 0.0050 \ln\,(\widehat{PYHR/PCE})$$
$$(3.5034)\ (1.2740)$$
$$+0.3350\,\{0.1810 \ln\,[YPD\$/(HHS)(PCE)]$$
$$(5.9695)$$
$$+\ln\,(HHS/HH_{-1})\} + 0.9655\ \hat{u}_{-1}; \qquad (2.40)$$

$$\bar{S}_e = 0.0030.$$

(3) *Non-farm Private Housing Starts*
     1925–40, 1950–66

$$\ln HSPR = -4.14059 + 0.71317 \ln [PYHR/(RL)(PHGIN)]$$
$$\qquad\qquad (3.6998) \quad (3.1702)$$
$$\qquad\quad + 1.69815 \ln (YPD\$/HH) + 12.7564 \ln (HH/HU)_{-1}$$
$$\qquad\qquad (10.4804) \qquad\qquad\qquad (5.0839)$$
$$\qquad\quad + 0.12607\, DHOUS + 0.46856\,[0.5 \ln (RL/RS)$$
$$\qquad\qquad (2.3313) \qquad\qquad (2.3717)$$
$$\qquad\quad + 0.5 \ln (RL/RS)_{-1}](DRLRG) + 0.6262\, \hat{u}_{-1}; \qquad (2.41)$$
$$\bar{S}_e = 0.1076.$$

(4) *Value Per Non-farm Private Housing Start*
     1925–40, 1950–66

$$\ln HCCA = -2.40505 + 0.63526 \ln [YPD\$/(PCE)(HH)]$$
$$\qquad\qquad (3.5205) \quad (4.1429)$$
$$\qquad\quad - 0.05412 \ln RS + 1.73273 \ln (NF/HH)$$
$$\qquad\qquad (2.2064) \qquad\qquad (3.8168)$$
$$\qquad\quad + 0.63324 \ln (HKN/HU)_{-1} + 0.3139\, \hat{u}_{-1}; \qquad (2.42)$$
$$\qquad\qquad (1.7322)$$
$$\bar{S}_e = 0.0435.$$

(5) *Housing Identities*

$$HGIND = (1 - WT_{-1})(HCCA_{-1})(HSPR_{-1})$$
$$\qquad\quad + (WT)(HCCA)(HSPR), \qquad\qquad\qquad (2.43)$$

$$HGIN = HGIND + HGAA + HGNH + HGBC + HGUS, \quad (2.44)$$

$$HSPR = \exp (\ln HSPR), \qquad\qquad\qquad\qquad (2.45)$$

$$PYHR = \exp (\ln PYHR), \qquad\qquad\qquad\qquad (2.46)$$

$$HH = \exp (\ln HH), \qquad\qquad\qquad\qquad\qquad (2.47)$$

$$HCCA = \exp (\ln HCCA), \qquad\qquad\qquad\qquad (2.48)$$

$$HU = HU_{-1} + HA + HSPU_{-1} + 0.5\, HSPR + 0.5\, HSPR_{-1}, \quad (2.49)$$

$$HKN = 0.98\, HKN_{-1} + HGIND + HGP + HGAA, \qquad (2.50)$$

$$HO = HH/HU_{-1}. \qquad\qquad\qquad\qquad\qquad (2.51)$$

5. Government Purchases of Goods and Services[9]

Federal purchases of goods and services are treated as an exogenous policy instrument in the model, but state and local expenditures are endogenous.

The principle explanatory variables for state and local expenditure are personal income, federal grants-in-aid, and the school-age population. The income variable is relevant both as a source of tax revenue and a determinant of the perceived demand for public services. Grants-in-aid are included on the basis of Osman's (1966, 1968) evidence that federal aid stimulates the state and local functions to which it is directed and is not merely a substitute for state and local funds. School-age population is included to account for the changing educational component of state and local expenditure, again on the hypothesis that school expenditures may independently affect the total. All variables are expressed in real per capita terms, using the implicit deflator for state and local expenditure as the price index.

Extensive statistical experimentation with lag distributions and adjustment hypotheses resulted in the following final specification. First, desired expenditure is related to a weighted average of the incomes, aid, and school-age populations of the preceding two years, with the weights for each variable determined by the data. Second, the desired amount of expenditure is only partially achieved during the current year, so the lagged dependent variable is included on the right-hand side to measure the speed of adjustment. The estimated equation (2.52) implies an adjustment speed of 0.736. Income lagged one year has less weight (31 percent) than income lagged two years, whereas the reverse is true of grants-in-aid (65 percent the first year). School-age population enters only with a one-year lag. A dummy variable shifts the level of the regression in the post-war years, and a time variable is included to capture unexplained elements in the long-standing uptrend in state and local spending per capita.

The government sector is completed with a number of identities. Separate identities for the federal and state and local branches relate income originating in general government to the number of govern-

---

[9] John M. Gemello and Margaret Sims collaborated on the state and local sector.

ment employees. Similarly, identities are included to measure the budget surpluses for both branches. Many of the variables in the identities are determined endogenously in the price and tax-transfer blocs.

5.1. *Estimated Equations: Government Purchases of Goods and Services (GOVT)*

(1) *State and Local Government Expenditures 1924–40, 1949–66*

$$GSL/N = 0.1592 - 0.03838 \, DUMMY1$$
$$ (6.8135) \quad (4.2129)$$
$$+ 0.001766 \, TIME2$$
$$(3.4080)$$
$$+ 0.0212 \, \{[YPE\$/(PGSL)(N)]_{-1}$$
$$(2.5176)$$
$$- [YPE\$/(PGSL)(N)]_{-2}\}$$
$$+ 0.06949 \, [YPE\$/(PGSL)(N)]_{-2}$$
$$(7.6834)$$
$$+ 0.7089\{[GAID\$/(PGSL)(N)]$$
$$(4.5157)$$
$$- [GAID\$/(PGSL)(N)]_{-1}\}$$
$$+ 1.0939 \, [GAID\$/(PGSL)(N)]_{-1}$$
$$(5.7996)$$
$$+ 0.5060 \, (NIT/N)_{-1} + 0.2744 \, (GSL/N)_{-1}; \qquad (2.52)$$
$$(4.4700) \qquad\qquad (2.4354)$$
$$\bar{R}^2 = 0.9932, \qquad \bar{S}_e = 0.0040, \qquad DW = 2.01.$$

(2) *Government Expenditure Identities*

$$GSL = (GSL/N)N, \tag{2.53}$$

$$GF = GGF + YGF, \tag{2.54}$$

$$G = GSL + GF. \tag{2.55}$$

(3)   *Income Originating in Government Identities*

    (a) *State and Local*

$$YGSL = 3.9156\,(EGSNW) + YSLWR, \tag{2.56}$$

$$YGSL\$ = 3.9156\,(EGSNW)(PYSLNW) + YSLWR\$. \tag{2.57}$$

    (b) *Federal*

$$YGF = 5.9818\,(EGFNW) + YLA + YFWR, \tag{2.58}$$

$$YGF\$ = 5.9818\,(EGFNW)(PYFNW) + (YLA)(PYLA) + YFWR\$. \tag{2.59}$$

(4)   *Identities for Government Budget Surplus*

    (a) *State and Local*

$$GRECSL\$ = TXPSL\$ + TXCSL\$ + TXISL\$ + TXSSL\$ + GAID\$, \tag{2.60}$$

$$GEXPSL\$ = (PGSL)(GSL) + YIGSL\$ + TPSLG\$ + SUBSL\$, \tag{2.61}$$

$$GBSSL\$ = GRECSL\$ - GEXPSL\$. \tag{2.62}$$

    (b) *Federal*

$$GRECF\$ = TXPF\$ + TXCF\$ + TXIF\$ + TXOAS\$ + TXUN\$ + TXSFO\$, \tag{2.63}$$

$$GEXPF\$ = (PGGF)(GGF) + YGF\$ + TPUC\$ + TPGFO\$ + TPGFF\$ + GAID\$ + YIGF\$ + SUBF\$, \tag{2.64}$$

$$GBSF\$ = GRECF\$ - GEXPF\$. \tag{2.65}$$

6. Foreign Trade [10]

The import equation is a structural demand function, with import price given exogenously. Real import demand is assumed to vary positively with real domestic production and negatively with the ratio

---

[10] Richard Freeman participated in the work on the import function.

of import and domestic prices. Relative price was not significant in the pre-war sample, however, and does not appear in the equation for 1924–40. The pre-war and post-war equations also differ in that the latter allows for a (Koyck) distributed lag in the response to changes in product and price. Finally, the post-war equation also has a longer sample period (1949–70) than is usual in the model. An equation fitted to data through 1966 goes badly astray thereafter, in part because of the U.S.–Canadian automobile agreement of 1965. In order to take account of this sharp structural change, the sample was extended to 1970, and the coefficients on the price and activity variables were allowed to take on different values in 1965–70 by the inclusion of slope dummies.

With regard to exports, their value in current dollars is given exogenously. Since the export price index is endogenous, real exports are also endogenous and are determined by the expenditure identity. This treatment implicitly assumes a unitary price elasticity of demand for exports.

6.1. Estimated Equations: Foreign Trade (FORT)

(1) *Imports*
    1924–40

$$FIM = 1.7867 + 0.03790\,(XGNP - FIM) + 0.40526\,\hat{u}_{-1};$$
$$\qquad\quad (0.9077)\ (3.4722) \qquad\qquad\qquad\qquad (2.66)$$
$$\bar{S}_e = 0.7164.$$

1949–70

$$FIM = 1.30409 + 0.04014\,(XGNP - FIM)$$
$$\qquad\quad (0.2643)\ (5.3969)$$
$$\qquad\quad - 6.02696\,(PFIM/PXGNP)$$
$$\qquad\qquad (1.818)$$
$$\qquad\quad + 0.05471\,(XGNP - FIM)(D65)$$
$$\qquad\qquad (4.6307)$$
$$\qquad\quad - 33.9192\,(PFIM/PXGNP)(D65)$$
$$\qquad\qquad (4.3255)$$
$$\qquad\quad + 0.39905\,FIM_{-1}; \qquad\qquad\qquad\qquad (2.67)$$
$$\qquad\qquad (3.8972)$$
$$\bar{R}^2 = 0.995, \qquad \bar{S}_e = 0.770, \qquad DW = 2.27.$$

(2)   *Trade Identities*

$$FEX = FEX\$/PFEX, \qquad (2.68)$$

$$FIM\$ = (FIM)(PFIM), \qquad (2.69)$$

$$F = FEX - FIM, \qquad (2.70)$$

$$F\$ = FEX\$ - FIM\$. \qquad (2.71)$$

CHAPTER 3

Factor Inputs and Production

1. Introduction

This chapter is concerned with firms' decisions with regard to factor inputs and production in the short and long runs. The supply side of the labor market and the determination of employment and potential output will be discussed in Chapter 4.

2. Labor Demand

The theoretical specification of the labor demand function is set forth in Chapter 1, section 3. The equation to be estimated is (1.6), repeated here for convenience and using full variable names,

$$MH = \{[(\alpha/\beta)^{\alpha} A^{-1}]^{1/(\alpha+\beta)} \times [(Q4/W)^*]^{\alpha/(\alpha+\beta)} (XNR^*)^{1/(\alpha+\beta)} e^{-[\gamma/(\alpha+\beta)]t}\}^{\lambda_1} (MH_{-1})^{1-\lambda_1}.$$

Labor input is measured in man-hours (MH). The rental price of capital ($Q4$) is a compound variable measuring the imputed rental rate for the use of the productive services of a unit of the capital stock, and W is the money wage rate. (Both $Q4$ and W are discussed more fully in Chapter 5.) The output variable (XNR) is gross private non-residential product and is equal to GNP minus income originating in general government employment and in housing rent.

The estimated equation for the case of constant returns to scale ($\alpha + \beta = 1$) is shown below [equation (3.1)]. As mentioned in Chapter 2, section 3, the implicit production parameters from (3.1) were imposed on the estimated investment demand function (2.15) to achieve the necessary a priori consistency between the two factor demand functions. Experimentation with alternative expectations hypotheses for output and relative factor prices suggested that actual current values were the best proxies for expected values. The constant-returns constraint was imposed by forcing the estimated coefficient on output to be the same as on lagged man-hours. Apart from a level shift and different rates of technical progress, the equation is the same before and after World War II.

The implicit Cobb–Douglas production function parameters as inferred from the labor coefficients are as follows. The elasticity of output with respect to capital stock is 0.316 and the corresponding elasticity for man-hours is 0.684. The pre-war and post-war rates of technical progress are 1.5 and 2.0 percent per annum. The estimated speed of adjustment of actual to desired man-hours is 0.56.

For comparison we also include the unconstrained-returns variant of the labor demand function [equation (3.1a)]. The implicit Cobb–Douglas parameters for this case are a capital elasticity of 0.283 and a labor elasticity of 0.977, implying returns to scale of 1.260. The estimated pre-war and post-war rates of technical progress are, respectively, 2.0 and 1.9 percent per annum, and the speed of adjustment is 0.69 per annum.

The choice between constant or increasing returns in the underlying production function is problematic. Increasing returns yields a better fit in the case of the labor demand equation (the standard error of estimate is 0.0165 versus 0.0190 for constant returns), but the reverse is true of the investment function [the standard errors of estimate are 0.0085 and 0.0090 for constant and increasing returns, respectively, from equations (2.15) and (2.15a)]. In view of this ambiguity, we decided to include both sets of factor demands in the complete model, with an option to use either set. This allows us to compare the alternatives in the context of the complete model's performance, where hopefully a decisive judgment in favor of one or the other may emerge. Our findings on this point are presented in Chapter 10. Since the evidence contained in Chapter 10 generally supports the constant returns hypothesis, we have adopted this as the standard option for the simulation and multiplier analyses to be reported in this book.

2.1. Estimated Equations: Labor Input (LBIN)

(1) *Constant Returns Production Function Constraint*
     1924–40, 1949–66

$$\ln MH - \ln MH_{-1} = 0.10313 - 0.03431\ DUMMY1$$
$$(0.5563)\quad(0.4224)$$
$$+0.17689\ \ln(Q4/W) - 0.00867\ TIME3$$
$$(1.5849)\qquad\qquad(6.7105)$$
$$-0.01095\ TIME5$$
$$(3.7076)$$
$$+0.55917\ (\ln XNR - \ln MH_{-1});\qquad(3.1)$$
$$(13.2204)$$

$$\bar{R}^2 = 0.852,\qquad \bar{S}_e = 0.0190,\qquad DW = 2.28.$$

(1a) *Increasing Returns Production Function*
      1924–40, 1949–66

$$\ln MH - \ln MH_{-1} = 0.73944 - 0.03118\ DUMMY1$$
$$(2.9084)\quad(0.4420)$$
$$+0.15507\ \ln(Q4/W) + 0.54855\ \ln XNR$$
$$(1.5961)\qquad\qquad(14.8753)$$
$$-0.01124\ TIME3 - 0.01069\ TIME5$$
$$(8.1731)\qquad\qquad(4.1652)$$
$$-0.69118\ \ln MH_{-1};\qquad(3.1a)$$
$$(4.1652)$$

$$\bar{R}^2 = 0.888,\qquad \bar{S}_e = 0.0165,\qquad DW = 2.4723.$$

3. Production

Prices and production are simultaneously determined in the model. On the assumption of constant returns to scale, long-run average cost is independent of output, but even in this case, the markup is a function of demand pressures as proxied by the rate of capacity utilization (see Chapter 1, section 6). Hence product prices are an increasing function of output in the short-run for given plant capacity. For given prices, including wages and interest rates, real purchases of goods and services are determined by sectoral demands (see Chapter

2) and total production is obtained from the real *GNP* identity [equation (3.2)]. Additional identities yield estimates of privately produced product (*XP*) and private non-residential product (*XNR*). As explained in Chapter 1, section 4, *XNR* satisfies the short-run production function (1.8) when the measured inputs of labor and capital are adjusted for current rates of factor utilization. The factor utilization indexes are discussed in Chapter 4, section 4.

The output bloc also contains the identity for permanent income per capita (3.17), a variable used in the money bloc, plus a number of analytical ratios and growth rates which are by-products of the model solution. The growth rates of full-employment, potential and capacity output are available for either the constant or increasing returns options.

3.1. *Output Identities and Analytical Ratios and Growth Rates (OUT)*

$$XGNP = CE + IGPD + GSL + GGF + YGF + FEX - FIM, \tag{3.2}$$

$$XP = XGNP - YGSL - YGF, \tag{3.3}$$

$$XNR = XP - YHR, \tag{3.4}$$

$$XGNP\$ = (PXGNP)(XGNP), \tag{3.5}$$

$$XP\$ = (PXP)(XP), \tag{3.6}$$

$$XNR\$ = (PXNR)(XNR), \tag{3.7}$$

$$XN\$ = XGNP\$ - CC\$, \tag{3.8}$$

$$GROUT = [(XGNP - XGNP_{-1})/XGNP_{-1}](100), \tag{3.9}$$

$$GRX7C = [(XNR7C - XNR7C_{-1})/XNR7C_{-1}](100), \tag{3.10}$$

$$GRX7 = [(XNR7 - XNR7_{-1})/XNR7_{-1}](100), \tag{3.10a}$$

$$GRX8C = [(XNR8C - XNR8C_{-1})/XNR8C_{-1}](100), \tag{3.11}$$

$$GRX8 = [(XNR8 - XNR8_{-1})/XNR8_{-1}](100), \tag{3.11a}$$

$$GRX9C = [(XNR9C - XNR9C_{-1})/XNR9C_{-1}](100), \tag{3.12}$$

$$GRX9 = [(XNR9 - XNR9_{-1})/XNR9_{-1}](100), \qquad (3.12a)$$

$$KLRA = KNB/MH, \qquad (3.13)$$

$$KYRA = KNB/XGNP, \qquad (3.14)$$

$$PROD = XNR/MH, \qquad (3.15)$$

$$QWRAT = Q4/W, \qquad (3.16)$$

$$XNPR = XNPRT + \sum_{j=0}^{6} (W_j)(XNP - XNPRT)_{-j}, \qquad (3.17)$$

where

$W_0 = 0.33,$ $W_4 = 0.07,$

$W_1 = 0.22,$ $W_5 = 0.05,$

$W_2 = 0.15,$ $W_6 = 0.03,$

$W_3 = 0.10,$ $XNP = \dfrac{XN\$ (1000)}{(N)(PXGNP)}.$

CHAPTER 4

Labor Supply and Potential Output

1. Introduction

In a growth-oriented model, explicit attention must be given to the determinants of aggregate supply. Our production function (1.1) relates the long-run growth of aggregate output to the rate of technical progress and to the rates of growth of capital and labor inputs. While we assume that technical progress occurs at an exogenously given rate, the growth rates of capital and labor are endogenously determined. The investment function for business fixed capital, which specifies the immediate determinants of capital stock growth, was already discussed in Chapter 2. Regarding labor supply growth, population developments are not explained within the model, but the labor force participation rate (the ratio of labor force to population) and average annual hours per worker are endogenous. The equations pertaining to these labor supply variables are described in section 2 of this chapter.

While the participation rate and average hours respond cyclically to changes in the state of the job market, at full employment they are determined essentially by the real wage rate. On the assumption that full employment exists at an unemployment rate of four percent, an admittedly arbitrary but nonetheless popular assumption, we are able to express the full-employment supply of man-hours as a function of the size of the population and the level of the real wage (see section 3 below). With full-employment man-hours so determined, and with technical knowledge and the existing capital stock given, the production function is used to calculate potential output, a central variable for analyses of economic growth. It should be noted that the development of potential output over time is not rigidly fixed in our model; rather, the general performance of the economy will influence potential growth through the channels of capital accumulation and real wage behavior.

Our measure of full-employment man-hours is also used in conjunction with the demand function for man-hours to determine full-employment output, defined as the level of output which, at existing relative prices, technical knowledge, and population, would equate man-hours demanded to the full-employment supply.

Actual output may diverge from potential in a given year for any or all of three reasons: (a) the existing capital stock is being used at an abnormal intensity, (b) currently employed man-hours are being used at an abnormal intensity, and (c) currently employed man-hours are not equal to full-employment man-hours. Since we estimate potential from the same production function that underlies our factor demand relations and factor intensity indexes, we are able not only to measure the utilization rate of potential output but also to identify the contributions of each of the above three sources to deviations of actual from potential output. The algebraic relation appropriate to this analysis was derived in Chapter 1 [see equation (1.25)]. The last section of this chapter takes up the empirical implementation of our framework for measuring potential utilization, as well as the capacity, labor, and full-employment utilization rates on which potential utilization depends.

2. Labor Force and Hours per Worker [1]

The equations in this bloc describe the secular and cyclical behavior of labor supply. Aggregate labor supply depends on the willingness of individuals to enter the labor force and on the number of hours of work they desire per year. We conceive of these decisions under full-employment conditions essentially as a choice between income and leisure, given the level of the real wage and subject to the various institutional constraints posed by such things as social mores regarding family life and the nature of labor contracts. During business

---

[1] This section is based on two papers by Coen (1971b, 1973a).

fluctuations, however, both labor force participation and average hours may be influenced by existing conditions in the labor market. A number of empirical studies have found evidence that participation tends to decline as unemployment rises and job opportunities grow scarce – the so-called discouraged-worker phenomenon.[2] The search for work is, after all, a costly undertaking, and eagerness to engage in search ought to depend on the probability of success of the venture. Also, average hours in the short run may diverge from those desired by workers owing to fluctuations in the demand for labor. These are the basic hypotheses underlying our specifications of the participation and hours equations, which we shall now examine in greater detail.

Our development of the participation equation begins with the notion of the "potential civilian labor force", i.e., the civilian labor force that would be supplied at full employment. We treat the potential labor force relative to the non-institutional, working-age population as a function of the after-tax real wage and a time trend, the latter serving as a proxy for institutional changes which are difficult to quantify. Demographic variables pertaining to the age or sex composition of the working-age population or to the ratio of the working-age population to total population are likely candidates for inclusion in the potential labor force equation, but such variables were not found to be statistically significant in our analyses of post-war data. We do, however, include military employment as a determinant of the potential civilian labor force, since military employment is not likely to be a perfect substitute for civilian employment and it is not entirely voluntary. Designating the potential labor force by L^p, we then have

$$\frac{L^p}{NNI} = a_0 + a_1 \frac{W1}{PCE} + a_2 t + a_3 \frac{LA}{NNI}. \tag{4.1}$$

The difference between the actual and potential participation rates depends upon conditions in the job market as they affect the perceived probability of obtaining work. In a cyclical downturn,

---

[2] See, for example, Bowen and Finegan (1969), Dernburg and Strand (1966), and Tella (1965).

employers generally reduce both the number of employees and average hours, so that deviations of either of these variables from their full-employment levels might serve as job-market indicators to workers. We utilize both indicators in our actual participation relation. Denoting potential, or full-employment, employment and hours as E^p and H^p, respectively, we have

$$LPC - \frac{L^p}{NNI} = a_4 \left(\frac{E}{NNI} - \frac{E^p}{NNI} \right) + a_5 (AH1 - H^p), \qquad (4.2)$$

where the parameters a_4 and a_5 measure the strength of discouraged-worker effects. Previous studies indicate that a_4 is positive, but the influence of cyclical changes in hours has never been examined. Our estimates confirm a positive value of a_4, but indicate a negative value for a_5, suggesting an added-worker effect with respect to hours; that is, when workers' incomes are reduced in a downturn by a cut in hours, they apparently respond by sending other family members out to seek work, in an effort to maintain family income. However, our estimates of the magnitudes of a_4 and a_5, in conjunction with the typical amplitudes of fluctuations in employment and hours, lead us to conclude that the discouraged-worker phenomenon is dominant.

To complete the specification of the participation equation, we need to express potential employment and hours in terms of observable variables. To define potential employment, we assume that e^p is the proportion of the labor force that would be employed at full employment, that is, the employment rate which *workers* consider to be the full-employment employment rate; then

$$E^p = e^p L^p. \qquad (4.3)$$

Potential hours, like potential labor force, are assumed to be determined by the real wage and a time trend,

$$H^p = b_0 + b_1 \frac{W1}{PCE} + b_2 t. \qquad (4.4)$$

Combining (4.1)–(4.4), we obtain the following participation equation:

$$LPC = c_0 + c_1 \frac{E}{NNI} + c_2 \frac{LA}{NNI} + c_3 \frac{W1}{PCE} + c_4 AH1 + c_5 t, \qquad (4.5)$$

where

$$
\left.
\begin{aligned}
c_0 &= (1 - a_4 e^p) a_0 - a_5 b_0 \\
c_1 &= a_4 \\
c_2 &= (1 - a_4 e^p) a_3 \\
c_3 &= (1 - a_4 e^p) a_1 - a_5 b_1 \\
c_4 &= a_5 \\
c_5 &= (1 - a_4 e^p) a_2 - a_5 b_2
\end{aligned}
\right\} \qquad (4.6)
$$

While a_4 and a_5 are identifiable from estimates of the c's, the other "structural parameters" are not.

Since annual data on the labor force are not available prior to 1940, the participation relation could be fitted only to post-war observations. The result is shown below as equation (4.11). The time trend was not found to be statistically significant and was therefore omitted from the final equation. We might also note that a distributed-lag form of the basic equation was tested and rejected. In addition to the discouraged-worker finding with respect to employment and the added-worker finding with respect to hours, our equation indicates that, ceteris paribus, larger armed forces and higher real wages have a substantial and significant negative impact on the size of the civilian labor force.

Lacking pre-war labor force data, we were faced with the problem of how to handle this period. One possibility was to make use of Stanley Lebergott's (1964) annual estimates of the pre-war labor force, which are carefully constructed and have frequently been employed in analyses of the pre-war period. However, his estimates have the drawback of being on a very different footing from the measured labor force series beginning in 1940, in that they do not fully reflect the influence of labor market conditions on participation. His procedure essentially involved interpolating participation rates by age and sex between the decennial censuses and then applying these interpolated rates to population data for the intercensoral years. As one might expect, the resulting labor force series displays almost no cyclical variation.

We chose instead to construct our own annual estimates of the pre-war labor force by "backcasting" participation rates from our post-war participation equation. Initial application of this procedure resulted in underestimates of participation rates for 1930 and 1940, the two census years for which enumerations are available; but the errors were roughly of the same magnitude in both years, suggesting that a simple adjustment of the constant term in the participation equation would correct the level of our estimates.[3] Equation (4.10) below is the constant-term adjusted form of the post-war participation equation used in this analysis. It should be noted that the slope coefficients in (4.10) differ somewhat from those in (4.11), since the former pertains to individuals 14 years of age and older, which was the definitional basis for labor force and working-age population statistics in the pre-war period, while the latter pertains to individuals 16 years of age and older. Our final labor force estimates imply substantially higher unemployment rates in the 1920's and somewhat lower unemployment rates in the 1930's as compared with Lebergott's. For example, Lebergott's estimates of unemployment rates in the 1922–29 period peak at 5.0 percent in 1924 and reach a low of 1.8 percent in 1926, whereas our series has its peak and trough in the same years, but the levels are 6.0 percent and 4.1 percent, respectively. Since very low unemployment rates have typically been accompanied by high inflation rates in the U.S. economy, our higher unemployment rates appear to be more consistent with the observed stability of wages and prices in the 1922–29 period. Appendix C presents our estimates of labor force and unemployment in the pre-war period and compares them with Lebergott's.

Turning now to average hours, we combine the hypothesis in (4.4) regarding potential hours with the notion that actual hours may diverge from potential owing to cyclical fluctuations in labor de-

---

[3] Coen (1973a) explores possible explanations for underestimates of the 1930 and 1940 participation rates and provides some reasonable grounds for the constant term adjustment. The strengths and weaknesses of our approach are discussed in Lebergott (1973) and Coen (1973b).

mand.[4] We have in mind here not a discouraged- or added-worker phenomenon, as was the case with labor force participation, but involuntary reductions in hours in downturns below levels desired by workers and overtime hours in upturns, perhaps induced by premium rates of pay for extra hours. Thus, our actual hours equation must be regarded as a hybrid relation embodying a desired supply function and a cyclical demand function. The variable selected to capture cyclical fluctuations in demand is the deviation of the unemployment rate, $U1$, from the full-employment unemployment rate, $U7$. Assuming that the difference between actual and potential hours is proportional to this deviation, we have

$$AH - H^p = b_3(U1 - U7). \tag{4.7}$$

Upon substituting (4.4) for H^p, we obtain

$$AH = b_0 - b_3 U7 + b_1 \frac{W3}{PCE} + b_2 t + b_3 U1, \tag{4.8}$$

or, assuming that $U7$ does not vary over time,

$$AH = b_0' + b_1 \frac{W3}{PCE} + b_2 t + b_3 U1.^5 \tag{4.9}$$

Estimates of this equation led to rejection of a common structure for the pre-war and post-war samples; in particular, the trend was significant in the earlier period but not in the later period, and the autoregressive pattern of the disturbances differed markedly. Hence, we settled on separate relations for the two eras, although the regression coefficients for both eras indicate strong negative influences of real wages and unemployment on average hours.

The equations in this bloc are completed by a set of identities

---

[4] The average hours variable entering the participation equation relates to all civilian employment, public and private. Since we assume, however, that hours of public-sector employees are constant through time at 2,000 per year, the hours variable we seek to explain relates only to private employees.

[5] The after-tax money wage here is $W3$ rather than $W1$, because the average hours variable on the left-hand side pertains only to employees in the private sector.

defining (a) the civilian labor force as the product of the participation rate and the non-institutional, working-age population, (b) private employment as the ratio of private man-hours to private average hours, (c) total civilian employment as the sum of private employment and public civilian employment, (d) the number of unemployed persons as the excess of the civilian labor force over civilian employment, (e) the conventionally measured unemployment rate, and (f) average hours for all civilian employees as a weighted average of private- and public-sector average hours, the weights being proportional to employment in the two sectors. In light of the importance accorded the unemployment rate in popular discussions of economic performance, special note should be made of how it is determined in the present model. We do not explain the unemployment rate directly, for example, by linking it to the deviation between actual and potential output à la Okun's law (1962); rather, it is derived from our predictions of labor force and employment, the latter variable in turn depending on our predictions of man-hours and average hours. Thus, prediction errors in these three variables will jointly determine the accuracy of our predictions of the unemployment rate. While at times the errors in the underlying variables can be large but offsetting, at other times they can be small but reinforcing. This is an inescapable and somewhat discomforting aspect of our approach.

2.1. Estimated Equations: Labor Force and Hours per Worker (EMLF)

(1) *Labor Force Participation Rate*
     1924–40

$$LPC = 0.6348 + 0.6084\,(E/NNI) - 0.6168\,(LA/NNI)$$
$$\quad\quad - 0.0234\,(W1/PCE) - 0.1502\,AH1. \quad\quad\quad (4.10)$$

1949–66

$$LPC = 0.6438 + 0.5414\,(E/NNI) - 0.6290\,(LA/NNI)$$
$$\quad\quad (11.572)(6.9008) \quad\quad\quad (6.9847)$$
$$\quad\quad - 0.0197\,(W1/PCE) - 0.1511\,AH1; \quad\quad\quad (4.11)$$
$$\quad\quad (5.3095) \quad\quad\quad\quad (5.4402)$$
$$\bar{R}^2 = 0.8590, \quad\quad \bar{S}_e = 0.0017, \quad\quad DW = 2.1824.$$

(2) *Average Hours, Private Sector*
     1925–40

$AH = 3.4349 + 0.0197 \ TIME3 - 1.0195 \ (W3/PCE)$
$\qquad$ (24.963) (3.5813) $\qquad$ (5.7549)
$\qquad - 0.0157 \ U1 - 0.2247 \ \hat{u}_{-1};$ $\qquad\qquad\qquad$ (4.12)
$\qquad$ (11.251)
$\bar{S}_e = 0.0241.$

1950–66

$AH = 2.2641 - 0.0830 \ (W3/PCE) - 0.0115 \ U1 + 0.7482 \ \hat{u}_{-1};$
$\qquad$ (47.487) (3.8441) $\qquad\qquad$ (7.2682) $\qquad\qquad$ (4.13)
$\bar{S}_e = 0.0070.$

(3) *Labor Force, Employment, Unemployment, and Average Hours*
     Identities

$$LC1 = (LPC)(NNI), \tag{4.14}$$

$$EP = MH/AH, \tag{4.15}$$

$$E = EP + EGSWR + EGSNW + EGFWR + EGFNW, \tag{4.16}$$

$$UN1 = LC1 - E, \tag{4.17}$$

$$U1 = (UN1/LC1)(100), \tag{4.18}$$

$$AH1 = [(AH)(EP) + 2.000 \ (E - EP)]/E. \tag{4.19}$$

3. Labor Supply at Full Employment[6]

Our measures of full-employment and potential output require estimates of private man-hours that would be supplied at full employment, *MH7*, which is the product of average hours of private employees at full employment, *AH7*, and private employment at full employment, *EP7*.[7] Full-employment average hours in the private

---

[6] The equations described in this section are part of the *UTIL* bloc, which is listed in full at the end of the next section.

[7] A "7" attached to the end of a variable name generally denotes a full-employment value of the variable.

sector are derived directly from equation (4.7), which gives

$$AH7 = AH + b_3(U7 - U1). \tag{4.20}$$

Calculation of $EP7$ is not so straightforward, because our labor force equation pertains to all civilian workers, private and public. If $E7$ and $LC17$ are the full-employment levels of civilian employment and labor force, respectively, then we have

$$EP7 = (WHT1)(E7) = (WHT1)[1 - (U7)/100](LC17), \tag{4.21}$$

where $WHT1$ is the ratio of private to total civilian employment at full employment. Our estimate of $WHT1$ is a trend measure of the actual ratio of private to total civilian employment. To implement (4.21), we need to estimate the full-employment civilian labor force, $LC17$.

Our measure of $LC17$ is derived from equation (4.5) above, after setting the appropriate right-hand variables–employment, average hours, and the wage rate–equal to their full-employment values, and allowing for the stochastic character of the fitted equation. As (4.21) indicates, civilian employment at full employment can be expressed as the product of the full-employment employment rate and $LC17$.[8] Full-employment average hours for all civilian employees are calculated as a weighted mean of $AH7$ and average hours of civilian government workers, which we assume to be 2,000 per year. The weights reflect the proportions of private and public employment in total civilian employment at full employment. Thus,

$$AH17 = (WHT1)(AH7) + (1 - WHT1)(2.0). \tag{4.22}$$

The full-employment after-tax money wage of civilian employees, $W17$, is likewise taken to be a weighted average of the after-tax wage rates in the private and public sectors, but with weights proportional

---

[8] Note that our assumed full-employment employment rate here, $1 - (U7)/100$, may differ from workers' views of the full-employment employment rate, e^p, which appeared in the specification of the participation equation. Because of this possibility, in this section we use a different notation to indicate full-employment values of variables.

to full-employment man-hours in the two sectors. Defining $EG7$ as civilian government employment at full employment and WG as the public-sector money wage,[9] we have

$$W17 = (1 - TXRW)\frac{(MH7)(W) + (EG7)(2.0)(WG)}{MH7 + (EG7)(2.0)}; \qquad (4.24)$$

or noting that $WHT1 = (EP7)/(EP7 + EG7)$,

$$W17 = (1 - TXRW)\frac{(WHT1)(AH7)(W) + (1 - WHT1)(2.0)(WG)}{(WHT1)(AH7) + (1 - WHT1)(2.0)}. \qquad (4.25)$$

Substituting $E7$, $AH17$ and $W17$ for E, $AH1$ and $W1$ in (4.5), and denoting the error in our prediction of the actual participation rate as $\hat{u}$, we can write the participation rate at full employment as

$$\frac{LC17}{NNI} = c_0 + c_1\frac{[1 - (U7)/100]LC17}{NNI} + c_2\frac{LA}{NNI} + c_3\frac{W17}{PCE}$$
$$+ c_4AH17 + c_5t + \hat{u}. \qquad (4.26)$$

Solving for $LC17$ gives

$$LC17 = \left\{\frac{1}{1 - c_1[1 - (U7)/100]}\right\}$$
$$\times \left[c_0NNI + c_2LA + c_3\left(\frac{W17}{PCE}\right)(NNI) + c_4(AH17)(NNI)\right.$$
$$\left. + c_5(t)(NNI) + \hat{u}(NNI)\right]^{10}, \qquad (4.27)$$

---

[9] The public-sector civilian money wage is the ratio of income originating (compensation of employees) in civilian government to civilian government employment; that is

$$WG = [YGF\$ + YGSL\$ - (PYLA)(YLA)]/EG. \qquad (4.23)$$

[10] From (4.22), (4.20) and (4.8), we see that $AH17$ could be expressed in terms of the public- and private-sector wage rates and a time trend. Thus, $LC17$ is basically just a function of wage rates, population, armed forces, and a time trend.

which can be expressed more conveniently as

$$LC17 = \left\{ \frac{1}{1 - c_1[1 - (U7)/100]} \right\}$$
$$\times \left[LC1 - c_1E + c_3\left(\frac{NNI}{PCE}\right)(W17 - W1) + c_4(NNI) \right.$$
$$\left. \times (AH17 - AH) \right]. \tag{4.28}$$

We include in our model a measure of the utilization rate of full-employment private man-hours, which is given by

$$UTMH = MH/MH7. \tag{4.29}$$

Given the manner in which $MH7$ is constructed, $UTMH$ will be approximately unity (100 percent) when the conventional unemployment rate is 4 percent.[11] In general, however, this utilization rate is a more appealing indicator of over- or underemployment of labor than the conventional unemployment rate for two reasons.[12] First, it measures labor utilization in terms of *full-employment* labor supply, whereas the conventional rate measures employment relative to the *existing* rather than the full-employment labor force. Since, as we have seen, the size of the labor force itself varies pro-cyclically, the conventional rate fails to take account of potential workers who withdraw from the labor force during recessions, for example. Second, $UTMH$ gives consideration both to the number of employees and to hours per employee in assessing labor utilization, whereas the conventional rate is solely concerned with the number of persons employed.

---

[11] We say "approximately", because the use of $WHT1$ in constructing $MH7$ introduces the possibility that the actual distribution of employment between the private and public sectors when the conventional unemployment rate is 4 percent may differ slightly from that given by $WHT1$. In practice, this qualification is of negligible importance.

[12] It should be noted that $UTMH$ is not comparable in terms of coverage to the conventional unemployment rate, since it pertains only to the private sector.

4. Capacity, Full-employment, and Potential Output, and Their Utilization Rates

Our basic expressions defining capacity and full-employment output were presented in equations (1.14) and (1.22). However, we do not use these equations to calculate capacity and full-employment output, but instead compute the utilization ratios according to equations (1.16) and (1.23), and then multiply the utilization ratios by actual output. Our reason for proceeding in this way stems from the stochastic nature of the fitted investment and labor demand functions, a point which we ignored in Chapter 1 for the sake of simplicity. Since both the numerator and denominator of the capacity utilization ratio were derived by inversions of the investment function to get output on the left-hand side, the disturbance term which ought to appear in the investment function would occur in the same form in both elements of the ratio and would therefore cancel out. A similar argument holds for the utilization rate of full-employment output, whose numerator and denominator were arrived at by inversions of the labor demand function. Thus, calculation of the utilization ratios first avoids the awkward problem of appending error terms to the definitional relations for capacity and full-employment output and then using these relations directly.

Measurement of potential output encounters special difficulties, because equation (1.24) defining potential was derived from the short-run production function (1.8), as opposed to inversions of the factor demand equations. As we have seen, estimates of the investment and labor demand functions were constrained to yield the same values of the production function parameters α, β and γ, but not the production function parameter A. Thus, we have two different estimates of A, A_K from the investment function, and A_L from the labor demand function. Furthermore, the short-run production function (1.8) ignored stochastic elements in the fitted investment and labor demand functions. And finally, our discussion in Chapter 1 of the short-run and potential production functions proceeded on the assumption that expected relative factor prices are formed in the same way for both investment and labor input decisions, whereas our empirical estimates of the investment and labor equations indicate that expected factor prices are best approximated by current prices in the labor equation and by lagged prices in the investment equation.

Recognition of these features of our empirical system of interrelated factor demands leads to a more complicated form of the short-run production function and therefore to a somewhat modified potential equation. Recalling equations (1.9) and (1.10), which define the factor intensity indexes k_t and m_t, we see that the short-run production function can be written as

$$X_t = A \ e^{\gamma t} (K_t^*)^\alpha (M_t^*)^\beta. \tag{4.30}$$

The desired inputs K_t^* and M_t^* were originally given by (1.2) and (1.3), which must now be amended to read[13]

$$M_t^* = [(\alpha/\beta)^{-\alpha} A_L^{-1}]^{1/(\alpha+\beta)} [(Q/W)_t]^{\alpha/(\alpha+\beta)} X_t^{1/(\alpha+\beta)} \ e^{-[\gamma/(\alpha+\beta)]t}, \tag{4.31}$$

and

$$K_t^* = [(\alpha/\beta)^\beta A_K^{-1}]^{1/(\alpha+\beta)} [(Q/W)_{t-1}]^{-\beta/(\alpha+\beta)} X_t^{1/(\alpha+\beta)} \ e^{-[\gamma/(\alpha+\beta)]t}. \tag{4.32}$$

Substitution of (4.31) and (4.32) into (4.30) should result in an identity in X_t, but this will be true only if

$$A = A_K^{\alpha/(\alpha+\beta)} A_L^{\beta/(\alpha+\beta)} [(Q/W)_{t-1}/(Q/W)_t]^{\alpha\beta/(\alpha+\beta)}. \tag{4.33}$$

Hence, the short-run production function becomes

$$X_t = A_K^{\alpha/(\alpha+\beta)} A_L^{\beta/(\alpha+\beta)} [(Q/W)_{t-1}/(Q/W_t]^{\alpha\beta/(\alpha+\beta)} \ e^{\gamma t} (K_t^*)^\alpha (M_t^*)^\beta. \tag{4.34}$$

The desired inputs on the right-hand side of (4.34) were implicitly defined in terms of observable current and past inputs by the factor adjustment relations (1.4) and (1.5). However, (1.4) and (1.5) should include error terms and read

$$M_t/M_{t-1} = (M_t^*/M_{t-1})^{\lambda_1} \ e^{u_t}, \tag{4.35}$$

---

[13] We make use here of our empirical finding that $X_t^* = X_t$, which was common to both the estimated investment and labor demand functions.

and

$$K_t/K_{t-1} = (K_t^*/K_{t-1})^{\lambda_2} e^{v_t}, \tag{4.36}$$

where u_t and v_t are the disturbances. Solving (4.35) and (4.36) for M_t^* and K_t^*, and recalling expressions (1.16) and (1.18) for the capacity and labor utilization ratios, we have

$$M_t^* = (M_t/M_{t-1})^{1/\lambda_1}M_{t-1} e^{-u_t/\lambda_1} = (X/X^m)_t^{1/(\alpha+\beta)}M_t e^{-u_t/\lambda_1}, \tag{4.37}$$

and

$$K_t^* = (K_t/K_{t-1})^{1/\lambda_2}K_{t-1} e^{-v_t/\lambda_2} = (X/X^c)_t^{1/(\alpha+\beta)}K_{t-1} e^{-v_t/\lambda_2}. \tag{4.38}$$

Substituting (4.37) and (4.38) into (4.34) yields the final, exact form of the short-run production function, namely,

$$X_t = A_K^{\alpha/(\alpha+\beta)}A_L^{\beta/(\alpha+\beta)}[(Q/W)_{t-1}/(Q/W)_t]^{\alpha\beta/(\alpha+\beta)} e^{\gamma t}$$
$$\times [(X/X^c)_t^{1/(\alpha+\beta)}K_{t-1}]^{\alpha}[(X/X^m)_t^{1/(\alpha+\beta)}M_t]^{\beta} e^{-[(\alpha v_t/\lambda_2)+(\beta u_t/\lambda_1)]}. \tag{4.39}$$

In line with our discussion in Chapter 1, we estimate potential output from the short-run production function by substituting full-employment man-hours M_t^f for M_t, the normal capacity utilization ratio n_c for $(X/X^c)_t$, and the normal labor utilization rate n_m for $(X/X^m)_t$. Additionally, if we think of potential as an equilibrium, non-stochastic concept, which seems natural, then in measuring potential from (4.39) we should abstract from temporary differences in expected factor prices affecting input decisions and from disturbances in factor adjustment relations.[14] These considerations lead us

---

[14] If in defining potential we ignore disturbances in the factor demand equations, then potential utilization must assume a stochastic character (see the following footnote). By contrast, our measures of capacity and full-employment utilization are non-stochastic, whereas the levels of capacity and full-employment output do include stochastic elements. Just as we prefer to think of potential as a non-stochastic concept, so we prefer to think of capacity and full-employment utilization, rather than the levels of capacity and full-employment output, as non-stochastic. Our basic hypothesis regarding factor adjustments is that they are related to utilization rates. It seems implausible to allow disturbances in factor adjustment relations to influence measured factor utilization rates. Instead, such disturbances ought to appear in the relationship between the utilization rates and observed output.

to specify the potential output equation as

$$X_t^P = A_K^{\alpha/(\alpha+\beta)} A_L^{\beta/(\alpha+\beta)} e^{\gamma t} (n_c^{1/(\alpha+\beta)} K_{t-1})^{\alpha} (n_m^{1/(\alpha+\beta)} M_t^f)^{\beta}. \tag{4.40}$$

After computing potential from this equation, we express the utilization rate of potential as the ratio of X_t to X_t^{P}.[15]

As we noted earlier, estimation of our factor demand equations did not lead to a clear-cut choice between constant and increasing returns to scale for the underlying production function. Since we have set up our model to accommodate either case, we include both constant and increasing returns to scale versions of the full-employment, capacity, and potential utilization rates. Moreover, since potential output is calculated directly from the production function, we must have separate pre-war and post-war potential equations to allow for our empirical findings of different rates of technical progress and different constants in the production function in the two eras. Potential output also depends on the normal rates of utilization of capacity and labor optimizing output, which differ between the two eras.

Appendix D presents and analyzes estimates of our various utilization rates calculated from actual (as opposed to predicted) values of the variables on which they depend. The discussion there includes consideration of the utilization rate of labor-optimizing output, a utilization measure which we introduced in Chapter 1 but do not carry as a separate variable within the model.

4.1. Estimated Equations: Full-employment Man-hours and Utilization Rates (UTIL)

(1) *Full-employment Average Hours, Private Sector 1924–40*

$$AH7 = AH - 0.0157 (U7 - U1). \tag{4.41}$$

---

[15] Division of (4.39) by (4.40) and use of (1.23) leads to an expression similar to (1.26) relating potential utilization to the utilization rates of capacity, labor-optimizing, and full-employment output, but we now see that the modified version of (1.26) must include two additional terms – one involving the ratio of lagged to current relative factor prices, the other the disturbances from the investment and labor demand functions. The first of the additional terms would disappear if price expectations were formed in the same way for investment and employment decisions, whereas the second would be eliminated if potential were given a stochastic definition.

1949–66

$$AH7 = AH - 0.0115\,(U7 - U1). \tag{4.42}$$

(2) *Full-employment Civilian Labor Force*
    1924–40

$$LC17 = [1/(1 - 0.6084 - 0.6084\,(0.01)\,U7)]$$
$$\times [LC1 - 0.6084E - 0.0234\,(NNI)(W17 - W1)/(PCE)$$
$$- 0.1502\,(NNI)(AH17 - AH1)], \tag{4.43}$$

where

$$W17 = \{(1 - TXRW)[(EG)(WHT1)(W)(AH7)$$
$$+ (1 - WHT1)(YGF\$ + YGSL\$ - YLA\$)]\}$$
$$/[(EG)(WHT1)(AH7) + (EG)(1 - WHT1)(2)], \tag{4.44}$$

$$AH17 = (WHT1)(AH7) + (1 - WHT1)(2). \tag{4.45}$$

1949–66

Form is same as for 1924–40, but parameters change:

From	To
-0.6084	-0.5414
-0.0234	-0.0197
-0.1502	-0.1511

(3) *Identities for Private Employment and Man-hours at Full*
    Employment

$$EP7 = (WHT1)[1 - (0.01)U7](LC17), \tag{4.46}$$

$$MH7 = (AH7)(EP7). \tag{4.47}$$

(4) *Utilization Rate of Full-employment Man-hours, Private Sector*

$$UTMH = MH/MH7. \tag{4.48}$$

(5) *Utilization Rate of Full-employment Output, Private Sector*
Constant Returns

$$UTXNR7C = (MH/MH7)^{1.788374}. \tag{4.49}$$

Increasing Returns

$$UTXNR7 = (MH/MH7)^{1.822998}. \tag{4.50}$$

(6) *Utilization Rate of Capacity Output, Private Sector*
Constant Returns

$$UTXNR9C = (KNB/KNB_{-1})^{5.686535}. \tag{4.51}$$

Increasing Returns

$$UTXNR9 = (KNB/KNB_{-1})^{6.356019}. \tag{4.52}$$

(7) *Potential Output, Private Sector*
Constant Returns
1924–40

$$XNR8C = (1.230128)\, e^{0.015498(TIME3)}[(1.2026)(KNB_{-1})]^{0.316340} \times [(1.0517)(MH7)]^{0.683660}. \tag{4.53}$$

1949–66

$$XNR8C = (1.169923)\, e^{0.019587(TIME5)}[(1.2280)(KNB_{-1})]^{0.316340} \times [(1.0151)(MH7)]^{0.683660}. \tag{4.54}$$

Increasing Returns
1924–40

$$XNR8 = (0.36886)\, e^{0.020490(TIME3)}[(1.1588)^{0.793639}(KNB_{-1})]^{0.282690} \times [(1.0351)^{0.793639}(MH7)]^{0.977328}. \tag{4.55}$$

1949–66

$$XNR8 = (0.354466)\, e^{0.019488(TIME5)}[(1.2503)^{0.793639}(KNB_{-1})]^{0.282690} \times [(1.0136)^{0.793639}(MH7)]^{0.977328}. \tag{4.56}$$

(8) *Identities for Potential Utilization, Full-employment Output, and Capacity Output*

$$UTXNR8C = XNR/XNR8C, \tag{4.57}$$

$$UTXNR8 = XNR/XNR8, \tag{4.58}$$

$$XNR7C = XNR/UTXNR7C, \tag{4.59}$$

$$XNR7 = XNR/UTXNR7, \tag{4.60}$$

$$XNR9C = XNR/UTXNR9C, \tag{4.61}$$

$$XNR9 = XNR/UTXNR9. \tag{4.62}$$

CHAPTER 5

Money, Wages and Prices

1. Introduction

The links between money and prices in the model are as follows. The proximate determinants of prices are average costs and the pressure of demand as reflected in capacity utilization. Real money balances do not appear in the expenditure functions. For given values of unborrowed reserves and other monetary instruments, the demand and supply of money determine the money stock and interest rates. Interest rates affect real expenditures in the housing and consumption sectors and influence output and employment through the multiplier process. Labor demand directly affects money wages, and hence average unit costs and prices. At the same time, production levels influence prices via capacity utilization and also, in the case of increasing returns to scale, by affecting unit costs.[1] The circle is closed by the feedback of nominal *GNP* on the demand for money.

Thus prices, production and employment are determined by the simultaneous interaction of the real and monetary sectors. The linkages between sectors can be identified, but in a non-recursive, interdependent system the idea of a uni-directional causal flow loses its meaning. It is preferable to stress the distinction between controllable and non-controllable variables, or the closely related distinction between instruments and targets. In later chapters we investigate the

---

[1] Thus if increasing returns are assumed, the cost-raising effects of an induced wage increase will be partly offset by the induced productivity gain accompanying output expansion, but this offset will be missing under our preferred specification of constant returns.

effects of changes in monetary and fiscal instruments on the nominal and real levels of economic activity, in a dynamic context and over the short- and long-runs. In the meantime, discussion of the structural hypotheses underlying the money, wage and price blocs will lay the groundwork for greater understanding and better judgment of the simulation properties of the full system.

2. The Monetary Sector [2]

This bloc contains a demand and supply model to determine the money stock (including time deposits other than large certificates of deposit), the interest rate paid on time deposits, and the 90-day Treasury bill rate, plus a term structure model to link short- and long-term interest rates. The term structure model is adapted from the earlier work of Nelson (1972) but the model of the money supply mechanism–the creation of John Scadding–is new. It is developed and analyzed in Scadding (1974), to which the reader is referred for a richer and more enlightening discussion than is possible in this volume. In particular, he provides an explicit profit-maximizing theory of the portfolio behavior of the individual commercial bank and shows how that differs from, and in full equilibrium is reconciled with, the portfolio behavior of the entire banking system. That is to say, the portfolio of the individual bank is chosen subject to its deposit constraint, whereas the corresponding constraint for the banking industry as a whole is not deposits at all, but rather unborrowed reserves, a control variable of the central bank. It is this macro-model of the banking system which is summarized below.

The complete system consists of eight equations:[3]

$$RESRD/(RESU - RESRT) = a_{10} + a_{11} \ln RSGB$$
$$+ a_{12} \ln RD + a_{13} \ln RRDB, \quad (5.1)$$

---

[2] The monetary sector was built by John Scadding with the collaboration of Jae-ik Kim especially on the time deposit and term structure portions of the model.

[3] Equations (5.4) and (5.5) are written in different, but equivalent form to those given in Scadding (1974). Equation (5.8), Scadding's partial adjustment money demand function, is used instead of the unlagged function reported by him in the cited reference.

$$RESX/(RESU - RESRT) = a_{20} + a_{21} \ln RSGB$$
$$+ a_{22} \ln RD + a_{23} \ln RRDB, \qquad (5.2)$$

$$-RB/(RESU - RESRT) = a_{30} + a_{31} \ln RSGB$$
$$+ a_{32} \ln RD + a_{33} \ln RRDB, \qquad (5.3)$$

$$RESRD + RESX - RB = RESU - RESRT, \qquad (5.4)$$

$$MDD = RESRD/RRDB, \qquad (5.5)$$

$$RT = \beta_0 + \beta_1 RSGB + \beta_2 RQ + \beta_3 RT_{-1}, \qquad (5.6)$$

$$MTDR = \gamma_0 + \gamma_1 \ln RT + \gamma_2 \ln [M2S/(N)(PXGNPR)], \qquad (5.7)$$

where

$$MTDR = MTDS/M2S,$$

$$\ln V = \delta_0 + \delta_1 \ln RSGB + \delta_2 \ln XNPR$$
$$+ \delta_3[\ln V_{-1} - (\ln M2S - \ln M2S_{-1})], \qquad (5.8)$$

where

$$V = (PXGNPR)(XNPR)(N)/M2S.$$

The first three equations describe the desired quantities of required reserves against demand deposits ($RESRD$), excess reserves ($RESX$) and borrowed reserves (RB) as functions of the Treasury bill rate ($RSGB$), the Federal Reserve discount rate (RD), the demand deposit reserve ratio ($RRDB$), and unborrowed reserves ($RESU$) less reserves required for time deposits ($RESRT$). The desired reserve quantities are specified to be linear homogenous in the reserve constraint ($RESU - RESRT$), as was indicated by preliminary estimations, and hence the ratio form is used for the dependent variables. These three equations, plus the reserve accounting identity (5.4), constitute a portfolio balance model with wealth constraint ($RESU - RESRT$). As is well known in such models [see Brainard and Tobin (1968)], all interest rates appear in all demand functions and the sum of the coefficients of each interest rate across all equations must equal zero. Equations (5.1)–(5.3) were estimated by 2SLS to avoid simultaneous equation bias, and this estimation technique shares with OLS the property of automatically imposing the adding-up constraint with respect to the interest variables.

The determination of bank supplies of time deposits is separable in the model. This is because time deposits appeared to have no measurable effect on the demands for excess or borrowed reserves in preliminary estimation. Hence, reserves required for time deposits are determined independently of the portfolio balance model and netted out of the unborrowed reserve constraint in equations (5.1)–(5.3). The stock of time deposits is determined as follows. The interest rate that banks are willing to pay on time deposits (RT) is explained by equation (5.6), and this rate, together with the level of real money balances, determines the proportion of the money supply that the public will hold as time deposits, $MTDR$ [equation (5.7)], and thus the portion of unborrowed reserves available to support demand deposits. The latter, plus the banks' demands for excess and borrowed reserves [equations (5.2) and (5.3)], determine the final amount left for demand deposit requirements [equation (5.1)], and hence the supply of demand deposits for the given reserve ratio [equation (5.5)].

The monetary sector is completed with the addition of a partial adjustment demand function for money, estimated in velocity form [equation (5.8)]. In contrast with the usual partial adjustment hypothesis, which would require only lagged velocity on the right-hand side, Scadding's formulation also includes the change in the nominal money stock in the lagged term. This is because measured velocity has a transitory component owing to the use of measured money stock rather than permanent money stock in its denominator. Hence, some of the variation in measured velocity reflects transitory changes in money stock in addition to the partial adjustments in desired or permanent velocity. The change in money stock is included as an explanatory variable to account for this transitory component of velocity.

The estimated versions of equations (5.1), (5.6), (5.7) and (5.8) are listed below as equations (5.9)–(5.14), with (5.9) and (5.10) the pre-war and post-war versions of (5.1), and (5.12) and (5.13) the corresponding versions of (5.7). The equations for RT and $MTDR$ were estimated by OLS, but 2SLS was used for the required reserves and money demand equations, employing the exogenous and predetermined variables of the money bloc, rather than of the entire macro-model, as the instruments. As noted above, the parameters of the equation for required reserves implicitly reflect the demands for excess and borrowed reserves, so that the latter equations are redundant insofar as the predictions of the endogenous variables in the bloc are concerned and are not listed below.

Identities (5.15)–(5.31) are included to provide detail on components of the money stock and some analytical ratios and growth rates. The basic definition of the money stock is currency plus demand deposits plus time deposits other than large certificates of deposit. This variable is named *M2S* in the model, but it is the same as the conventional definition of *M2* in the literature. The ratio of currency to the money stock is presumed to be exogenously determined.

The estimated parameters of the required reserve demand function (i.e., the demand deposit supply function) are significantly different in the pre-war and post-war samples [see equations (5.9) and (5.10)]. The discount rate was insignificant in the pre-war period, reflecting the fact that member bank borrowing "went out of fashion" during the 1930's because the discount rate consistently exceeded market rates and also because of increased resistance of the Federal Reserve to such borrowing during the banking crises of the period.[4] After World War II, member bank borrowing returned as a viable option, so that the discount rate again becomes a significant determinant of demand deposits. In contrast, the required reserve ratio on demand deposits is insignificant post-war, since banks were loaned up throughout the period, whereas it was a significant influence pre-war owing to the large proportion of excess reserves during the Thirties. As Scadding (1974) has stressed, these large excess reserves of the Thirties were drawn upon as needed to provide interest elasticity to the supply of bank credit and demand deposits, in the same way as borrowed reserves were used before and after the period.

In contrast to the supply side, the demand function for money (*M2* definition) is statistically stable between the pre-war and post-war periods, according to the Chow test at the five percent significance level, and hence the parameters are estimated over the entire sample. The estimated coefficients imply an adjustment speed of 0.4 per year

---

[4] For this reason, total instead of unborrowed reserves were used as the constraint on reserve demands in the pre-war model and the demand equation for borrowed reserves was eliminated from the system. Hence the portfolio choice underlying equation (5.9) is that between excess and required reserves.

and long-run elasticities of real money balances with respect to the interest rate of -0.36 and to real permanent income per capita of 0.87.

2.1. The Term Structure Model

The link between the monetary and the real sectors of the model is provided by the private short and long interest rates, as measured by the four-to-six month commercial paper rate (RS) and Moody's corporate bond average (RL). The private short rate is linked to the Treasury bill rate–the endogenous rate predicted by the supply and demand for money–by regression (5.32), and the purpose of the term structure equations is to connect the private short and long rates.

Since Moody's corporate bond rate (RL) is an average of different maturities, the term structure equations are used to predict the Durand (1942) five-year corporate bond rate $(RLM5)$ and the latter is then related to (RL) by regression equation (5.44).

The equations used to predict $RLM5$ are taken from Nelson (1972). The key stochastic relations are in effect reduced-form equations expressing the relationship between the "price" of forward loans and the determinants of the excess supply of forward loans. The price in this case is the difference between the forward rate and the expected spot rate, which Nelson calls the term premium. The supply of forward loans is the outcome of utility maximization by risk-averse portfolio holders. Nelson shows that the supply of forward loans is an increasing function of the term premium, the short-term spot rate, and the level of business activity. In the empirical implementation, the unemployment rate $(U1)$ is a proxy for business activity in the equations for the 1-year and 4-year term premiums, $RLP1$ [equation (5.39)] and $RLP4$ [equation (5.42)]. The expected sign on $U1$ is positive whereas that on RS is negative. These expectations are met for $U1$ in both regressions and for RS in equation (5.39). In the equation for the 4-year premium, RS has the wrong sign but is insignificant.

Since the term premiums are defined as the difference between the corresponding forward and expected spot rates, it is necessary to determine those rates endogenously. By definition, the forward rates are implicit in the comparison of the current yields on securities of differing maturities, as shown for the 1-year and 4-year maturities in equations (5.35) and (5.36).[5] Following Nelson, the expected spot rates are taken to be conditional expectations of future realizations of the linear stochastic process assumed to generate the spot rates. Autoregressive and mixed autoregressive-moving average schemes of different dimensions were fitted to the *RS* and *RLM1* series to find their time series representations. The best results in terms of maximizing R^2 were equations (5.33) and (5.40). The first of these equations provided the coefficients for estimating the expected rate on commercial paper, *RSX1* [equation (5.34)], whereas the second performed the same role in the estimation of the average of expected 1-year bond rates over the next four years, *RLM1X4A* [equation (5.41)]. These are the expected spot rates that enter the definitions of the 1-year and 4-year term premiums in equations (5.37) and (5.38).

Finally, *RLM5* is calculated from the identity relating it to the term premiums and expected spot rates [equation (5.43)],[6] and then fed into equation (5.44) to predict *RL*.

2.2. Estimated Equations: Money and Interest Rates (MONY)

(1)   *Required Reserves Demand Equation*

   1924–40 [2SLS]

$$RESRD/(RESU + RB - RESRT) = 2.35300 + 0.13810 \ln RSGB$$
$$ (4.9782) \quad (4.5062)$$
$$+ 0.02421 \ln RD$$
$$(0.2146)$$
$$+ 0.36550 \ln RRDB; \quad (5.9)$$
$$(3.3543)$$

$$\bar{R}^2 = 0.890, \qquad \bar{S}_e = 0.070, \qquad DW = 1.2988.$$

_____

[5] All of the rates are annual rates. Thus in equation (5.35), $(1 + RS) = (1 + RS_{1/2})^2$, where $RS_{1/2}$ is the rate on 6-month money. For convenience it was assumed that all commercial paper had a 6-month maturity.

[6] This identity is derived by combining equations (5.35)–(5.38).

1949–66 [2SLS]

$$RESRD/(RESU - RESRT) = 0.65510 + 0.20670 \ln RSGB$$
$$(1.7262) \quad (2.7354)$$
$$- 0.26000 \ln RD$$
$$(2.2565)$$
$$- 0.08902 \ln RRDB; \qquad (5.10)$$
$$(0.6912)$$

$\bar{R}^2 = 0.993, \qquad \bar{S}_e = 0.021, \qquad DW = 2.2758.$

(2)　*Interest Rate on Time Deposits*
1924–40, 1949–66

$$RT = -0.00088 + 0.89214\, RT_{-1} + 0.04105\, RQ + 0.13137\, RSGB;$$
$$(1.3370) \quad (35.1035) \qquad (3.2137) \qquad (8.2618)$$

$\bar{R}^2 = 0.988, \qquad \bar{S}_e = 0.001, \qquad DW = 1.9037. \qquad (5.11)$

(3)　*Public's Desired Time Deposit Ratio*
1922–40

$$MTDR = 0.38766 + 0.14051 \ln RT$$
$$(1.4590) \quad (8.0712)$$
$$+ 0.07618 \ln [M2S/(N)(10^{-3})(PXGNPR)]; \qquad (5.12)$$
$$(1.6489)$$

$\bar{R}^2 = 0.825, \qquad \bar{S}_e = 0.020, \qquad DW = 0.619.$

1949–66

$$MTDR = -1.47804 + 0.13694 \ln RT + 0.00453\, DUMAC$$
$$(2.3616) \quad (13.8981) \qquad (0.6304)$$
$$+ 0.32798 \ln [M2S/(N)(10^{-3})(PXGNPR)]; \qquad (5.13)$$
$$(4.3540)$$

$\bar{R}^2 = 0.989, \qquad \bar{S}_e = 0.008, \qquad DW = 0.786.$

(4)　*Money Demand (velocity form)*
1924–40, 1949–66 [2SLS]

$$\ln V = -0.00710 - 0.03771\, DUMAC + 0.01431 \ln RSGB$$
$$(0.0722) \quad (3.8485) \qquad (5.3106)$$

$$+ 0.04892 \ln XNPR + 0.59890 [\ln V_{-1}$$
$$(4.5793) \qquad (20.6380)$$
$$- (\ln M2S - \ln M2S_{-1})];$$ (5.14)
$$\bar{R}^2 = 0.980, \qquad \bar{S}_e = 0.013, \qquad DW = 1.46.$$

Note: $V = (PXGNPR)(XNPR)(N)/M2S$.

(5) *Money Stock Identities*

$$RSGB = \exp(\ln RSGB),$$ (5.15)

$$M2S = \exp(\ln M2S),$$ (5.16)

$$MTDS = (MTDR)(M2S),$$ (5.17)

$$MTD = MTDS + MTCD,$$ (5.18)

$$MDD = (1 - MTDR - MCR)M2S,$$ (5.19)

$$MC = (MCR)(M2S),$$ (5.20)

$$M1 = MDD + MC,$$ (5.21)

$$RESRD = (RRDB/SRD)MDD,$$ (5.22)

$$RESRT = (RRT/SRT)MTDS + (RRT)(MTCD),$$ (5.23)

$$RESF = RESU - RESRD - RESRT,$$ (5.24)

$$RESX = RESF + RB,$$ (5.25)

$$MMR = M2S/(RESU + RB), \qquad \text{[Pre-war]}$$ (5.26)

$$MMR = M2S/RESU, \qquad \text{[Post-war]}$$ (5.27)

$$MV1 = XGNP\$/M1,$$ (5.28)

$$MV2S = XGNP\$/M2S,$$ (5.29)

$$GRM1 = [(M1 - M1_{-1})/M1_{-1}](100),$$ (5.30)

$$GRM2 = [(M2S - M2S_{-1})/M2S_{-1}](100).$$ (5.31)

(6) *Relation between Commercial Paper and Treasury Bill Rates 1924–40, 1950–65*

$$RS = 0.00290 + 1.02681\ RSGB + 0.00036\ U1 + 0.66220\ \hat{u}_{-1};$$
$$\quad (0.9295)\quad (15.7734)\qquad\qquad (1.7984)\qquad (5.0766)\qquad (5.32)$$
$$\bar{R}^2 = 0.9790,\qquad \bar{S}_e = 0.0021,\qquad DW = 1.9899.$$

(7) *Time Series Representation of Commercial Paper Rate 1924–40, 1950–65*

$$RS = 0.00328 + 0.87426\ RS_{-1};\qquad\qquad\qquad\qquad (5.33)$$
$$\quad (1.1022)\quad (9.3489)$$
$$\bar{R}^2 = 0.7320,\qquad \bar{S}_e = 0.00762,\qquad DW = 1.9936.$$

Note: This is an intermediate relationship used in the estimation of the coefficients of equation (5.34) and is not itself included in the model.

(8) *Expected Rate on Commercial Paper*

$$RSX1 = 0.00171 + 0.93504\ RS.\qquad\qquad\qquad\qquad (5.34)$$

Note: Coefficients are calculated from parameters of regression (5.33). Coefficients adjusted to correct for compounding error in using annual equivalent rates for a less-than-one-year rate. The adjustments are (a) $0.93504 = (0.87426)^{\frac{1}{2}}$ and (b) $0.00171 = (0.00328)/[1 + (0.87426)^{\frac{1}{2}}]$.

(9) *Definitions of Forward Rates and Term Premiums*

$$RSF1 = (1 + RLM1)^2/(1 + RS),\qquad\qquad\qquad\qquad (5.35)$$

$$RLF4 = [(1 + RLM5)^5/(1 + RLM1)]^{\frac{1}{4}} - 1,\qquad\qquad (5.36)$$

$$RLP1 = RSF1 - RSX1,\qquad\qquad\qquad\qquad\qquad (5.37)$$

$$RLP4 = RLF4 - RLM1X4A.\qquad\qquad\qquad\qquad (5.38)$$

(10)   *One-year Term Premium*
       1924–40, 1950–65

$RLP1 = 0.00895 - 0.20895\ RS + 0.00325\ (U1 - U1_{-1})$
          (2.2034)   (1.5948)   (4.0172)
          $+ 0.16924\ \hat{u}_{-1};$ (5.39)
$\bar{R}^2 = 0.3915,$ $\bar{S}_e = 0.0090,$ $DW = 2.1004.$

(11)   *Time Series Representation of Durand One-year Bond Rate*
       1924–40, 1950–65

$RLM1 = 0.00236 + 0.64742\ RLM1_{-1} + 0.24812\ RLM1_{-2};$ (5.40)
          (0.7026)   (3.6260)   (1.3913)
$\bar{R}^2 = 0.7266,$ $\bar{S}_e = 0.0075,$ $DW = 1.9621.$

Note: This is an intermediate relationship used to provide the
        coefficients for predicting the expected 1-year to 4-year
        bond rates involved in equation (5.41) and is not itself
        included in the model.

(12)   *Geometric Average of Expected One-year Bond Rates over
       Next Four Years*

$RLM1X4A = [(1 + RLM1X1)(1 + RLM1X2)(1 + RLM1X3)$
              $\times (1 + RLM1X4)]^{\frac{1}{4}} - 1;$ (5.41)

where

$RLM1X1 = 0.00236 + 0.64742\ RLM1 + 0.24812\ RLM1_{-1},$

$RLM1X2 = 0.00236 + 0.64742\ RLM1X1 + 0.24812\ RLM1,$

$RLM1X3 = 0.00236 + 0.64742\ RLM1X2 + 0.24812\ RLM1X1,$

$RLM1X4 = 0.00236 + 0.64742\ RLM1X3 + 0.24812\ RLM1X2.$

Note: These coefficients are taken from regression (5.40).

(13) *Four-year Term Premium*
      1924–40, 1950–65

$$RLP4 = -0.000001 + 0.05231\ RS + 0.00055\ U1 + 0.50301\ \hat{u}_{-1};$$
$$\quad\quad\quad (0.0006)\quad (1.1247)\quad\quad (4.3414)\quad\quad\quad\quad\quad (5.42)$$
$$\bar{R}^2 = 0.7605,\quad \bar{S}_e = 0.0018,\quad DW = 1.8543.$$

(14) *Identity for Estimated Durand Five-year Commercial Bond Rate*

$$RLM5 = [\{(RLP1 + (1+RSX1))(1+RS)\}^{\frac{1}{2}}$$
$$\times \{RLP4 + (1+RLM1X4A)\}^4]^{\frac{1}{5}} - 1. \quad\quad\quad (5.43)$$

(15) *Relation between Moody's Corporate Bond Average Rate and Durand's Five-year Commercial Bond Rate*
      1924–40, 1950–65

$$RL = 0.00925 + 0.93450\ RLM5 + 0.000014\ U1$$
$$\quad (51.4436)\ (19.3926)\quad\quad\quad (0.0546)$$
$$\quad + 0.01320\ D31; \quad\quad\quad\quad\quad\quad\quad\quad (5.44)$$
$$\quad (3.8927)$$
$$\bar{R}^2 = 0.9413,\quad \bar{S}_e = 0.0024,\quad DW = 1.9440.$$

3. Wages [7]

Most macro-economic models explain wage rates by some form of Phillips (1958) curve. The theoretical basis, as originally developed by Lipsey (1960) and later by Hansen (1970), consists of a stable relationship between wage changes and excess demand for labor, and a stable relationship between excess demand for labor and unemployment. Hansen assumes, for example, that

$$\dot{w}/w = k(q_x/q), \quad\quad\quad\quad\quad\quad\quad\quad (5.45)$$

---

[7] The wage equation was specified and estimated by Michael Hurd.

where q_x = excess demand for labor, q = supply, and $\dot{w} = dw/dt$, and then uses the unemployment rate as a proxy for (q_x/q). The wage equation in our model contains both a measure of short-run excess demand and a measure of unemployment, and hence it is possible to estimate the independent influence of unemployment which was previously obscured because of its correlation with excess demand.

The general hypothesis underlying the wage equation may be stated in the following form:

$$W = k(W_e, U/E, P)(M^D/M_{-1})^\beta. \tag{5.46}$$

In this expression, W_e is the expected wage as viewed by employers, U is the number of unemployed workers, E is employment, P is the price level, M^D is the desired short-run labor input measured in man-hours, and M is actual man-hours. This general specification, plus the additional assumptions leading to the estimating form of the equation, is developed rigorously in Hurd (1974). The approach incorporates elements of the search theory of unemployment [see Phelps et al. (1970)]. All that can be done here is to summarize the basic rationale of the approach, leaving it to the interested reader to consult the original derivation for details on the micro-economic foundations and estimating techniques used by Hurd.

Employers are assumed to be wage setters who have a target level of employment and adjust their wage offers to achieve the target by influencing quits and hires. Desired man-hours are given by the labor demand function described in section 3 of Chapter 1 and in section 2 of Chapter 3. Thus firms have a desired long-run labor input of M^*, but adjustment costs lead them to adjust gradually according to

$$M^D = (M^*)^{\lambda_1}(M_{-1})^{1-\lambda_1},$$

where M^D is desired short-run man-hours, and

$$M = M^D \cdot v,$$

where M = actual man-hours and v is a random disturbance. Thus the last term in expression (5.46) is the ex-ante shortfall in man-hours, which measures the "excess demand for labor" from the employers' viewpoint.

Employers may attempt to achieve the desired short-run labor input in part by adjusting average hours rather than the number of employees. They may also alter wage rates to change the flows of quits and hires, however. At what level must wages be set to achieve the employment target? After abstracting from some unmeasurable influences, Hurd postulates that the wage offer is a function of the three variables determining the proportionality constant in (5.46). The higher the average wage level expected by employers, the higher must be the wage offer to induce acceptance by job seekers or avoid quits by present employees. Since the real wage may influence labor force participation, the current price level must also be considered. Finally, for given wage offers and price level, the expected number of hires is proportional to the pool of unemployed and the expected number of quits to the level of employment, and hence the higher is the ratio of U to E, the lower is the necessary wage offer.

Notice that expression (5.46) relates the current wage level to the excess labor demand, whereas the Phillips curve (5.45) refers to the rate of change of wages. This is because the hypothesis underlying (5.46) assumes that wage offers depend on ex-ante job vacancies and the expected wage as viewed by employers, rather than on market disequilibrium between demand and supply (or perhaps on a theory of collective bargaining) as in the conventional Phillips curve framework. If it is assumed that the expected wage depends on past wage experience, however, the basis is laid for a systematic relationship between W and W_{-1} in the search theory framework. This was Hurd's approach.

The estimating equation was derived as follows. First, the log-linear form was chosen to represent the general hypothesis of equation (5.46),

$$\ln W = a + \alpha \ln W_e + \beta (\ln M^D / M_{-1}) + \gamma \ln (U/E) + \delta \ln P + u,$$
(5.47)

where u is a disturbance term. Second, it was assumed that the expected (relative) rate of change of wages is determined by adaptive expectations,[8]

---

[8] Adaptive expectations in the level of wages was also tried but did not fit the data as well.

$$\dot{W}_e - \dot{W}_{-1} = \lambda (\dot{W}_{e-1} - \dot{W}_{-1}).\tag{5.48}$$

However, for moderate inflation,

$$\dot{W}_e = (W_e - W_{-1})/W_{-1} \simeq \ln (W_e/W_{-1}),$$

and similarly for the other variables, so that

$$\ln W_e \simeq \lambda \ln W_{e-1} + (2 - \lambda) \ln W_{-1} - \ln W_{-2} + v_e,\tag{5.49}$$

where the disturbance term (v_e) has been added to represent unsystematic factors affecting wage expectations.

Lagging (5.47) one period, multiplying by λ and subtracting the resulting expression from (5.47) yields an equation in $\ln W_e - \lambda \ln W_{e-1}$ and other terms. Equation (5.49) may then be substituted to eliminate the term in expected wages. Finally, since $M = M^D v$, where $E(\ln v) = 0$, M^D may be replaced by M/v, resulting in an equation in observable variables for estimation,

$$\begin{aligned}
\ln W - \lambda \ln W_{-1} = a &+ \alpha[(2 - \lambda) \ln W_{-1} - \ln W_{-2}] \\
&+ \beta[\ln (M/M_{-1}) - \lambda \ln (M_{-1}/M_{-2})] \\
&+ \gamma[\ln (U/E) - \lambda \ln (U/E)_{-1}] \\
&+ \delta(\ln P - \lambda \ln P_{-1}) + (u - \lambda u_{-1}) \\
&- \beta(\ln v - \lambda \ln v_{-1}) + \alpha v_e.
\end{aligned}\tag{5.50}$$

The equation was estimated for the 1925–40, 1950–66 sample by a modified version of Amemiya's (1974) two-stage nonlinear method using 10 principal components of the exogenous variables of the complete macro-model as first stage instruments [see Hurd (1974)].

The wage expectations parameter λ was not constrained to be the same pre-war and post-war and was estimated to be 0.2 pre-war and 1.0 post-war [see equation (5.51)]. This means that there were unchanging expectations of $\dot{W}$ in the post-war period, which in view of the rather stable prices that prevailed apart from the Korean War, seems reasonable. Wage expectations may have changed in the late Sixties and early Seventies, however, and it would be desirable to estimate a separate λ for the new inflationary environment of that period and to test for possible changes in the other wage parameters.

The coefficient of price was constrained to be zero post-war for two reasons. First, cross-section studies of labor force participation in the post-war period show that the participation of the dominant group of primary workers (21–64) is relatively insensitive to changes in the real wage rate, and this means that when firms set the wage rate they are not influenced by the expected real rate. Second, an approximate test of the null hypothesis that the price coefficient was zero post-war led to its acceptance.

In the post-war period, with $\lambda = 1$, (5.51) is approximately a first-order difference equation in $\dot{W}$. It is damped rather strongly, so that 58 percent of the ultimate change in the equilibrium level of $\dot{W}$ owing to a once-for-all change in the level of one of the other right-hand variables would occur in the first year of adjustment, and 93 percent would be accomplished within three years. This is of particular interest in connection with the influence of unemployment on wage inflation. The right-hand variable involving unemployment is approximately the rate of change of the unemployment rate. A permanent change in the unemployment rate will cause the rate of change of unemployment to be different from zero for one period only. This in turn will cause wage inflation to differ from its long-run level for that period and for several periods after, but by sharply decreasing magnitudes. For all practical purposes $\dot{W}$ will have returned to its long-run value after three periods at the new permanently different unemployment rate. The equation implies, therefore, that in the long run, the rate of wage inflation is independent of the unemployment rate (a horizontal long-run Phillips curve), and that the short-run trade-off diminishes rapidly over time. Of course, these implications hold only if the other right-hand variables are constant. Since they are endogenous variables, they will generally respond to government policy, and it is possible that a more substantial and permanent trade-off between unemployment and wage inflation would be found in policy simulations of the entire model. This question will be examined in Chapter 8.

The influence of changes in the growth rate of desired manhours on wage inflation is also transitory, for the same reason. However, the elasticity of $\dot{W}$ with respect to M^D/M_{-1} is much greater than it is for unemployment (0.46 as compared with -0.06). An implication of the substantial coefficient on M^D/M_{-1} is that it is costly for firms to increase their work force rapidly. There is not a perfectly elastic short-run labor supply. It may be optimal to hire during one year only part of the increment in work force desired in the long run. This hypothesis is confirmed by the demand function for labor in Chapter 3, which implies an adjustment speed of actual to desired man-hours of 0.56 under constant-returns.

3.1. Estimated Equations: Money Wage Rate (WAGE)

(1) *Money Wage Rate, Private Sector*
     1925–40, 1950–66 [nonlinear 2SLS]

$$\ln W - \lambda \ln W_{-1} = -0.43373 + \alpha \left[(2 - \lambda) \ln W_{-1} - \ln W_{-2}\right]$$
$$\qquad (2.18)$$
$$\qquad + \delta (\ln PCE - \lambda \ln PCE_{-1})$$
$$\qquad + 0.45521[\ln (MH/MH_{-1})$$
$$\qquad (1.96)$$
$$\qquad - \lambda \ln (MH_{-1}/MH_{-2})]$$
$$\qquad - 0.05709[\ln (UN1/E) - \lambda \ln (UN1_{-1}/E_{-1})]$$
$$\qquad (1.22)$$
$$\qquad + 0.15758(D34 - \lambda D34_{-1})$$
$$\qquad (3.33)$$
$$\qquad + 0.46376\, DUMMY1 ; \qquad\qquad\qquad (5.51)$$
$$\qquad (2.23)$$

where

$\lambda = 0.2$ pre-war and 1.0 post-war,
$\delta = -0.36184$ pre-war and 0.0 post-war,
$\qquad (1.25)$
$\alpha = 0.78165$ pre-war and 0.41988 post-war,
$\qquad (2.17) \qquad\qquad\qquad (1.89)$
$S_e = 0.039.$

(2) *After-tax Wage Rate Identities*

$$W1 = (1.0 - TXRW)\{[(W)(MH) + YGF\$ + YGSL\$$$
$$\qquad - (PYLA)(YLA)]/(AH1)(E)\}, \qquad\qquad (5.52)$$

$$W3 = (1.0 - TXRW)(W). \qquad\qquad\qquad (5.53)$$

4. Prices

As described in Chapter 1, section 6, firms are assumed to base price on normal or long-run average cost, but may vary the markup from year to year according to current demand pressures as measured by the rate of capacity utilization. The estimating equation for the basic price variable of the model, the implicit price deflator for gross private non-residential product, is the logarithmic form of equation (1.29),

$$\ln PXNRNT1 - \ln PXNRNT1_{-1}$$
$$= \epsilon \ln \mu_0 + \delta\epsilon \ln UTXNR9C + \epsilon \ln AC - \epsilon \ln PXNRNT1.$$

$$(5.54)$$

Here $PXNRNT1$ is the output price deflator net of indirect business taxes, $UTXNR9C$ is the rate of capacity utilization, and AC is the average cost as determined from identity (1.27). Thus in the estimation of (5.54), AC is a known variable. The equation was estimated for both the constant and the increasing returns assumptions and is adjusted for serial correlation of the residuals.

Given the estimated value of $PXNRNT1$, the price gross of taxes ($PXNR1$) is obtained by adding an estimate of indirect taxes per unit of output [identity (5.88)]. This two-step procedure was adopted on the assumption that indirect business taxes are fully shifted to buyers. Sectoral deflators are then linked to $PXNR1$ through auxiliary equations (5.58) to (5.68), which also include capacity utilization and trend variables as proxies for systematic cyclical and secular influences on relative prices. Since the logarithms of our capacity utilization indexes under constant and increasing returns must be proportional to one another [see equation (1.16)], we show only the increasing-returns versions of the sectoral price equations–those based on $UTXNR9$. When $UTXNR9C$ is substituted for $UTXNR9$, the statistical properties of these equations are not changed, but all the coefficients on the logarithm of the capacity utilization index must be multiplied by the (constant) ratio of $\ln UTXNR9$ to $\ln UTXNR9C$.

Two estimates of the implicit GNP deflator are available in the model. The first, $PXGNP$, is derived as the weighted average of the sectoral deflators, (5.84). The other, $PXGNP1$, is calculated as a weighted average of the directly estimated deflator for gross private non-residential product (*PXNR1*) and the deflators for income originating in housing and government, (5.89). As it turns out, errors in the sectoral deflators are not offsetting, so that *PXGNP1* is predicted with smaller error than the alternative prediction from the sectoral indexes.

The bloc also contains the identity for the permanent price level, (5.92), a variable used in the money bloc.

4.1. Rental Price of Capital

The rental price of capital is a key variable affecting factor substitution and investment demand. It measures the price per annum for the services of a unit of business fixed capital and is a complex function of several variables,

$$Q = p_k (e^r - 1 + \delta)[1 - s - u(1 - ms)B]/(1 - u), \qquad (5.55)$$

where p_k is the price of newly produced capital goods, δ is the real depreciation rate, s is the rate of tax credit for gross investment expenditure, u is the rate of direct taxation on business income, m is the proportion of the investment tax credit which must de deducted from the depreciable base of assets on which the credit is claimed, B is the discounted value of the stream of depreciation charges for tax purposes generated by a dollar of current investment, and r is the discount rate. Equation (5.55) is derived from the conditions for firms' minimizing the discounted value of outlays for factors and taxes over an infinite planning horizon.[9]

Several features of the empirical implementation of (5.55) are worth noting [see equation (5.93)]. First, different rates of depreciation are used pre-war and post-war, in conformity with the marked reduction in average useful lives of assets after World War II (see Chapter 2, section 3). Second, the estimated discounted value of depreciation charges for tax purposes is a weighted average of the

---

[9] The seminal conceptualization of the rental price of capital appears in Jorgenson (1963), who called it the user cost of capital. On our derivation, see Coen (1971a) and Coen and Hickman (1970).

discounted values under four allowable depreciation schemes: straight-line, declining-balance, sum-of-years-digits, and accelerated amortization. Third, and most important, we have experimented with three alternative measures of r: the nominal after-tax rate of interest on private bonds, the corresponding real rate of interest (the nominal rate corrected for the expected rate of price inflation), and a constant, after-tax required rate of return of 10 percent. The last assumption yields smaller errors of prediction of investment alone and better performance of the entire model and hence has been adopted herein.[10] Hence, variations in market rates of interest have no direct influence on business fixed investment in our model.

4.2. Estimated Equations: Prices (PRIC)

(1) *Price of Private Non-residential Product Net of Indirect Business Taxes, Direct Estimate, Constant Returns to Scale 1925–40, 1950–66*

$$\ln PXNRNT1 - \ln PXNRNT1_{-1} = 0.42331 - 0.07395\, DUMMY1$$
$$(12.3751)\ (3.8649)$$
$$+ 0.09652 \ln UTXNR9C$$
$$(3.1375)$$
$$+ 0.92226\,[0.31634 \ln Q4$$
$$(13.1697)$$
$$+ 0.68366 \ln W$$
$$- 0.06550\, TIME3$$
$$- 0.01959\, TIME5$$
$$- \ln PXNRNT1_{-1}]$$
$$+ 0.6620\, \hat{u}_{-1}; \qquad (5.56)$$

$\bar{S}_e = 0.017.$

(1a) *Price of Private Non-residential Product Net of Indirect Business Taxes, Direct Estimate, Increasing Returns to Scale*

---

[10] A similar assumption–a constant before-tax rate of return of 20 percent in the evaluation of investment opportunities–has been adopted by Hall and Jorgenson (1971) in a study of tax policy and investment.

1925–40, 1950–66

$$\ln PXNRNT1 - \ln PXNRNT1_{-1} = 1.19226 - 0.07950\ DUMMY1$$
$$(13.5541)\ (5.7174)$$
$$+ 0.18692\ \ln UTXNR9$$
$$(7.8629)$$
$$+ 0.88146\ [0.22435\ \ln Q4$$
$$(13.6231)$$
$$+ 0.77565\ \ln W$$
$$- 0.20636\ \ln XNR$$
$$- 0.01626\ TIME3$$
$$- 0.01547\ TIME5$$
$$- \ln PXNRNT1_{-1}]$$
$$+ 0.5114\ \hat{u}_{-1}; \qquad (5.57)$$

$\bar{S}_e = 0.016.$

(2) *Price of Consumer Non-durables*
1925–40, 1950–66

$$\ln PCND = 0.26784 + 1.1674\ \ln PXNR1$$
$$(5.1351)\quad(16.9643)$$
$$+ 0.06060\ \ln UTXNR9 - 0.00674\ TIME3$$
$$(2.7216)\qquad\qquad(4.7032)$$
$$- 0.00770\ TIME5 + 0.5701\ \hat{u}_{-1}; \qquad (5.58)$$
$$(5.7147)$$

$\bar{S}_e = 0.011.$

(3) *Price of Consumer Services*
1925–40, 1950–66

$$\ln PCS = -0.29398 + 0.41238\ \ln PXNR1$$
$$(1.9101)\quad(3.1669)$$
$$+ 0.01384\ \ln UTXNR9$$
$$(0.3112)$$
$$- 0.00684\ TIME3 + 0.00983\ TIME5 + 0.8622\ \hat{u}_{-1};$$
$$(0.8521)\qquad\qquad(2.5267)\qquad\qquad(5.59)$$

$\bar{S}_e = 0.021.$

(4) *Price of Automobiles*
   1924–40, 1949–66

$$\ln PCA = -0.03759 + 0.98201 \ln PXNR1$$
$$\qquad\qquad (0.2920)\quad (5.7460)$$
$$\qquad -0.18450 \ln UTXNR9$$
$$\qquad (3.5217)$$
$$\qquad -0.00288\ TIME3 - 0.00504\ TIME5$$
$$\qquad (1.3827)\qquad\qquad (1.4750)$$
$$\qquad +0.22865\ DUMMY1\ ;$$
$$\qquad (4.1882)\qquad\qquad\qquad\qquad\qquad (5.60)$$
$$\bar{R}^2 = 0.9941,\qquad \bar{S}_e = 0.034,\qquad DW = 1.5906.$$

(5) *Price of Other Consumer Durables*
   1925–40, 1950–66

$$\ln PCOD = 0.38904 + 1.1582 \ln PXNR1 + 0.02818 \ln UTXNR9$$
$$\qquad (4.1754)\quad (9.409)\qquad\qquad (0.7407)$$
$$\qquad -0.00811\ TIME3 - 0.01781\ TIME5$$
$$\qquad (4.4326)\qquad\qquad (7.2045)$$
$$\qquad +0.24294\ DUMMY1$$
$$\qquad (4.4369)$$
$$\qquad +0.3097\ \hat{u}_{-1};\qquad\qquad\qquad\qquad\qquad (5.61)$$
$$\bar{S}_e = 0.020.$$

(6) *Price of Gross Business Fixed Investment*
   1925–40, 1950–66

$$\ln PIGB = -0.44990 + 0.85476 \ln PXNR1$$
$$\qquad (5.1683)\quad (8.8771)$$
$$\qquad -0.01818 \ln UTXNR9$$
$$\qquad (0.6444)$$
$$\qquad +0.01425\ TIME3 + 0.00404\ TIME5$$
$$\qquad (3.8478)\qquad\qquad (1.1520)$$
$$\qquad +0.29567\ DUMMY1$$
$$\qquad (2.0944)$$
$$\qquad +0.7747\ \hat{u}_{-1};\qquad\qquad\qquad\qquad\qquad (5.62)$$
$$\bar{S}_e = 0.015.$$

(7) *Price of Non-farm Residential Construction*
1925–40, 1950–66

$$\ln PHGIN = -0.38631 + 0.99086 \ln PXNR1$$
$$\qquad (2.9606) \quad (6.0723)$$
$$\qquad + 0.08420 \ln UTXNR9$$
$$\qquad (1.5860)$$
$$\qquad + 0.00145 \ TIME3 + 0.00044 \ TIME5$$
$$\qquad (2.7642) \qquad\qquad (0.1019)$$
$$\qquad + 0.37877 \ DUMMY1$$
$$\qquad (2.5809)$$
$$\qquad + 0.6572 \ \hat{u}_{-1}; \qquad\qquad\qquad (5.63)$$
$$\bar{S}_e = 0.025.$$

(8) *Price of Gross Private Domestic Investment*
1924–40, 1949–66

$$\ln PIGPD = 0.64486 + 2.2977 \ln PXNR1 + 0.00145 \ln UTXNR9$$
$$\qquad (3.4417) \quad (9.1973) \qquad\qquad (0.0188)$$
$$\qquad + 0.02171 \ TIME3 - 0.01794 \ TIME5; \qquad (5.64)$$
$$\qquad (7.1379) \qquad\qquad (3.7502)$$
$$\bar{R}^2 = 0.9920, \qquad \bar{S}_e = 0.0493, \qquad DW = 1.9059.$$

(9) *Price of Exports*
1925–40, 1950–66

$$\ln PFEX = 0.43417 + 1.6491 \ln PXNR1 + 0.11005 \ln UTXNR9$$
$$\qquad (3.1465) \quad (11.0212) \qquad\qquad (2.1995)$$
$$\qquad + 0.01111 \ TIME3 - 0.01982 \ TIME5$$
$$\qquad (1.8475) \qquad\qquad (3.5014)$$
$$\qquad + 0.25782 \ DUMMY1$$
$$\qquad (1.1170)$$
$$\qquad + 0.7841 \ \hat{u}_{-1}; \qquad\qquad\qquad (5.65)$$
$$\bar{S}_e = 0.023.$$

(10) *Price of Federal Purchases of Goods and Services (excluding*
wages and salaries of government employees)
1925–40, 1950–66

$$\ln PGGF = 0.38171 + 1.61911 \ln PXNR1$$
$$\quad (1.2125) \quad (4.0686)$$
$$\quad + 0.06459 \ln UTXNR9 - 0.00473 \ TIME3$$
$$\quad (0.4907) \qquad\qquad (0.4164)$$
$$\quad - 0.01169 \ TIME5 + 0.6995 \ \hat{u}_{-1}; \qquad\qquad (5.66)$$
$$\quad (1.4255)$$

$\bar{S}_e = 0.063.$

(11) *Price of State and Local Purchases of Goods and Services (excluding wages and salaries of government employees)*

$$\ln PGGSL = -0.22420 + 0.78904 \ln PXNR1$$
$$\quad (1.7419) \quad (4.6315)$$
$$\quad + 0.04205 \ln UTXNR9 - 0.00027 \ TIME3$$
$$\quad (0.7664) \qquad\qquad (0.0798)$$
$$\quad + 0.00603 \ TIME5 + 0.5458 \ \hat{u}_{-1}; \qquad\qquad (5.67)$$
$$\quad (1.8162)$$

$\bar{S}_e = 0.027.$

(12) *Price of Income Originating in State and Local Government (excluding work relief)*
1925–40, 1950–66

$$\ln PYSLNW = 0.98044 + 0.29374 \ln PXNR1$$
$$\quad (7.8909) \quad (2.3111)$$
$$\quad - 0.01284 \ln UTXNR9 + 0.00461 \ TIME3$$
$$\quad (0.3022) \qquad\qquad (0.9592)$$
$$\quad + 0.03811 \ TIME5 - 0.4217 \ DUMMY1; \quad (5.68)$$
$$\quad (8.3539) \qquad\qquad (2.3061)$$

$\bar{S}_e = 0.020.$

(13) *Price Identities*

$$PXNRNT1 = \exp(\ln PXNRNT1), \qquad\qquad (5.69)$$

$$PCND = \exp(\ln PCND), \qquad\qquad (5.70)$$

$$PCS = \exp(\ln PCS), \qquad\qquad (5.71)$$

$$PCA = \exp(\ln PCA), \qquad\qquad (5.72)$$

$$PCOD = \exp(\ln PCOD), \qquad\qquad (5.73)$$

$$PIGB = \exp(\ln PIGB), \tag{5.74}$$

$$PIGPD = \exp(\ln PIGPD), \tag{5.75}$$

$$PHGIN = \exp(\ln PHGIN), \tag{5.76}$$

$$PFEX = \exp(\ln PFEX), \tag{5.77}$$

$$PYSLNW = \exp(\ln PYSLNW), \tag{5.78}$$

$$PGGF = \exp(\ln PGGF), \tag{5.79}$$

$$PGGSL = \exp(\ln PGGSL), \tag{5.80}$$

$$PCE = [(PCND)(CND) + (PCS)(CS) + (PCA)(CA) \\ + (PYLA)(YLA) + YFGWR\$]/GF, \tag{5.81}$$

$$PGF = [(PGGF)(GGF) + (5.9818)(EGFNW)(PYFNW) \\ + (PYLA)(YLA) + YFGWR\$]/GF, \tag{5.82}$$

$$PGSL = [(PGGSL)(GSL - YGSL) + YSLWR\$ \\ + (3.9156)(EGSNW)(PYSLNW)]/GSL, \tag{5.83}$$

$$PXGNP = [(PCE)(CE) + (PIGPD)(IGPD) + (PGF)(GF) \\ + (PGSL)(GSL) + (PFEX)(FEX) \\ - (PFIM)(FIM)]/XGNP, \tag{5.84}$$

$$PXP = [(PXGNP)(XGNP) - YGSL\$ - YGF\$]/XP, \tag{5.85}$$

$$PXNR = [(PXP)(XP) - (PYHR)(YHR)]/XNR, \tag{5.86}$$

$$PXNRNT = PXNR - (TXI\$/XNR), \tag{5.87}$$

$$PXNR1 = PXNRNT1 + (TXI\$/XNR), \tag{5.88}$$

$$PXGNP1 = [(PXNR1)(XNR) + (PYHR)(YHR) + YFGWR\$ \\ + (5.9818)(EGFNW)(PYFNW) + (PYLA)(YLA) \\ + (3.9156)(EGSNW)(PYSLNW) \\ + YSLWR\$]/XGNP, \tag{5.89}$$

$$INFL = [(PXGNP - PXGNP_{-1})/PXGNP_{-1}](100), \tag{5.90}$$

$$INFLC = [(PCE - PCE_{-1})/PCE_{-1}](100), \tag{5.91}$$

$$PXGNPR = PXGNPRT + \sum_{j=0}^{6}(W_i)(PXGNP - PXGNPRT)_{-j}, \tag{5.92}$$

where

$$W_0 = 0.33, \qquad W_1 = 0.22, \qquad W_2 = 0.15, \qquad W_3 = 0.10,$$

$$W_4 = 0.07, \qquad W_5 = 0.05, \qquad W_6 = 0.03.$$

(14)   *Rental Price of Capital*

$$
\begin{aligned}
Q4 = {} & [PIGB/(1 - TXBR)] \\
& \times [0.1071 + 0.0319 \, DUMMY1 + \exp(RDISC) - 1] \\
& \times [1 - ITCR - \{(1 - (ITCD \times ITCR)) \times TXBR \\
& \times (WHTSL \times DVSL + WHTDB \times DVDB + WHTSYD \\
& \times DVSYD + WHTACAM \times DVAM)\}], \tag{5.93}
\end{aligned}
$$

where

$$RDISC = 0.1,$$

$$
\begin{aligned}
DVSL = {} & [\exp(-RDISC)] \\
& \times [1 - \exp(-RDISC \times KGBLIF)] \\
& /(RDISC \times KGBLIF),
\end{aligned}
$$

$$
\begin{aligned}
DVDB = {} & \{[\exp(-RDISC)] \times 2 \\
& \times [1 - \exp\{(-0.5 \, RDISC \times KGBLIF) - 1\}] \\
& /[(RDISC \times KGBLIF) + 2]\} \\
& + \{[\exp(-RDISC)] \times 2 \\
& \times [\exp\{(-0.5 \, RDISC \times KGBLIF) - 1\} \\
& - \exp\{(-RDISC \times KGBLIF) - 1\}] \\
& /[RDISC \times KGBLIF]\},
\end{aligned}
$$

$$
\begin{aligned}
DVSYD = {} & [\exp(-RDISC)] \times 2 \\
& \times [(RDISC \times KGBLIF) \\
& - (1 - \exp\{-RDISC \times KGBLIF\})] \\
& /(RDISC \times KGBLIF)^2,
\end{aligned}
$$

$$
\begin{aligned}
DVAM = {} & [\exp(-RDISC)] \\
& \times [1 - \exp(-5 \times RDISC)]/(5 \times RDISC).
\end{aligned}
$$

CHAPTER 6

Income and Taxes

1. Introduction

The principal purpose of the income and tax-transfer blocs is to provide an endogenous determination of disposable personal income, a prominent variable in several of our expenditure equations (see Chapter 2). With current-dollar gross national product built up from the expenditure side of the accounts [see equation (3.2) and (3.5) above], national income and personal income are arrived at by the addition and subtraction of appropriate items. In brief outline, national income is current-dollar *GNP* less capital consumption allowances and indirect business taxes; personal income is national income less corporate profits taxes, corporate retained earnings, and social insurance taxes, plus transfer payments; and disposable personal income is personal income less personal taxes. The income bloc contains equations for corporate profits, dividends, and capital consumption allowances, as well as the various income identities required in the model. The tax-transfer bloc provides equations for major federal taxes and for unemployment benefits. All taxes and transfers of state and local governments are exogenous.

Our procedure for determining national and personal income does not require explanatory equations for the conventional income flows comprising the national income, except for corporate profits. Thus, the model does not account for the shares of compensation of employees, proprietors' income, and rental income in national income. There is, however, a functional distribution of income generated by the model, namely, that between "labor income" and "property income". Our measure of labor income consists of compensation

of employees (exclusive of that paid by sole proprietors and partnerships) and an imputed labor share of proprietors' income;[1] property
income is the difference between national income and labor income.
Labor income in the private sector is determined by the product of
the endogenous private wage rate[2] and endogenous private man-
hours, while labor income in the public sector (income originating in
government) is largely exogenous.[3] Identities pertaining to the shares
of private labor income, corporate profits, and other income in
national income are contained in the income bloc.

Finally, personal saving is obtained by subtracting personal consumption expenditures, net interest paid by consumers (exogenous),
and personal transfers to foreigners (exogenous) from disposable
personal income, and an identity defining the personal saving rate is
included in the income bloc.

2. Income

Corporate profits before taxes, including inventory valuation adjustment, plus corporate capital consumption allowances are related to
the level of private non-residential output, the excess of price over
unit labor cost in the private non-residential sector, and the unemployment rate. The basic notion here is that profits depend on the level
of output and profit per unit of output. The unemployment rate
appears in the equation to capture the relative decline in the corporate
share of private output normally observed during overall business
contractions. It should be noted that this approach to explaining
corporate profits relies on accounting relationships rather than behavioral postulates. Price, wage, and productivity behavior are dealt

---

[1] As explained in Appendix B, the imputation is based on the assumption that the
proportions of labor and property income in proprietors' income are the same as those
observed in the corporate sector.

[2] It should be noted that our private wage rate is not a wage index of the usual sort.
Rather, it is the wage rate implicit in our estimates of private labor income and private
man-hours. See Appendix B for details.

[3] Income originating in federal employment is entirely exogenous. Employment in
state and local governments is exogenous, but the wage rate of state and local employees
(*PYSLNW*) is endogenous.

with elsewhere in the model. The identities (6.9)–(6.12) define corporate profits before and after taxes and corporate cash flow.

Our specification of the dividend equation follows Brittain's (1966) study of dividend behavior. Let α be the desired, or target, ratio of dividends to corporate cash flow. The target level of dividends is then $\alpha\ YCFC\$$, and we assume that actual dividends are adjusted toward the target level at a rate β. Thus,

$$YD\$ - YD\$_{-1} = \beta\,(\alpha\ YCFC\$ - YD\$_{-1}). \tag{6.1}$$

The target payout ratio is assumed to be negatively related to the excess of the tax rate on dividends over the tax rate on long-term capital gains, reflecting the strength of shareholders' desires to receive income in the form of more lightly taxed capital gains. Since the tax rate on capital gains did not vary much over the sample period, the marginal statutory tax rate on ordinary income at the \$50,000 level ($TXRD$) is used as a surrogate for the differential tax rate on dividends. The target dividend ratio is also assumed to be negatively influenced by the cost of long-term borrowing to firms (RL), reflecting management and shareholders' preferences to finance larger portions of capital expenditures from internal sources when debt issue is expensive.

Hence,

$$\alpha = \alpha_0 + \alpha_1\ TXRD + \alpha_2 RL, \qquad \alpha_1, \alpha_2 < 0, \tag{6.2}$$

and

$$
\begin{aligned}
YD\$ - YD\$_{-1} = {} &\beta\alpha_0\ YCFC\$ + \beta\alpha_1\,(TXRD)(YCFC\$) \\
&+ \beta\alpha_2(RL\,)(YCFC\$) - \beta YD\$_{-1}.
\end{aligned} \tag{6.3}
$$

We omit the period 1936–38 in fitting this equation, since these years were disturbed by federal legislation allowing corporations to exclude dividend payments from their taxable income. The special variable $DYD\$$ adjusts dividends predicted for 1936–38 by our estimated equation to the actual levels of dividends in those years.

Corporate and non-corporate capital consumption allowances are treated separately, each being related to an approximate measure of the stock of capital goods to which it pertains. While capital consumption allowances are endogenous, they are not obtained from fitted, stochastic equations.

Corporate capital consumption allowances, which in the U.S. national accounts largely reflect depreciation charges reported on corporation tax returns, are expressed as a depreciation rate multiplied by the gross stock of business fixed capital valued at historical costs and assuming a service life of 15 years.[4] The depreciation rate is set equal to the ratio of actual corporate capital consumption to our measure of the gross stock; thus, the depreciation rate varies from year to year, primarily as a result of changes in tax depreciation policy and enforcement practices. This approach facilitates simulations involving alternative tax depreciation policies, since policy changes may be introduced by simply modifying the depreciation rate.

Non-corporate capital consumption allowances are related in a similar fashion to the stock of non-farm residential structures. In this case, however, we use the net stock existing at the end of the previous year valued at last year's price level.

2.1. Estimated Equations: Income (INC)

(1) *Corporate Profits before Taxes, Including Inventory Valuation Adjustment, plus Corporate Capital Consumption Allowances 1924–40, 1949–66*

$$\ln YCFCG\$ = 0.66865 + 0.90821 \ln XNR$$
$$ (0.4239) \quad (4.1128)$$
$$ + 1.45607 \ln [PXNR - (YL\$/XNR)]$$
$$ (5.2549)$$
$$ - 0.11616 \ln U1; \tag{6.4}$$
$$ (2.1593)$$
$$\bar{R}^2 = 0.9905, \quad \bar{S}_e = 0.1036, \quad DW = 0.8134.$$

---

[4] In our measurement of the gross stock, we also make use of the so-called half-year convention; that is, only one-half the value of assets acquired in a given year are included in the depreciable stock for that year.

(2) *Dividends*
1924–35, 1939–40, 1949–66

$$YD\$ - YD\$_{-1} = 0.4490 + 0.1921 \ YCFC\$$$
$$(1.9105) \ (6.2196)$$
$$-0.1142 \ (TXRD)(YCFC\$)$$
$$(3.3100)$$
$$-0.5198 \ (RL)(YCFC\$)$$
$$(1.6000)$$
$$-0.4146 \ YD\$_{-1} + DYD\$; \tag{6.5}$$
$$(6.0178)$$
$$\bar{R}^2 = 0.8180, \qquad \bar{S}_e = 0.3263, \qquad DW = 1.4743.$$

(3) *Corporate Capital Consumption Allowances*

$$CCC\$ = (CCCR)[0.5 \ (PIGB)(IGB) + \sum_{i=1}^{14} (PIGB_{-i})(IGB_{-i})$$
$$+ 0.5 \ (PIGB_{-15})(IGB_{-15})]. \tag{6.6}$$

(4) *Non-corporate Capital Consumption Allowances*

$$CCNC\$ = (CCNCR)(PHGIN_{-1})(HKN_{-1}). \tag{6.7}$$

(5) *Income Identities*

$$YCFCG\$ = \exp(\ln YCFCG\$), \tag{6.8}$$

$$YC\$ = YCFCG\$ - CCC\$, \tag{6.9}$$

$$YCB\$ = YCFCG\$ - CCC\$ - IVAC\$, \tag{6.10}$$

$$YCBT\$ = YCB\$ - TXC\$, \tag{6.11}$$

$$YCFC\$ = YCFCG\$ - IVAC\$ - TXC\$, \tag{6.12}$$

$$CC\$ = CCC\$ + CCNC\$, \tag{6.13}$$

$$YN\$ = XGNP\$ - CC\$ - TXI\$ - TPB\$ - ERR\$ + SUB\$, \tag{6.14}$$

$$YPE\$ = YN\$ - YCFCG\$ + CCC\$ - TXS\$ - SW\$ + TPG\$$$
$$+ YIG\$ + YIC\$ + YD\$ + TPB\$, \tag{6.15}$$

$$YPD\$ = YPE\$ - TXP\$, \tag{6.16}$$

$$YPD = YPD\$/PCE, \tag{6.17}$$

$$YL\$ = (W)(MH), \tag{6.18}$$

$$SHLAB = YL\$/YN\$, \tag{6.19}$$

$$SHPRO = YC\$/YN\$, \tag{6.20}$$

$$SHOTH = (YN\$ - YL\$ - YC\$)/YN\$, \tag{6.21}$$

$$SP\$ = YPD\$ - CE\$ - YIC\$ - TPPF\$, \tag{6.22}$$

$$SAVRATE = SP\$/YPD\$. \tag{6.23}$$

3. Taxes and Transfers [5]

Unemployment insurance benefits,[6] the only endogenous component of transfer payments, are expressed as the product of the average payment per beneficiary and the number of beneficiaries. The mean level of benefits is related to a simple average of the private-sector wage rate over the past three years. This equation accurately captures the endogenous behavior of policy-makers attempting to keep unemployment benefits in line with the growth of employee earnings. The change in the number of beneficiaries depends on current and past changes in the number of unemployed persons, the negative coefficient on the lagged unemployment change reflecting exhaustion of benefits by individuals who have been unemployed for long periods.[7] The identity (6.39) defining total benefits includes a special

---

[5] David Waterman and George Green were primarily responsible for the construction of this bloc.

[6] The unemployment insurance program referred to here is the so-called state unemployment insurance system. This program was established by the federal government in the 1930's, although it has always been administered by state governments, subject to broad federal regulations. For national accounting purposes, benefits paid and taxes collected under the program are attributed to the federal government. Railroad unemployment insurance benefits, another federally sponsored program, are not included in our variable *TPUC\$*.

[7] The maximum duration of benefits has been about 26 weeks in most states.

adjustment (*ADJUC$*) to account for emergency benefits provided during periods of particularly high or prolonged unemployment (1958–59 and 1961–62, for example). Although the unemployment insurance program was initiated in the 1930's, we have endogenized benefits only for the post-war period.

The tax equations take the general form of a rate times a base, so that the logarithms of receipts are linearly related to the logarithms of tax rates and tax bases. Since statutory rate schedules and definitions of bases of most taxes are quite complex, and since the broad categories of receipts with which we deal often include several types of levies, our measures of rates and bases are necessarily somewhat rough approximations. Furthermore, the model does not always generate the best variables with which to construct tax bases, which introduces further inaccuracies in these measures. For these reasons, our estimates of elasticities of receipts with respect to changes in rates and bases diverge from unity in many instances. Also, major changes in tax codes from time to time require separate tax equations for different eras, which we sometimes accomplish by the use of shift and slope dummies in the relations.

Unemployment insurance contributions are payroll taxes levied on private employers at rates which vary according to the employer's past contributions–benefit experience. If unemployed workers are collecting benefits which are high relative to their previous employer's contributions to the program, his tax rate will be increased, and conversely. We relate total contributions to a regularly published estimate of the national-average tax rate and, as a proxy for the base, to our own measure of private labor income. The tax rate is in turn determined by its own lagged value and by the ratio of lagged benefits to an average of the base over the past three years. This is the only instance in which we have attempted to provide an endogenous explanation of a tax rate. As with unemployment benefits, contributions to the program are endogenous only in the post-war period.

Old-age, survivors, and disability insurance contributions, commonly referred to as social security taxes, also take the form of a payroll levy.[8] This flat-rate tax, half borne by employers and half by

---

[8] Self-employed individuals have also made contributions to this program beginning in 1952. We have included these contributions in our measure of total receipts.

employees, applies to annual earnings only up to a specified maximum. Our equation relates total receipts to the tax rate, to an
approximate measure of the base, and to maximum taxable earnings
relative to annual private labor income per worker. The proxy
measure for the base is composed of three elements: (1) the share of
private labor income representing compensation of employees covered by the program; (2) military pay beginning in 1957 when
coverage of the program was extended to the armed forces; and (3)
the share of private labor income representing earnings of self-
employed persons to whom coverage was extended in 1952.[9] Having
explained the total of employee, employer, and self-employed contributions in our basic equation, we specify subsidiary relations to
account for the employee share of the total, a variable required to
define the base of the personal income tax (see below). Until 1952, the
employee share was simply one-half the total; thereafter, the employee share fell to about 47 percent of the total, reflecting the
extension of coverage to the self-employed.

Federal personal tax receipts consist predominantly of revenues
generated by the personal income tax. Marked changes in the
structure of the income tax between the pre-war and post-war periods
preclude specifying a single equation for both eras. In the pre-war
period there was no withholding system, and personal exemptions
were relatively large. Our rate proxy for this period is the average tax
rate on an income of $50,000, and our base proxy is adjusted personal
income. The adjustments to personal income account for the exclu-
sion of government transfers from taxable income and for the
inclusion of employee contributions to social security and net realized capital gains in taxable income. Both the rate and base are lagged
one year, since in the absence of withholding, current-year receipts
are tax liabilities on last year's income.

With the introduction of withholding in the early 1940's, current-
year personal tax receipts appearing in the national accounts include
current-year withholding net of refunds on last year's withholding.

---

[9] Contributions of the self-employed are not withheld from pay checks; rather, these
individuals make payments to the program when they file their annual tax returns in
April for their previous year's income. Hence, we introduce a one-year lag in entering
earnings of the self-employed into the tax base.

Thus, actual tax liabilities on current-year income are best approximated as current-year receipts plus current-year refunds (on last year's withholding) less next year's refunds. It is this measure of tax liabilities which we choose as our dependent variable for the post-war period. Identity (6.45) relates this variable to personal tax receipts. Our rate proxy for the post-war period is the statutory marginal tax rate on taxable income of $2,000 to $4,000, and our base proxy is once again adjusted personal income, although we found the capital gains adjustment to be unimportant here and therefore omitted it. We did, however, include the personal exemption level per capita[10] as an additional determinant of tax liabilities but constrained the elasticity on the exemption to be the same as that on the tax base. Thus, either a one percent rise in our measure of the base or a one percent decline in the exemption level will raise tax liabilities by 1.8 percent, according to our relation.

As was the case with personal tax receipts, structural differences between the pre-war and post-war periods required separate corporate profits tax equations for the two eras. Our strategy for the pre-war period was first to construct our own measure of the tax base (*ECB$*) by dividing corporate taxes by the top-bracket statutory rate and then to specify an equation to account endogenously for the size of this base. In our formulation, the base is determined by (a) corporate profits before taxes (with a coefficient constrained to unity), (b) a variable measuring the exemption level on corporate profits,[11] (c) a dummy variable for 1936–37 capturing the influence of dividend deductability in those years, and (d) the change in the unemployment rate, which is intended to account for corporate losses occurring in business contractions. With the base explained by

---

[10] Per capita personal exemption is calculated as a weighted average of exemption levels for different population groups, the weights reflecting the importance of each group in the total population.

[11] This variable, which we refer to as the "equivalent corporate tax exemption", reflects both the amount of profits exempted from tax, if any, and the progressivity of the rate structure for taxable profits. For example, if all profits above $10,000 are taxed at a flat rate of ten percent, then the equivalent exemption is simply $10,000. However, if the first $10,000 of profits is taxed at five percent and the remainder at ten percent, then the equivalent exemption is $5,000. In this latter case, a firm with $20,000 in profits would pay the same tax under the graduated rate structure as it would under a flat ten-percent rate with a $5,000 exemption.

equation (6.34), the identity (6.47) expresses corporate taxes as the top-bracket rate times the base.

The corporate tax equation for the post-war period is more straightforward. Tax liabilities are directly regressed on the statutory top-bracket rate and corporate profits before taxes, with a slope dummy introduced in 1951–53 on the tax rate to account for the excess profits tax in those years. We measure tax liabilities here before subtraction of the investment tax credit, which was introduced in 1962. Equation (6.36) determines the amount of the credit as the product of the effective credit rate and the value of non-residential fixed investment. This is not an estimated equation; rather, the effective credit rate is simply set equal each year to the ratio of the actual credit claimed by corporations to the value of non-residential fixed investment. Finally, identity (6.48) gives us corporate taxes net of the investment credit.

Indirect business tax receipts encompass a multitude of commodity levies whose coverage and rate structures have been subject to rather frequent changes. Our approach has been to relate these receipts to the value of private non-residential output (net of indirect taxes), allowing the regression coefficients to determine the overall effective average and marginal tax rates. Upon inspecting scatter diagrams of receipts against the value of output, and bearing in mind the legislative history of these taxes, we were able to identify subperiods displaying relatively stable structures. Using appropriate shift and slope dummies to demarcate these subperiods, we estimated separate pre-war and post-war relationships with reasonable success.

In developing these tax-transfer equations, we sought not only to provide accurate endogenous predictions of receipts and expenditures but also to include in the relationships the major federal policy parameters which might be altered in simulation analyses or post-sample projections. The translation of complex tax-transfer policies into a small number of parameters is admittedly a difficult and inexact undertaking; our aspiration has been to strike a satisfactory balance between attentiveness to statutory details on the one hand and the benefits of plausible simplifications on the other, while recognizing the inherent limitations of an aggregative model. Although the tax-transfer bloc is economical in structure, it nonetheless allows us to study an extensive and interesting set of policy options.

3.1. *Estimated Equations: Taxes and Transfers (TXTR)*

(1) *Average Benefit for Unemployment Compensation* (post-war only)
1949–66

$$ABUC\$ = 5.4491 + 12.1644 \times \tfrac{1}{3} \sum_{i=1}^{3} W_{-i}; \qquad (6.24)$$
$$(8.7316) \ (39.1325)$$
$$\bar{R}^2 = 0.9890, \qquad \bar{S}_e = 0.6489, \qquad DW = 1.6387.$$

(2) *Number of Beneficiaries for Unemployment Compensation* (post-war only)
1949–66

$$NBUC - NBUC_{-1} = 0.5184 \, (UN1 - UN1_{-1})$$
$$(20.30)$$
$$- 0.1122 \, (UN1_{-1} - UN1_{-2}); \qquad (6.25)$$
$$(4.35)$$
$$\bar{R}^2 = 0.9670, \qquad \bar{S}_e = 0.0882, \qquad DW = 2.3961.$$

(3) *Contributions to Unemployment Insurance Programs* (post-war only)
1949–66

$$\ln TXUN\$ = -3.7172 + 0.9529 \ln UNCR$$
$$(37.07) \quad (41.45)$$
$$+ 0.7006 \ln YL\$; \qquad (6.26)$$
$$(35.69)$$
$$\bar{R}^2 = 0.9984, \qquad \bar{S}_e = 0.0162, \qquad DW = 2.0398.$$

(4) *Contribution Rate for Unemployment Insurance Programs* (post-war only)
1949–66

$$\ln UNCR = 1.6966 + 0.8133 \ln UNCR_{-1}$$
$$(7.60) \quad (16.09)$$
$$+ 0.2698 \ln \left(\frac{TPUC\$_{-1}}{YL\$_{-1} + YL\$_{-2} + YL\$_{-3}} \right); \quad (6.27)$$
$$(7.33)$$
$$\bar{R}^2 = 0.9575, \quad \bar{S}_e = 0.0506, \quad DW = 1.7824.$$

(5) *Employer, Employee and Self-employed Contributions to Old-age, Survivors, and Disability Insurance Programs 1937–40, 1949–66*

$$\ln TXOAS\$ = -7.2505 + 0.8648 \ln OASR$$
$$(8.47) \quad (17.57)$$
$$+ 1.1739 \ln OASB\$$$
$$(18.62)$$
$$+ 0.2184 \ln \frac{MTOAS\$}{AH \times W}, \quad (6.28)$$
$$(2.59)$$

where

$$OASB\$ = DYLOAS \times YL\$ + DMOAS \times YLA\$$$
$$+ DSEOAS \times (YL\$)_{-1}; \quad (6.29)$$
$$\bar{R}^2 = 0.9984, \quad \bar{S}_e = 0.0293, \quad DW = 1.1940.$$

(6) *Employee Contributions to OASDHI Programs 1937–51*

$$TXOASE\$ = 0.5\ TXOAS\$. \quad (6.30)$$

1952–66

$$TXOASE\$ = 0.47\ TXOAS\$. \quad (6.31)$$

(7) *Federal Personal Taxes 1924–40*

$$\ln TXPF\$ = -14.6391 + 1.4694 \ln (TXR50)_{-1}$$
$$(8.5830) \quad (7.6690)$$
$$+ 2.5438 \ln (YPE\$ - TPG\$$$
$$(8.0434)$$
$$+ TXOASE\$ + KG\$)_{-1}; \quad (6.32)$$
$$\bar{R}^2 = 0.8187, \quad \bar{S}_e = 0.1857, \quad DW = 1.1820.$$

1949–66

$$\ln TXPFR\$ = -1.4833 + 1.00565 \ln TXRPF$$
$$(5.0581) \quad (11.0148)$$
$$-1.8078 \ln \left[\frac{TXEPF\$}{(YPE\$ - TPG\$ + TXOASE\$)}\right];$$
$$(69.70)$$
$$\bar{R}^2 = 0.9941, \quad \bar{S}_e = 0.0270, \quad DW = 1.2677. \tag{6.33}$$

(8) *Federal Corporate Tax Base* (pre-war)
1924–40

$$ECB\$ - YCB\$ = 1.9220 - 0.3482\, TXCQE\$$$
$$(6.47) \quad (3.71)$$
$$+ 1.2959\, D3637 + 0.4237\,(U1 - U1_{-1}); \tag{6.34}$$
$$(1.92) \qquad (4.99)$$
$$\bar{R}^2 = 0.6877, \quad \bar{S}_e = 0.7440, \quad DW = 1.4865.$$

(9) *Federal Corporate Taxes* (post-war)
1949–66

$$\ln TXCFI\$ = -3.4293 + 0.0283\,(D5153 \times \ln TXCR)$$
$$(12.40) \quad (6.42)$$
$$+ 0.9818 \ln YCB\$ + 0.6730 \ln TXCR; \tag{6.35}$$
$$(37.28) \qquad (8.85)$$
$$\bar{R}^2 = 0.9915, \quad \bar{S}_e = 0.0249, \quad DW = 2.1085.$$

(10) *Corporate Investment Tax Credit*

$$ITC\$ = (ITCRAT)(PIGB)(IGB). \tag{6.36}$$

(11) *Federal Indirect Business Taxes*
1924–40

$$TXIF\$ = 1.56603 - 0.003252\,(PXNRNT1)(XNR)$$
$$(3.9390) \quad (0.5452)$$
$$- 0.992744\, DTXI3$$
$$(2.2694)$$
$$+ 0.010948\,(DTXI3)(PXNRNT1)(XNR)$$
$$(1.6653)$$

$$-0.555235 \, DTXI4$$
$$(1.2786)$$
$$+0.024815 \, (DTXI4)(PXNRNT1)(XNR); \qquad (6.37)$$
$$(3.7064)$$

$\bar{R}^2 = 0.9705, \qquad \bar{S}_e = 0.09748, \qquad DW = 2.4543.$

$DTXI3 \begin{cases} 1, & \text{for 1927–32;} \\ 0, & \text{otherwise.} \end{cases} \qquad DTXI4 \begin{cases} 1, & \text{for 1933–40;} \\ 0, & \text{otherwise.} \end{cases}$

1949–70

$$TXIF\$ = 1.15635 + 0.034649(PXNRNT1)(XNR)$$
$$(0.9334) \quad (6.7687)$$
$$-0.238304 \, DTXI5$$
$$(0.1756)$$
$$-0.001388(DTXI5)(PXNRNT1)(XNR)$$
$$(0.2603)$$
$$-0.395798 \, DTXI6$$
$$(0.1860)$$
$$-0.006968(DTXI6)(PXNRNT1)(XNR); \qquad (6.38)$$
$$(1.1916)$$

$\bar{R}^2 = 0.9907, \qquad \bar{S}_e = 0.3244, \qquad DW = 1.9248.$

$DTXI5 \begin{cases} 1, & \text{for 1954–65;} \\ 0, & \text{otherwise.} \end{cases} \qquad DTXI6 \begin{cases} 1, & \text{for 1966–70;} \\ 0, & \text{otherwise.} \end{cases}$

(12)   *Tax and Transfer Identities*

$$TPUC\$ = 0.052 \times NBUC \times ABUC\$ + ADJUC\$, \qquad (6.39)$$

$$TPG\$ = TPUC\$ + TPGFO\$ + TPSLG\$, \qquad (6.40)$$

$$TXUN\$ = \exp(\ln TXUN\$), \qquad (6.41)$$

$$TXOAS\$ = \exp(\ln TXOAS\$), \qquad (6.42)$$

$$TXS\$ = TXUN\$ + TXOAS\$ + TXSFO\$ + TXSSL\$, \qquad (6.43)$$

$$TXPF\$ = \exp(\ln TXPF\$), \qquad [1924–40] \quad (6.44)$$

$$TXPF\$ = \exp(\ln TXPFR\$) - RFNDL\$_{-1} + RFNDL\$,$$
$$[1949–66] \quad (6.45)$$

$$TXP\$ = TXPF\$ + TXPSL\$, \tag{6.46}$$

$$TXCF\$ = TXCR \times ECB\$, \qquad [1924\text{--}40] \tag{6.47}$$

$$TXCF\$ = \exp{(\ln TXCFI\$)} - ITC\$, \qquad [1949\text{--}66] \tag{6.48}$$

$$TXC\$ = TXCF\$ + TXCSL\$, \tag{6.49}$$

$$TXI\$ = TXIF\$ + TXISL\$. \tag{6.50}$$

CHAPTER 7

Prediction Errors in Dynamic Simulations

1. Introduction

Errors made in simulations of the complete model are investigated for several historical periods and forecasting horizons in this chapter.[1] Error measures are presented and discussed for predictions of levels and annual changes of 21 important variables. The simulations discussed here, like those to be presented in Chapters 8 and 9, pertain to the constant-returns-to-scale version of the model.

2. Errors in Dynamic Simulations

In table 7.1 we present error measures for the three time spans 1926–40, 1951–66 and 1967–72. The measures are for complete dynamic simulations of the model with initial conditions given at the beginning of each historical period. In the second and subsequent years of each period, the values of the lagged endogenous variables are those generated in the solution for the preceding year or years. Even though known values of the exogenous variables are used in every year, a dynamic simulation is a stringent test of the tracking ability of a model, since errors can cumulate over time through the lagged endogenous variables. This is true even of the sample period, which covers the first two time spans in the table. The 1967–72

---

[1] The computer programs to solve the model and compute the error statistics and multipliers in Chapters 7–10 were written by George R. Green, John Taylor, Carl van Duyne, Michael D. Hurd and Robert M. Coen. Most of the computations in these chapters were made by Andrea Kusko and Anthony Lima.

TABLE 7.1
Prediction errors for dynamic solutions.

	RMSE[a]			RMSE/Mean[b]		
Variable	1926–40	1951–66	1967–72	1926–40	1951–66	1967–72
GNP	4.5	9.6	29.5	5.3	2.0	3.1
Real *GNP*	6.4	10.0	16.9	3.5	2.1	2.3
Real consumption	3.6	4.9	8.1	2.7	1.6	1.7
Real business fixed investment	2.3	4.0	3.5	13.4	8.2	4.6
Real residential construction	1.2	2.7	3.8	16.1	12.6	15.1
Real inventory investment	1.8	2.9	4.6	735.0	67.2	81.5
Real state and local purchases	0.5	0.8	2.8	2.3	1.9	3.7
Real exports	0.7	0.9	2.0	7.8	3.3	4.0
Real imports	0.7	0.8	2.4	7.7	3.4	4.9
Implicit price deflator (1958 = 100)[c]	1.6	2.3	5.1	3.5	2.3	3.9
Civilian labor force	1.2	0.5	2.2	2.3	0.7	2.7
Employment	1.2	1.1	1.6	2.7	1.6	2.0
Unemployment rate	1.1	1.1	1.1	8.2	22.2	22.2
Wage rate	0.02	0.05	0.25	3.5	2.3	6.3
Labor income	2.1	6.1	31.8	4.5	2.3	6.1
Personal income	2.7	4.8	49.8	3.9	1.2	6.4
Corporate profits before taxes	2.3	6.9	35.4	44.1	13.0	41.8
Commercial paper rate (percent)	0.8	0.3	2.2	32.1	9.1	36.1
Corporate bond rate (percent)	0.5	0.3	2.7	10.8	6.0	37.7
Money stock (*M1*)	1.1	2.4	24.7	4.2	1.7	11.4
Money stock (*M2*)	1.8	5.1	32.5	4.3	2.3	7.7

[a] Root-mean-square-error.
[b] Root-mean-square-error as a percent of the mean of the variable.
[c] Prediction of *PXGNP1* (see Chapter 5, section 4).

solution of the model can be expected to yield even larger errors as the system is extrapolated beyond the period of fit.

Columns 1–3 give the root-mean-square-errors for each interval, calculated for each variable as

$$RMSE_i = \left\{ \sum_{t=1}^{T} (\hat{y}_{it} - y_{it})^2 / T \right\}^{1/2}, \tag{7.1}$$

where T is the number of observations in each prediction period and $\hat{y}_{it}$ and y_{it} are, respectively, the predicted and actual values of the ith endogenous variable for the tth observation. In columns 4–6, the *RMSE* for each variable is expressed as a percentage of the mean of the variable over the prediction period.

It is apparent from a glance at the table that the *RMSE*'s for most variables are smaller pre-war than post-war even apart from the post-sample errors for 1967–72. This is puzzling at first, since the fluctuations in economic activity were much larger during the 1930's than after World War II, and yet the model tracks the former better than the latter. Recall, however, that many of the behavioral functions of the model are specified in log-linear form with additive disturbance terms. The minimization of squared residuals is therefore implicitly performed on errors which are proportional to the dependent variables. A fit that was equally good in the pre-war and post-war periods in logarithmic terms would nonetheless imply larger *RMSE*'s for the arithmetic values in the later period, simply because the mean levels of the variables are so much higher.

For this reason, the pre-war and post-war fits are better compared after division of the *RMSE* for each variable by its mean. On this criterion, the sample-period fit is indeed better in 1951–66 than 1926–40. Thus real *GNP* was predicted with an average error of 2.1 percent post-war and 3.5 percent pre-war, and a similar improvement is observable for most other variables in table 7.1. A noteworthy exception is the unemployment rate, owing to the fact that it averaged much higher pre-war than post-war.

In the pre-war period the relative error in the implicit *GNP* deflator is the same as for real *GNP*, and the errors are reinforcing insofar as nominal *GNP* is concerned. The relative errors are slightly larger in prices than production during 1951–66, but during this period they are offsetting, so that the error in nominal *GNP* is smaller on average than for real *GNP*.

Among the principal expenditure components of *GNP*, real consumption has the largest *RMSE* in both halves of the sample period. This is because of its large size rather than its volatility, however. Investment expenditures, exports and imports have smaller *RMSE*'s, but these errors are much larger in percentage terms than those in consumer purchases. This is particularly true of inventory investment, which is poorly predicted in absolute terms and fluctuates about a mean level close to zero.

Comparatively small errors for labor force and employment result in large errors in unemployment, which is predicted as their difference. The percentage errors in money stock, interest rates and money incomes are smaller post-war than pre-war, in conformity with the predictions for *GNP* and its components.

Prediction errors are generally larger during the post-sample years, in line with the universal experience with econometric models.[2] The increases in percentage errors in the post-sample period are small for real *GNP* and its components, however. Thus the average percentage error in real *GNP* was 2.1 in 1951–66 and 2.3 in 1967–72. Extrapolation error increases were much larger for prices and nominal incomes, with the average percentage error for *GNP* rising from 2.0 to 3.1. The post-sample errors for interest rates, money stock and corporate profits are sharply higher than in the sample period. Of course, these relatively large errors may arise in part from the presence of federal controls on wages and prices in late 1971 and 1972.

2.1. Role of Inventory Investment

Inventory investment is a notoriously volatile component of *GNP* and is responsible for a large share of the year-to-year fluctuations in aggregate output. As noted in Chapter 1, our model is structured for

---

[2] To quote from a survey of prediction errors among econometric models of the U.S. economy by Fromm and Klein (1975), "Extrapolation error is . . . nearly two or three times as large as within-sample simultation error. When one does not have the confines of samples that contain only data to which the model has been 'fitted', one is subject to a much wider margin of error."

long-run analysis and subordinates those characteristics, including the processes of inventory accumulation and decumulation, which primarily affect short-run stability. Not surprisingly inventory investment is badly predicted, as is virtually inevitable in an annual model. This is largely irrelevant in a long-run model, however, since inventory investment is a small fraction of *GNP* and accounts for little of the change in *GNP* over spans of three or more years. For this reason, we have calculated error measures for the model with inventory investment exogenous, in order to abstract from its transitory destabilizing influence (table 7.2).

It is apparent from a comparison of tables 7.1 and 7.2 that the error in predicting real *GNP* is substantially lower when inventory investment is exogenous, falling by about one percentage point pre-war and 0.6 in both post-war periods. The improvement is partly due to the elimination of the error in inventory change itself, but the predictions of the other expenditure components are also improved in most cases by the reduction of error propagation through the system. Because of their close links to output, the errors for employment and labor force, and hence for unemployment, are also moderately reduced.

Unfortunately, a corresponding gain is not forthcoming for nominal variables. The prediction error is about the same for prices and money *GNP* in the two simulations. This is because unit costs in the constant-returns model are invariant to output changes, and the improvements in the predictions of labor demand and capacity utilization are insufficient to affect the wage and price predictions.

2.2. Errors in Predicting Annual Changes

Thus far we have considered the accuracy of level predictions of the variables. Where a significant bias component of error exists, however, predictions of changes may be more accurate, since errors in first differences are less likely to cumulate over time. Of course, the bias is zero for sample-period errors in single equations estimated by least-squares, but sample-period errors for levels of variables explained by log-linear relations may be biased even in single equations. Additionally, there may be biases in the complete-system solutions for the sample period. In our model, moreover, the sample period is

TABLE 7.2
Prediction errors for dynamic solutions with inventory investment exogenous.

Variable	RMSE[a]			RMSE/Mean[b]		
	1926-40	1951-66	1967-72	1926-40	1951-66	1967-72
GNP	4.0	9.4	31.7	4.8	1.9	3.3
Real GNP	4.8	7.3	12.0	2.6	1.5	1.7
Real consumption	3.3	4.3	7.4	2.5	1.4	1.6
Real business fixed investment	1.9	3.8	3.1	11.2	7.8	4.1
Real residential construction	1.2	2.7	3.8	16.6	12.4	15.2
Real inventory investment	0	0	0	0	0	0
Real state and local purchases	0.5	0.7	3.0	2.4	1.7	4.0
Real exports	0.7	0.9	2.3	7.9	3.6	4.7
Real imports	0.6	0.7	2.5	7.0	3.0	5.1
Implicit price deflator (1958 = 100)[c]	1.6	2.4	5.1	3.5	2.5	3.8
Civilian labor force	1.2	0.4	2.1	2.3	0.6	2.6
Employment	1.1	0.9	1.3	2.4	1.4	1.7
Unemployment rate	0.9	0.9	1.1	6.7	19.4	23.1
Wage rate	0.02	0.06	0.25	3.5	2.6	6.1
Labor income	1.9	5.9	31.3	4.1	2.2	6.0
Personal income	2.3	5.1	48.5	3.3	1.3	6.2
Corporate profits before taxes	2.2	6.6	35.0	42.0	12.5	41.3
Commercial paper rate (percent)	0.8	0.3	2.1	33.3	8.9	35.1
Corporate bond rate (percent)	0.5	0.3	2.7	10.6	6.4	37.4
Money stock (M1)	n.a.	n.a.	n.a.	n.a.	n.a.	n.a.
Money stock (M2)	1.8	5.0	33.3	4.3	2.3	7.9

[a] Root-mean-square-error.
[b] Root-mean-square-error as a percent of the mean of the variable.
[c] Prediction of PXGNPI (see Chapter 5, section 4).

split chronologically, and for equations estimated across both periods there may be non-zero sums of the residuals in either portion of the sample. Thus, the question of bias is worth investigating in reference to both the sample-period and the post-sample errors.

The error measure used is the root-mean-square-error in terms of changes,

$$RMSE\Delta_i = \left\{ \sum_{t=1}^{T} [(\hat{y}_{it} - \hat{y}_{i,t-1}) - (y_{it} - y_{i,t-1})]^2 / T \right\}^{1/2}. \tag{7.2}$$

The results are shown in table 7.3. As compared with the level errors in table 7.1, the errors in first differences of real *GNP* and its components are somewhat larger on balance in 1951–66 and much larger in 1926–40. There is a substantial improvement in the first-difference predictions of wages and prices, however. The same generalizations hold even more strikingly for the post-sample results, when the element of bias in the forecasts of wage and price levels was quite large. An average-level error of 6.3 percent for wages in 1967–72 was reduced to 2.5 percent in first-difference form, and the corresponding figures for the *GNP* deflator are 3.9 and 2.0. A similar marked improvement is present in the first-difference errors for corporate profits, interest rates and money stock during 1967–72, where the average errors are reduced by half or more when changes instead of levels are predicted.

3. Forecast Horizon and Error Cumulation

It is well known that simulation error grows with the length of the simulation period in econometric models [Fromm and Klein (1975)] and the present case is no exception. Table 7.4 contains the *RMSE* measures for one-to-six-year predictions during 1956–66. There are eleven predictions to be averaged for each prediction interval and variable, since the prediction horizon begins as early as 1951, allowing a six-year-ahead forecast for 1956 and all subsequent years, and similarly for the other prediction spans. For comparison, the *RMSE*'s for the 16-year simulations reported in table 7.1 are repeated in the last column.

TABLE 7.3
First-difference prediction errors, dynamic solutions.

Variable	RMSEΔ[a]			RMSEΔ/Mean[b]		
	1926–40	1951–66	1967–72	1926–40	1951–66	1967–72
GNP	4.8	10.2	27.5	5.7	2.1	2.9
Real *GNP*	8.7	10.5	19.0	4.7	2.2	2.6
Real consumption	4.5	4.7	8.4	3.4	1.5	1.8
Real business fixed investment	2.7	2.9	4.6	16.1	6.0	5.9
Real residential construction	1.0	1.8	3.9	14.2	8.3	15.4
Real inventory investment	2.8	4.0	5.0	1150.2	92.8	87.4
Real state and local purchases	0.7	0.6	1.6	3.6	1.5	2.1
Real exports	0.6	0.7	1.6	6.5	2.5	3.3
Real imports	0.9	0.9	2.1	10.0	4.0	4.3
Implicit price deflator (1958 = 100)[c]	1.2	1.4	2.6	2.7	1.4	2.0
Civilian labor force	0.8	0.4	0.7	1.6	0.5	0.8
Employment	1.3	0.9	1.0	2.9	1.3	1.3
Unemployment rate	1.7	1.1	0.9	12.4	22.6	19.4
Wage rate	0.02	0.03	0.10	3.4	1.3	2.5
Labor income	2.6	5.8	18.9	5.6	2.2	3.6
Personal income	3.5	5.5	18.0	5.0	1.4	2.3
Corporate profits before taxes	1.9	6.3	15.0	36.2	12.0	17.6
Commercial paper rate (percent)	1.0	0.3	1.0	44.0	10.6	16.7
Corporate bond rate (percent)	0.7	0.3	0.9	15.3	6.7	11.8
Money stock (*M1*)	1.3	1.9	7.1	4.9	1.3	3.3
Money stock (*M2*)	1.5	5.2	11.6	3.6	2.4	2.7

[a] Root-mean-square-error.
[b] Root-mean-square-error as a percent of the mean of the variable.
[c] Prediction of *PXGNP1* (see Chapter 5, section 4).

TABLE 7.4

RMSE measures for predictions, one to six years ahead, 1956–66.

Variable	Prediction interval						Long-run[a]
	(1)	(2)	(3)	(4)	(5)	(6)	
GNP	13.5	13.1	12.7	17.7	16.8	16.7	9.6
Real GNP	9.2	12.8	12.3	13.1	15.5	14.2	10.0
Real consumption	5.1	6.6	6.6	7.0	8.4	7.8	4.9
Real business fixed investment	3.4	4.6	4.7	4.7	5.0	5.0	4.0
Real residential construction	1.3	1.9	2.1	2.4	2.5	2.4	2.7
Real inventory investment	2.3	3.1	3.1	3.1	3.2	3.2	2.9
Real state and local purchases	0.5	0.6	0.8	0.9	0.9	0.9	0.8
Real exports	0.9	1.2	1.1	1.3	1.6	1.8	0.9
Real imports	0.9	1.1	1.1	1.1	1.0	0.9	0.8
Implicit price deflator (1958 = 100)[b]	1.2	1.9	2.4	2.9	3.4	3.4	2.3
Civilian labor force	0.3	0.4	0.4	0.4	0.4	0.4	0.5
Employment	0.8	1.1	1.0	0.9	1.1	1.1	1.1
Unemployment rate	0.9	1.2	1.1	0.9	1.2	1.2	1.1
Wage rate	0.04	0.06	0.08	0.09	0.11	0.12	0.05
Labor income	7.6	7.8	6.5	8.7	9.6	9.3	6.1
Personal income	8.6	8.9	8.6	10.8	11.3	11.3	4.8
Corporate profits before taxes	5.0	4.4	4.8	6.5	5.3	5.4	6.9
Commercial paper rate (percent)	0.5	0.4	0.5	0.5	0.6	0.5	0.3
Corporate bond rate (percent)	0.2	0.3	0.3	0.3	0.4	0.4	0.3
Money stock (M1)	3.2	3.4	3.7	4.2	4.0	4.3	2.4
Money stock (M2)	6.2	6.6	7.5	8.0	7.4	7.3	5.1

[a] RMSE for a single 16-year simulation, 1951–66.
[b] Prediction of PXGNP1 (see Chapter 5, section 4).

The largest error increments in real *GNP* and components occur between the first and second years. The errors are then essentially flat until the fifth and sixth years when another jump occurs. Error buildup in the implicit price deflator is steady through the fifth year and levels off in the sixth. Errors in nominal *GNP* follow still a different pattern, remaining stable during the first three years and jumping to a higher plateau for the last three. These divergent patterns partially reflect offsetting biases in real *GNP* and prices in the predictions for shorter horizons.

The growth of *RMSE* as the simulation period is lengthened is due primarily to error cumulation owing to persisting biases in the direction of prediction errors. Error-correcting mechanisms in the form of stock-adjustment processes and autoregressive error structures are built into many equations of the model, but these mechanisms operate sufficiently slowly that a large error in a particular year may require several years to reverse in its entirety. These biases are effectively "differenced-out" when annual changes are predicted, as may be seen from table 7.5.

Table 7.5 shows the *RMSE* measures for predictions of first differences over the same period and forecasting spans as in table 7.4. The error for the single-period changes is the same as for levels, since the lagged values of the endogenous variables are known without error in this case [see equation (7.2)]. Over the longer horizons, however, the annual changes are more accurately predicted than the levels for the vast majority of variables. The errors in most variables, whether nominal or real, are essentially flat over the one-to-six-year horizons.

4. Concluding Observations

The builder of a long-run model faces a dilemma in the evaluation of forecast error. His model is designed with an eye for its growth or trend properties, and yet part of the evidence on which the model may be judged is its ability to track cyclical fluctuations over the sample period. During 1951–66, real and nominal *GNP* were predicted with *RMSE*'s respectively of 9.6 and 10.0. These errors are in the same general range as long-run predictions with existing U.S.

TABLE 7.5

RMSE measures for predictions of first differences, one to six years ahead, 1956–66.

Variable	Prediction interval						Long-run[a]
	(1)	(2)	(3)	(4)	(5)	(6)	
GNP							
Real *GNP*	13.5	10.5	11.2	11.4	10.5	11.2	10.2
Real consumption	9.2	12.2	10.8	11.2	11.2	11.1	10.5
Real business fixed investment	5.1	5.3	5.1	5.1	5.1	5.1	4.7
Real residential construction	3.4	3.5	3.4	3.3	3.3	3.3	2.9
Real inventory investment	1.3	1.6	1.4	1.6	1.6	1.6	1.8
Real state and local purchases	2.3	4.1	4.0	4.0	4.1	4.0	4.0
Real exports	0.5	0.6	0.7	0.7	0.7	0.7	0.6
Real imports	0.9	0.6	0.5	0.5	0.6	0.6	0.7
Implicit price deflator (1958 = 100)[b]	0.9	1.0	1.0	0.9	0.9	0.9	0.9
Civilian labor force	1.2	1.0	0.8	0.9	1.0	1.0	1.4
Employment	0.3	0.4	0.3	0.3	0.3	0.3	0.4
Unemployment rate	0.8	1.0	0.8	0.8	0.8	0.8	0.9
Wage rate	0.9	1.1	1.1	1.1	1.0	1.1	1.1
Labor income	0.04	0.03	0.03	0.03	0.03	0.03	0.03
Personal income	7.6	5.3	5.6	5.8	5.3	5.6	5.8
Corporate profits before taxes	8.6	5.6	5.7	5.9	5.5	5.7	5.5
	5.0	5.4	5.9	5.8	5.6	5.8	6.3
Commercial paper rate (percent)	0.4	0.3	0.3	0.3	0.3	0.3	0.3
Corporate bond rate (percent)	0.2	0.3	0.3	0.3	0.3	0.3	0.3
Money stock (*M1*)	3.2	2.3	2.4	2.3	2.1	2.3	1.9
Money stock (*M2*)	6.2	4.3	4.5	4.2	4.0	4.2	5.2

[a] *RMSE* for a single 16-year simulation, 1951–66.
[b] Prediction of *PXGNP1* (see Chapter 5, section 4).

models, including one monthly and seven quarterly models [see Fromm and Klein (1975)]. Our errors are substantially higher than the other models over one and two year spans, however. This is partly because the annual time unit, although entirely appropriate for a long-run model, permits only a crude approximation to the short-term dynamics of the business cycle.

It should also be noted that the parameters of the HC model were estimated on data spanning the Great Depression, the Korean and Vietnam Wars, and several peacetime cycles of varying intensity. Thus, the errors in a dynamic simulation of our model for post-war years are not sample-period errors in the same sense as those generated by quarterly or monthly U.S. models, which are fitted solely to post-war data. Moreover, for many important sectors we have emphasized a priori constraints rather than goodness-of-fit in choosing among competing specifications. This search for structural stability at the expense of sample-period error minimization partly explains why the percentage errors increase comparatively little in the post-sample forecasts of the real variables in the system. The errors for the nominal variables unfortunately increase more substantially in the post-sample predictions, probably because of the inflationary environment of 1967–72, although it should be recalled that errors in the first differences of the nominal variables were much smaller than those for their levels. This suggests that constant-term adjustments which reflect past prediction errors in individual equations–a common practice in econometric forecasting–could substantially reduce the errors in our predictions of levels for 1967–72.

CHAPTER 8

Post-war Policy Simulations

1. Introduction

Cause and effect are impossible to specify in the model owing to its simultaneous structure. An exogenous change in a policy instrument has indirect as well as direct effects on the endogenous variables. The principal channels for the direct effects can be identified from the model's structure, but the total effect of a policy change can only be obtained by simulation of the complete system.

The model contains many policy instruments. The fiscal instruments include federal purchases of goods and services; federal employment; personal, corporate and indirect taxes; contributions for social insurance; the investment tax credit; and the parameters for tax depreciation policy. Incremental federal expenditures for goods purchased from the private sector are a direct contribution to aggregate demand, as are incremental expenditures for federal employment. Tax changes affecting receipts from personal or indirect taxes or from social security contributions affect incomes (and in the case of indirect taxes, prices) directly and consumer and housing demands indirectly. Changes in the various tax parameters affecting corporate income will directly influence business fixed investment expenditures and dividend contributions to personal incomes.

The monetary instruments include unborrowed reserves, regulation Q, the rediscount rate, and the required reserve ratios against demand and time deposits. Changes in these instruments affect the supply side of the money market and induce changes in the money stock and interest rates. The money stock is not an argument in any of the final demand functions of the model, but interest rates enter the behavioral equations for residential construction and expenditures on consumer durables.

Seven different policy simulations are analyzed in this chapter. We evaluate the effects of an independent increase of federal expenditures and an independent decrease in federal personal income taxes, in both cases with and without an accommodating monetary policy. We also assess the effects of an autonomous monetary stimulus in the form of an increase in unborrowed reserves. Finally, we investigate the consequences of an increase in the investment tax credit under two alternative assumptions about its impact on pricing decisions. As will be seen, the predicted effects of the various policies are far from uniform in the model.

2. Nature of the Simulations

All the multiplier runs in this chapter are based on a sample period control solution for 1951–66 and hence cover a period of 16 years. For each experiment, a given policy variable was incremented by a constant amount throughout the sample period, the model was re-solved, the difference between the new and control solutions was calculated for each year, and the calculated differences were normalized by the change in the policy variables to yield the dynamic multiplier estimates.

Thus the conceptual experiment is to study the time path of response of the system to a sustained shift in an exogenous variable rather than to an isolated shock in a single period. In a simultaneous system of linear difference equations, the normalized response path would be determined solely by the parameters of the model, and hence would be independent of the magnitude of the impulse or of the initial conditions in each year of the simulation. In a nonlinear model such as ours, however, initial conditions and size of shocks can make a difference. Experience suggests that the size of shock is not of great moment for our model, at least when it is confined to a range consistent with historical experience. Initial conditions are another matter, however. The results in this chapter refer to a control path during 1951–66 with an average unemployment rate of 4.2 percent and hence may be considered representative of high-employment conditions.

The following assumptions were made for the various multiplier runs:

(1) A sustained exogenous increase in federal purchases of goods and services of 1.0 billion dollars at current prices, with no change in monetary policy.
(2) A sustained exogenous increase in federal purchases of goods and services of 1.0 billion dollars at current prices, accompanied by an accommodating monetary policy to keep interest rates unchanged from the control solution.
(3) A sustained exogenous decrease of personal income tax receipts of 1.0 billion dollars at current prices, with no change in monetary policy.
(4) A sustained exogenous decrease of personal income tax receipts of 1.0 billion dollars at current prices, with an accommodating monetary policy.
(5) A sustained increase in unborrowed reserves of 0.5 billion dollars at current prices.
(6) A sustained increase in the rate of investment tax credit, with the credit deducted from the depreciable tax base [i.e., with $ITCD = 1$ in equation (5.93)]. The rate of investment tax credit [$ITCR$ in equation (5.93)] was set at zero in the control solution and 0.027 in the shocked solution.
(7) A variant of the previous simulation, in which the shock is the same, but the investment credit is assumed to have no direct effect on pricing decisions.

The difference between simulations (6) and (7) is as follows. The rental price of capital [equation (5.93)] affects not only the investment decision [equation (2.15)], but also labor input [equation (3.1)] and prices [equation (5.56)]. In the first variant of the investment credit multipliers, the credit is assumed to have its full effect on the rental price of capital in all three equations. In variant (2), however, it is assumed that entrepreneurs fail to treat the investment credit as a cost reduction insofar as pricing is concerned, so that the rental price of capital is unaltered in the price equation, although still changed in the investment and labor functions. The rationale for this distinction is discussed below.

Each of the foregoing experiments yields a measure of induced responses for the dependent variables of the model, in the form of differences between the shocked and control solutions. To form the corresponding multipliers, it is necessary to decide on normalization procedures.

One approach is to divide the induced responses by the corresponding exogenous impulses. In the first case, for example, the dynamic multipliers for gross national product may be calculated as $(\Delta XGNP\$)_t/(\Delta GGF\$)$, where the numerator is the induced response of current-dollar GNP in year t and the denominator is the increment in federal purchases at current dollars, shown without subscript since it is constant over time. We have adopted this procedure wherever it is meaningful – in particular for the results of the first 5 multiplier runs as shown in columns 1–5 of tables 8.1–8.3 – but we have used other normalizations as well, for several important reasons.

First, in the case of runs (6) and (7), the instrument variable is the rate of investment tax credit rather than the dollar stream of tax credits taken by business firms. The sustained increment in the rate implies a rising stream of dollar credits over the simulation period. We have normalized the investment credit multipliers in columns 7 and 8 of tables 8.1–8.3 by the value of the dollar credits generated each year by the increase from zero to 0.027 in the credit rate. An alternative would be to normalize by the dollar credits that would have been generated each year by a credit rate of 0.027 as applied to the gross business fixed investment stream from the control solution. This alternative would exclude incremental credits due to the induced rise of business investment itself and might be preferable on conceptual grounds. We have opted to include the induced component of tax credits in the normalization, however, since it corresponds to commonly used methods for tax and money multipliers.

Second, two normalizations were used with respect to simulation (5). As noted above, the first normalization is by the exogenous impulse itself, which in this instance is the 0.5 billion dollar increase of unborrowed reserves. The second normalization, used to derive the multipliers in column 6 of tables 8.1–8.3, employs the change in the money supply between the control and shocked solutions as the divisor. For gross national product, as an example, the two variants of the monetary policy multipliers are respectively $(\Delta XGNP\$)_t/(\Delta RESU)$ and $(\Delta XGNP\$)_t/(\Delta M1)_t$, where $\Delta RESU$ is the constant value of the change in unborrowed reserves and $(\Delta M1)_t$ is the varying amount of change in the money supply excluding time deposits. Once again, the second normalization includes an induced component of money supply response, in accord with common practice. Multipliers could also be calculated for the money stock including time deposits, but the *M1* definition is commonly used in econometric models and hence has been employed herein.

Third, there is an important question concerning the appropriate normalizations for induced responses of nominal and real variables to nominal or real impulses. In the first multiplier run, for example, the impulse is an increase in federal purchases of goods and services in current dollars. Should the response of a real variable, such as *GNP* in constant prices, be normalized by the increment in nominal government expenditure? The answer hinges on the purpose of the analysis.

From the standpoint of policy analysis, it is certainly meaningful to express the induced responses in either nominal or real variables as ratios to the policy injection in current dollars. The policy-maker, for example, could think in terms of so much stimulus to employment or real *GNP* per nominal dollar of sustained tax reduction or expenditure increase. It is with this interpretation in mind that Fromm and Taubman (1968) christened such measures "fiscal multipliers". In tables 8.1–8.3 all induced changes, whether of real or nominal variables, are normalized on injections measured in current dollars, and hence are fiscal multipliers in the Fromm–Taubman sense.

A constant annual injection measured in nominal dollars will represent a varying impulse in real terms as prices change over time, however. In order to appraise the induced responses of real variables to real impulses, it is necessary to normalize the former by the latter. This has been done in tables 8.4–8.9 for real *GNP* and its major components and for all the multiplier experiments except for monetary policy. Thus tables 8.4 and 8.5 refer to the real government expenditure multipliers implicit in the first two simulations. Instead of dividing the induced change in real *GNP* each year by the constant incremental flow of government expenditure in current dollars $(\Delta GGF\$)$, it is divided by the varying increment of real government expenditure as measured by $(\Delta GGF\$)/(PGGF)_t$, where $PGGF_t$ is the government purchases price deflator for year t. Similarly, the real multipliers for the personal tax simulation in tables 8.6 and 8.7 are normalized by $(\Delta\ TXPF\$)/(PCE)_t$, where *PCE* is the consumption deflator, and those for the investment tax credit in tables 8.8 and 8.9 are normalized by $(\Delta\ ITC\$)_t/(PIGB)_t$, where the numerator is the dollar flow of tax credits and the denominator is the implicit deflator for business fixed investment expenditure.

No constant-price normalization is presented for the money multiplier simulation. It is a basic tenet of monetary theory that the central bank can control the nominal money supply but not the real money stock. The conceptual experiment appropriate for monetary policy is to augment the nominal money stock through open market operations and to observe the effects on nominal income, the price level, and real income. The appropriate normalization is therefore by unborrowed reserves or the money supply in nominal units, as given in tables 8.1–8.3.

3. Policy Multipliers for 1951–66 [1]

Multiplier results for six key variables are presented in tables 8.1–8.3. All multipliers in these tables are normalized by nominal inputs, as discussed in section 8.2. The two columns headed $\Delta\ G$ refer to the effects of a sustained increase of federal spending in current dollars, without (1) and with (2) an accommodating monetary policy. Similarly, the columns headed $\Delta\ T$ refer to a sustained reduction in personal income taxes under the same alternative monetary assumptions. Next are shown the effects of an expansionary monetary policy $(\Delta\ M)$ consisting of a permanent increase in the level of unborrowed reserves, where variant (1) is normalized by unborrowed reserves, and variant (2) by the money stock. Finally the multipliers for a change in the rate of investment tax credit are shown with $(\Delta\ TC1)$ and without $(\Delta\ TC2)$ direct effects of the credit on prices.

A remarkable diversity in the predicted effects of alternative policies on nominal and real *GNP* is evident in table 8.1. A similar disparity appears in the predicted consequences of any given policy over time, so that its short-run and long-run effects may be strikingly

---

[1] Some of these results were published in Hickman, Coen and Hurd (1975).

TABLE 8.1
Multipliers–*GNP* in current and constant prices.

	GNP (current prices)							
	Δ *G*		Δ *T*		Δ *M*		Δ *TC*	
Year	(1)	(2)	(1)	(2)	(1)	(2)	(1)	(2)
1	2.73	2.87	1.47	1.51	2.90	1.49	− 2.85	− 2.38
2	2.51	3.07	1.91	2.27	4.00	1.36	− 0.47	− 1.81
3	2.93	3.21	2.36	2.54	2.51	0.87	− 0.64	− 2.74
4	3.54	3.53	2.85	2.85	0.40	0.14	− 0.22	− 2.63
5	3.73	3.89	3.06	3.25	0.44	0.14	0.26	− 2.29
6	3.55	3.79	2.89	3.10	0.73	0.21	0.62	− 1.79
7	3.59	3.77	2.95	3.12	0.81	0.22	0.80	− 1.57
8	3.87	3.85	3.26	3.26	0.34	0.08	0.96	− 1.64
9	3.87	3.95	3.28	3.39	1.08	0.25	1.21	− 1.39
10	3.90	3.91	3.38	3.40	0.31	0.07	1.39	− 1.23
11	4.09	4.02	3.60	3.59	0.06	0.01	1.55	− 1.26
12	4.30	4.22	3.83	3.84	0.10	0.02	1.81	− 1.33
13	4.33	4.27	3.90	3.91	− 0.12	− 0.02	2.00	− 1.18
14	4.35	4.46	4.16	4.12	− 0.17	− 0.03	2.30	− 1.18
15	4.24	4.12	3.90	3.86	− 0.14	− 0.03	2.23	− 1.01
16	4.25	4.15	4.00	3.96	0.16	0.03	2.44	− 1.02
	Real *GNP* (1958 prices)							
1	1.64	1.76	0.87	0.95	1.68	0.87	2.61	− 0.12
2	0.92	1.06	0.76	0.89	1.65	0.56	3.73	0.85
3	1.10	1.15	0.95	0.97	0.64	0.22	3.43	0.56
4	1.59	1.59	1.28	1.30	− 0.30	− 0.11	3.82	0.49
5	1.65	1.75	1.36	1.46	0.12	0.04	3.90	0.45
6	1.64	1.73	1.32	1.38	0.44	0.13	4.09	0.59
7	1.71	1.77	1.37	1.43	0.44	0.12	4.20	0.57
8	1.90	1.88	1.59	1.57	0.09	0.02	4.27	0.42
9	1.98	2.03	1.66	1.72	0.70	0.16	4.36	0.49
10	2.11	2.12	1.81	1.81	0.10	0.02	4.49	0.49
11	2.19	2.13	1.90	1.88	0.05	0.05	4.55	0.44
12	2.25	2.15	1.96	1.94	0.14	0.03	4.49	0.42
13	2.28	2.22	2.03	2.00	− 0.08	0.02	4.50	0.48
14	2.38	2.29	2.15	2.08	− 0.02	− 0.00	4.63	0.47
15	2.13	2.04	1.90	1.85	0.01	0.00	4.39	0.55
16	1.92	1.88	1.79	1.76	0.12	0.02	4.21	0.63

different. Cyclical fluctuations occur over the 16-year span in all cases, but with considerable variation in timing and amplitude according to type of shock.

The impact or first-year multipliers for real *GNP* range from − 0.1 to 2.6 when normalized per nominal dollar of exogenous input. The

TABLE 8.2

Multipliers–*GNP* implicit price index and unemployment rate.

Implicit price index (1958 = 100)

Year	Δ G (1)	(2)	Δ T (1)	(2)	Δ M (1)	(2)	Δ TC (1)	(2)
1	0.34	0.36	0.20	0.19	0.36	0.19	− 1.31	− 0.60
2	0.44	0.54	0.30	0.37	0.62	0.21	− 0.94	− 0.63
3	0.47	0.53	0.36	0.40	0.47	0.16	− 0.90	− 0.79
4	0.50	0.51	0.40	0.41	0.17	0.06	− 0.86	− 0.72
5	0.50	0.52	0.41	0.44	0.07	0.02	− 0.76	− 0.62
6	0.45	0.49	0.38	0.41	0.09	0.03	− 0.71	− 0.53
7	0.43	0.46	0.36	0.39	0.10	0.03	− 0.68	− 0.46
8	0.42	0.42	0.36	0.37	0.04	0.01	− 0.65	− 0.44
9	0.40	0.40	0.34	0.35	0.09	0.02	− 0.62	− 0.39
10	0.36	0.37	0.32	0.33	0.04	0.01	− 0.62	− 0.34
11	0.35	0.36	0.32	0.32	0.00	0.00	− 0.58	− 0.33
12	0.36	0.35	0.33	0.33	0.01	0.00	− 0.54	− 0.33
13	0.33	0.33	0.31	0.32	− 0.01	0.00	− 0.52	− 0.31
14	0.33	0.32	0.31	0.31	− 0.02	− 0.00	− 0.47	− 0.29
15	0.30	0.29	0.28	0.28	− 0.02	− 0.00	− 0.45	− 0.27
16	0.31	0.31	0.28	0.29	0.00	0.00	− 0.39	− 0.28

Unemployment rate (percent)

Year	Δ G (1)	(2)	Δ T (1)	(2)	Δ M (1)	(2)	Δ TC (1)	(2)
1	− 0.12	− 0.13	− 0.07	− 0.07	− 0.12	− 0.06	0.06	0.24
2	− 0.11	− 0.13	− 0.07	− 0.09	− 0.15	− 0.05	0.03	0.25
3	− 0.12	− 0.13	− 0.09	− 0.10	− 0.10	− 0.04	0.01	0.25
4	− 0.15	− 0.16	− 0.12	− 0.13	− 0.03	− 0.01	− 0.01	0.27
5	− 0.17	− 0.18	− 0.14	− 0.15	− 0.01	− 0.00	− 0.04	0.25
6	− 0.17	− 0.18	− 0.14	− 0.15	− 0.04	− 0.01	− 0.07	0.24
7	− 0.17	− 0.18	− 0.14	− 0.15	− 0.05	− 0.01	− 0.09	0.23
8	− 0.19	− 0.18	− 0.15	− 0.15	− 0.02	− 0.01	− 0.10	0.23
9	− 0.19	− 0.19	− 0.16	− 0.16	− 0.05	− 0.01	− 0.11	0.22
10	− 0.20	− 0.20	− 0.17	− 0.17	− 0.02	− 0.01	− 0.13	0.21
11	− 0.20	− 0.20	− 0.17	− 0.17	− 0.01	− 0.01	− 0.14	0.19
12	− 0.20	− 0.19	− 0.17	− 0.17	− 0.02	− 0.00	− 0.14	0.18
13	− 0.19	− 0.19	− 0.17	− 0.17	0.00	0.00	− 0.14	0.17
14	− 0.19	− 0.18	− 0.17	− 0.17	0.00	0.00	− 0.15	0.16
15	− 0.17	− 0.16	− 0.16	− 0.15	0.00	0.00	− 0.14	0.14
16	− 0.15	− 0.15	− 0.14	− 0.14	− 0.01	− 0.00	− 0.13	0.12

tax multipliers are only half as large initially as the federal expenditure multipliers, but they build to a peak nearly equalling the latter
over the long run. The money multipliers are also substantial during
the first two years, but they diminish toward zero or negative values
thereafter. An increase in the investment tax credit has the largest

impact of any of the policies on real *GNP* per nominal dollar of impulse, provided it is assumed to affect prices directly [variant (1)]. Otherwise, the impact multiplier is negative and the long-run effects small [variant (2)]. It will be shown below that conversion of the nominal tax credit impulse to real terms greatly moderates the rise in the real *GNP* multipliers for the first variant of the investment credit simulation.

For the most part, the multipliers for nominal *GNP* are larger than those for real *GNP* but of the same sign, since prices increase with output (tables 8.1 and 8.2). In sharp contrast to the other policies, however, the investment credit reduces nominal *GNP* temporarily [variant (1)] or permanently [variant (2)]. This is because the tax credit tends to reduce prices either indirectly [variant (2)] or both directly and indirectly [variant (1)]. The indirect effects operate through the labor market as follows. The tax-induced reduction in the rental price of capital increases the relative price of labor and hence reduces labor demand [equation (3.1)] while increasing investment demand [equation (2.15)]. The reduction in labor demand lowers the nominal wage rate and puts downward pressure on prices. As for the direct effects, the rational entrepreneur will recognize that a permanent increase in the tax credit is a permanent reduction in the price of capital services, and competition will induce the corresponding reduction in product price [equation (5.56)]. Put another way, the tax credit is equivalent to a reduction in the price of newly produced capital goods, and rational pricing policies plus competition should induce businessmen to reduce product prices accordingly.

To the extent that firms are irrational in their pricing decisions or competition is weak, however, the pricing model may overstate the direct effect on prices. If firms fail to value depreciation costs and profits at replacement cost, for example, they will make inadequate allowance for changing capital costs in their pricing decisions, contrary to our hypothesis in equation (5.56). Moreover, they may resist reducing prices when costs fall and imperfect competition prevails. For these reasons, we introduced variant (2), in which the reduction in rental price is completely ignored in the pricing decision. The truth probably lies between taking full account or no account of the direct reduction in the price of capital services, so that our simulations bracket the probable outcome.

Unfortunately, the range of probable outcomes is wide. Full pass-through of the direct price effects results in a sharp reduction of prices and a correspondingly large increase of output. Price reductions are smaller with no direct pass-through effects, and production gains are considerably weaker, as can be seen from tables 8.1 and 8.2.

All the other policies raise prices either permanently or for several years at least. This is because they have no direct effect on the rental price of capital or wage rate, and the indirect effects are in the inflationary direction as increased labor demand raises wages and increased capacity utilization raises profit mark-ups.

According to the model, a sustained exogenous increase in federal expenditures or reduction in personal income taxes will permanently reduce the level of unemployment, with most of the potential reduction accomplished within five years (table 8.2). An expansionary monetary policy will reduce unemployment temporarily, but after a few years the unemployment rate reverts to approximately its original level. The investment credit with direct price effects [variant (1)] reduces unemployment over the long run, but increases it during the first three years. This initial rise occurs because the fall in the rental price of capital increases the relative price of labor and reduces labor demand in the early years despite the rise of output. Without direct price effects, the investment credit permanently reduces labor demand and increases unemployment. This is because the growth of output is insufficient to offset the substitution of capital for labor in this case.

The trade-off between inflation and unemployment differs in the short and long runs. An expenditure increase or personal tax cut permanently raises the price level, but the inflation rate–the annual rate of change of prices–is largest in the first year, diminishes in each subsequent year, and turns negative after five years. The expansionary monetary policy also reduces unemployment at the expense of some inflation in the first two years, but prices fall thereafter as the decline of unemployment is reversed, and they eventually return to the original level. Thus neither the price nor unemployment levels are altered in the long run by monetary policy.

The inflation–unemployment trade-off in the case of the investment credit again differs sharply from the patterns of other policies. In the case with direct price effects, the initial impact is a sharp reduction in the price level accompanied by a substantial increase of unemployment. After the first year, however, prices gradually rise again, so that the inflation rate is positive even though prices are still far below the original level after 16 years have passed. Meanwhile, unemployment falls to a permanently lower level by about the tenth year. Thus this policy reduces both unemployment and prices over the long run, provided prices fully reflect the tax-induced change in rental costs of capital. Without direct price effects, however, unemployment is permanently increased by the investment credit, although it is still true that a permanent reduction is achieved for prices.

3.1. Budgetary Impacts of Alternative Policies

In the absence of an explicit government budget constraint, the sources of deficit finance are merely implicit in the model.[2] In the first simulation, the exogenous increase in federal expenditure is implicitly financed by borrowing from the public or from excess reserves of commercial banks. As a result, interest rates rise and residential construction is deterred, offsetting part of the expansionary stimulus of federal spending. In the second simulation, an accommodating monetary policy is assumed, in the sense that the Federal Reserve allows unborrowed reserves to increase enough to prevent interest rates from rising, and hence partly finances the increased government spending through creation of high-powered money. An accommodating monetary policy increases the *GNP* mutliplier comparatively little, however, since the degree of "crowding out" of residential construction is small when interest rates are allowed to rise. A similar observation holds for fiscal stimulus through tax reduction, as may be seen by comparing the third and fourth simulations. Given the uniformity of these results, no attempt was made to investigate the effects of an accommodating monetary policy on the investment credit multipliers.

The foregoing results indicate that fiscal policies have an important impact on aggregate economic activity and that this is true whether or

---

[2] See Christ (1967) on the desirability of including the government budget constraint in econometric models.

An Annual Growth Model of the U.S. Economy

TABLE 8.3
Multipliers–Federal surplus and net exports.

	Federal surplus (current prices)							
	ΔG		ΔT		ΔM		ΔTC	
Year	(1)	(2)	(1)	(2)	(1)	(2)	(1)	(2)
1	0.07	0.12	−0.42	−0.42	1.16	0.60	−1.74	−1.58
2	0.00	0.20	−0.27	−0.10	1.57	0.53	−0.70	−1.11
3	0.09	0.18	−0.12	−0.06	0.91	0.31	−0.72	−1.30
4	0.16	0.13	−0.06	−0.08	0.07	0.02	−0.71	−1.27
5	0.20	0.25	−0.01	0.05	0.14	0.04	−0.67	−1.27
6	0.10	0.19	−0.10	−0.02	0.27	0.08	−0.59	−1.14
7	0.11	0.17	−0.09	−0.03	0.31	0.08	−0.55	−1.08
8	0.19	0.18	0.01	0.01	0.15	0.04	−0.50	−1.11
9	0.17	0.20	0.00	0.04	0.44	0.10	−0.45	−1.05
10	0.17	0.17	0.03	0.03	0.16	0.04	−0.43	−1.03
11	0.23	0.21	0.10	0.10	0.09	0.02	−0.37	−1.05
12	0.29	0.27	0.17	0.18	0.13	0.03	−0.29	−1.09
13	0.29	0.28	0.18	0.20	0.06	0.01	−0.26	−1.06
14	0.30	0.28	0.22	0.21	0.06	0.01	−0.22	−1.07
15	0.15	0.12	0.08	0.08	0.10	0.02	−0.29	−1.03
16	0.19	0.18	0.14	0.15	0.24	0.05	−0.20	−1.05
	Net exports (current prices)							
1	−0.10	−0.11	−0.06	−0.05	−0.11	−0.05	−0.01	0.06
2	−0.11	−0.13	−0.07	−0.09	−0.15	−0.05	−0.07	0.04
3	−0.11	−0.13	−0.09	−0.10	−0.11	−0.04	−0.09	0.05
4	−0.14	−0.15	−0.11	−0.12	−0.04	−0.02	−0.12	0.05
5	−0.15	−0.16	−0.12	−0.14	−0.02	−0.01	−0.14	0.05
6	−0.16	−0.17	−0.13	−0.14	−0.04	−0.01	−0.16	0.03
7	−0.16	−0.17	−0.13	−0.14	−0.04	−0.01	−0.18	0.02
8	−0.16	−0.16	−0.13	−0.13	−0.02	−0.00	−0.19	0.02
9	−0.16	−0.16	−0.13	−0.14	−0.04	−0.01	−0.20	0.01
10	−0.16	−0.17	−0.14	−0.14	−0.02	−0.00	−0.21	0.01
11	−0.17	−0.17	−0.14	−0.15	−0.01	−0.00	−0.22	0.00
12	−0.17	−0.16	−0.15	−0.15	−0.01	−0.00	−0.22	0.00
13	−0.17	−0.16	−0.15	−0.15	0.00	0.00	−0.23	0.00
14	−0.17	−0.17	−0.16	−0.16	0.00	0.00	−0.24	0.00
15	−0.35	−0.33	−0.31	−0.31	0.01	0.00	−0.34	0.03
16	−0.40	−0.39	−0.36	−0.37	−0.01	0.00	−0.39	0.04

not the deficit is financed by a new injection of high-powered money. Another important issue concerns the effects of induced income expansion on tax revenue, and hence, on the ultimate state of budget balance resulting from an exogenous deficit.

It is important to note that the ex-ante deficit for the case of increased federal spending is converted to an ex-post surplus even during the first year (table 8.3). When allowance is made for the rise of tax receipts induced by income expansion, then, deficit financing is essentially transitory for this case. A deficit-financed personal tax reduction, in contrast, results in ex-post deficits of diminishing magnitude for five or six years before an ex-post surplus is generated. Even in this case, however, the ex-post deficit each year is considerably smaller than the amount of the exogenous tax reduction.

The net outcome of the investment credit simulations is a large deficit in the initial year which is decreased but never eliminated by the subsequent expansion of tax revenues from other sources. These cases are not directly comparable with the other fiscal policies, however, since they assume a permanent incremental credit rate, and hence an increasing dollar flow of tax credits over the simulation period. Thus the flow of credits generated in variant (1), with prices directly affected, rises from 0.85 billion dollars in the first year to 2.16 in the last. The corresponding figures for the second variant are 0.85 and 2.06. Hence the multiplier results in these cases embody a growing reduction in corporate tax revenue owing to the growing tax credit, in contrast to the fixed reduction in revenue assumed for the personal tax cut. Were the investment credit simulation to assume a fixed dollar increase in tax credits, it too would lead eventually to a budget surplus under variant (1), as the induced growth of nominal *GNP* increases revenue from other taxes. Since nominal *GNP* never rises in variant (2), however, the deficit would be permanent even for a fixed dollar increase of investment credits.

The monetary simulation involves an injection of unborrowed reserves by the central bank, typically through an open market purchase of government securities. It therefore has no direct effect on government expenditures or receipts. The resulting expansion of income generates a federal surplus, however, which gradually falls over time as the monetary stimulus weakens and national income returns to its original level.

With regard to net exports, the various policies reduce the nominal surplus and increase the nominal deficit on foreign account to the extent that real imports are raised by higher domestic incomes and prices (table 8.3). This is because nominal exports and the price of imports are exogenous. Real imports are reduced under variant (2) of the investment credit, however, inducing an export surplus. In this case, real income rises insufficiently to offset the reduction of real import demand induced by the fall of domestic prices relative to import prices. Any induced changes in the monetary base stemming from foreign transactions is assumed to be offset in all the simulations by appropriate Federal Reserve actions to control unborrowed reserves.

4. Real Multipliers and Spending Propensities, 1951–66

As explained earlier, the multipliers in the previous section, including those for real *GNP*, were normalized by the nominal value of the exogenous policy injections. While appropriate for some purposes, such multipliers can give a misleading impression of the response of real variables to real policy inputs. In this section we present the corresponding real input multipliers for *GNP*. We also include multipliers for the principal components of real national expenditure and some related marginal spending propensities, as aids for interpretation of the *GNP* multipliers for various fiscal policies.

The real input multipliers are shown in the top halves of tables 8.4–8.9 and refer to gross national product (*XGNP*), disposable personal income (*YPD*), personal consumption expenditure (*CE*), business fixed investment (*IGB*), residential construction (*HGIN*), non-farm inventory investment (*IINF*), exports (*FEX*), and imports (*FIM*). (For details on the normalization procedures, see Chapter 8, section 2.)

The spending propensities in the bottom halves must be interpreted with two points in mind. First, they are gross in the sense that the numerators refer to the change in a particular variable due to all relevant factors and not just to income change alone. The value for $\Delta CE/\Delta XGNP$, for example, reflects the effect on consumption expenditure of induced changes in prices and interest rates as well as the change in *GNP* itself. Despite this caveat, it is reasonable for the most part to interpret the propensities in the usual way, especially since the changes in prices and interest rates are themselves influenced by income change. Second, the marginal propensity for a given year refers to the cumulative effects on the numerator and denominator since the year in which the exogenous impulse was introduced. Thus this concept is the dynamic counterpart to the usual dichotomy between a short-run and long-run propensity, where the latter allows for complete adjustment of, say, consumer expenditure to a sustained change in income.

It is apparent from a comparison of the real *GNP* multipliers in tables 8.4–8.9 with their counterparts in table 8.1 that correction of the policy inputs for induced price changes has brought the multiplier values for the different policies closer together.

4.1. The Expenditure Multipliers

The simulations of the effects of an exogenous increase of federal expenditure reveal some interesting properties of the model (tables 8.4 and 8.5).

A pronounced inventory cycle occurs in the first two years in response to the shock. The fluctuations of inventory investment (*IINF*) and real national product (*XGNP*) are highly damped thereafter, owing to the speedy stock-adjustment mechanism for inventories [equation (2.17)].

Without an accommodating monetary policy, part of the expansionary impact of the new federal spending is offset by a loss of residential construction (*HGIN*) especially in the early years. Thus some crowding out occurs initially, but after the third year the difference between the *GNP* multipliers with and without monetary accommodation is small.

At first, the change in consumer expenditures accounts for only a small fraction of the change in *GNP*, but $\Delta CE/\Delta XGNP$ grows markedly over time. Consumers spend most of their incremental disposable income from the beginning and in some years spending actually increases more than income, so that $\Delta CE/\Delta YPD$ exceeds unity. In the early years, however, disposable income increases little relative to the increase in *GNP*, and it is not until $\Delta YPD/\Delta XGNP$ rises that $\Delta CE/\Delta XGNP$ can grow.

The small initial value of $\Delta YPD/\Delta XGNP$ is a measure of the strength of the economy's built-in stabilizers. Induced increases in tax receipts and undistributed profits severely limit the response of disposable income to increases in national income, just as they cushion the economy against income declines during contractions.

TABLE 8.4

Real multipliers and gross spending propensities, exogenous increase in government expenditure without accommodating monetary policy.

Year					Multipliers				
	XGNP	YPD	CE	IGB	HGIN	IINF	GSL	FEX	FIM
1	1.59	0.31	0.29	0.19	0.00	0.32	-0.00	-0.12	0.09
2	1.06	0.14	0.32	0.16	-0.07	-0.09	-0.01	-0.16	0.12
3	1.39	0.29	0.39	0.20	-0.04	0.06	0.08	-0.16	0.14
4	1.83	0.63	0.58	0.26	0.10	0.14	0.08	-0.18	0.16
5	1.87	0.75	0.70	0.28	0.09	0.06	0.10	-0.19	0.17
6	1.83	0.82	0.75	0.28	0.02	0.01	0.14	-0.20	0.17
7	1.96	0.88	0.84	0.30	0.01	0.04	0.16	-0.21	0.18
8	2.26	1.12	1.03	0.34	0.05	0.04	0.16	-0.19	0.19
9	2.32	1.16	1.07	0.35	0.04	0.05	0.17	-0.18	0.19
10	2.44	1.32	1.17	0.36	0.05	0.04	0.18	-0.18	0.19
11	2.62	1.42	1.30	0.38	0.07	0.03	0.20	-0.18	0.20
12	2.81	1.45	1.47	0.41	0.07	0.04	0.22	-0.19	0.21
13	2.86	1.58	1.53	0.43	0.07	0.01	0.23	-0.19	0.21
14	3.00	1.70	1.66	0.44	0.07	0.03	0.23	-0.21	0.21
15	2.70	1.58	1.67	0.41	0.05	-0.05	0.24	-0.19	0.43
16	2.60	1.45	1.74	0.41	0.01	-0.08	0.25	-0.21	0.51

Spending propensities

Year	$\dfrac{\Delta YPD}{\Delta XGNP}$	$\dfrac{\Delta CE}{\Delta YPD}$	$\dfrac{\Delta CE}{\Delta XGNP}$	$\dfrac{\Delta IGB}{\Delta XGNP}$	$\dfrac{\Delta HGIN}{\Delta XGNP}$	$\dfrac{\Delta IINF}{\Delta XGNP}$	$\dfrac{\Delta GSL}{\Delta XGNP}$	$\dfrac{\Delta FEX}{\Delta XGNP}$	$\dfrac{\Delta FIM}{\Delta XGNP}$
1	0.19	0.99	0.18	0.12	0.00	0.20	-0.00	-0.08	0.06
2	0.30	2.27	0.30	0.15	-0.06	-0.08	0.01	-0.15	0.11
3	0.21	1.38	0.28	0.15	-0.03	0.04	0.06	-0.12	0.10
4	0.35	0.92	0.32	0.14	0.06	0.08	0.04	-0.10	0.09
5	0.40	0.94	0.38	0.15	0.05	0.03	0.05	-0.10	0.09
6	0.45	0.92	0.41	0.15	0.01	0.01	0.08	-0.11	0.09
7	0.45	0.96	0.43	0.15	0.00	0.02	0.08	-0.11	0.09
8	0.49	0.92	0.46	0.15	0.02	0.02	0.08	-0.08	0.08
9	0.50	0.92	0.46	0.15	0.02	0.02	0.07	-0.08	0.08
10	0.54	0.88	0.48	0.15	0.02	0.02	0.07	-0.07	0.08
11	0.54	0.92	0.50	0.15	0.03	0.01	0.08	-0.07	0.08
12	0.52	1.01	0.52	0.15	0.02	0.01	0.08	-0.07	0.07
13	0.55	0.97	0.53	0.15	0.02	0.00	0.08	-0.07	0.07
14	0.57	0.98	0.55	0.15	0.02	0.01	0.08	-0.07	0.07
15	0.58	1.06	0.62	0.15	0.02	-0.02	0.09	-0.07	0.16
16	0.56	1.20	0.67	0.16	0.00	-0.03	0.10	-0.08	0.20

TABLE 8.5

Real multipliers and gross spending propensities, exogenous increase in government expenditure with accommodating monetary policy.

					Multipliers				
Year	XGNP	YPD	CE	IGB	HGIN	IINF	GSL	FEX	FIM
1	1.72	0.32	0.31	0.21	0.07	0.35	-0.00	-0.12	0.10
2	1.30	-0.04	0.36	0.22	0.02	-0.04	0.02	-0.19	0.15
3	1.53	0.28	0.42	0.27	0.10	0.02	0.08	-0.19	0.17
4	1.83	0.65	0.57	0.29	0.12	0.12	0.08	-0.18	0.17
5	1.99	0.78	0.74	0.32	0.14	0.07	0.11	-0.20	0.18
6	1.97	0.83	0.81	0.32	0.09	0.01	0.15	-0.22	0.18
7	2.07	0.90	0.90	0.34	0.05	0.03	0.17	-0.23	0.19
8	2.24	1.13	1.02	0.35	0.05	0.01	0.18	-0.19	0.19
9	2.39	1.18	1.10	0.37	0.06	0.01	0.19	-0.18	0.19
10	2.45	1.19	1.14	0.38	0.04	0.06	0.19	-0.18	0.19
11	2.54	1.28	1.27	0.40	0.04	0.01	0.20	-0.18	0.20
12	2.70	1.42	1.43	0.41	0.05	-0.01	0.21	-0.19	0.21
13	2.79	1.48	1.47	0.43	0.04	0.02	0.22	-0.19	0.21
14	2.89	1.58	1.59	0.44	0.04	0.02	0.22	-0.21	0.21
15	2.58	1.51	1.59	0.40	0.02	-0.07	0.23	-0.18	0.40
16	2.55	1.24	1.63	0.42	-0.01	-0.03	0.24	-0.20	0.51

Spending propensities

Year	$\dfrac{\Delta YPD}{\Delta XGNP}$	$\dfrac{\Delta CE}{\Delta YPD}$	$\dfrac{\Delta CE}{\Delta XGNP}$	$\dfrac{\Delta IGB}{\Delta XGNP}$	$\dfrac{\Delta HGIN}{\Delta XGNP}$	$\dfrac{\Delta IINF}{\Delta XGNP}$	$\dfrac{\Delta GSL}{\Delta XGNP}$	$\dfrac{\Delta FEX}{\Delta XGNP}$	$\dfrac{\Delta FIM}{\Delta XGNP}$
1	0.19	0.98	0.18	0.12	0.04	0.21	-0.00	-0.07	0.06
2	-0.03	-8.73	0.28	0.17	0.02	0.03	0.02	-0.15	0.12
3	0.18	1.51	0.27	0.17	0.07	0.01	0.05	-0.12	0.11
4	0.35	0.88	0.31	0.16	0.07	0.06	0.04	-0.10	0.09
5	0.39	0.95	0.37	0.16	0.07	0.03	0.06	-0.10	0.09
6	0.42	0.97	0.41	0.16	0.04	0.01	0.08	-0.11	0.09
7	0.43	1.00	0.43	0.16	0.03	0.01	0.08	-0.11	0.09
8	0.50	0.91	0.46	0.15	0.02	0.01	0.08	-0.08	0.08
9	0.49	0.93	0.46	0.16	0.02	0.03	0.08	-0.08	0.08
10	0.38	0.96	0.47	0.16	0.02	0.03	0.08	-0.07	0.08
11	0.50	0.99	0.50	0.15	0.02	0.01	0.08	-0.07	0.08
12	0.53	1.01	0.53	0.16	0.02	0.00	0.08	-0.07	0.08
13	0.53	0.99	0.53	0.15	0.02	0.01	0.08	-0.07	0.08
14	0.55	1.00	0.56	0.15	0.01	0.01	0.08	-0.07	0.07
15	0.59	1.05	0.62	0.15	0.01	0.03	0.08	-0.07	0.16
16	0.59	1.32	0.64	0.16	-0.00	0.01	0.09	-0.08	0.20

TABLE 8.6

Real multipliers and gross spending propensities, exogenous reduction in personal taxes without accommodating monetary policy.

Multipliers

Year	XGNP	YPD	CE	IGB	HGIN	IINF	GSL	FEX	FIM
1	0.77	1.09	0.57	0.10	0.10	0.17	-0.00	-0.05	0.05
2	0.69	1.14	0.79	0.08	0.11	-0.01	0.00	-0.08	0.06
3	0.89	1.20	0.93	0.13	0.13	0.06	0.03	-0.10	0.08
4	1.17	1.40	1.11	0.17	0.17	0.09	0.05	-0.11	0.10
5	1.27	1.49	1.26	0.19	0.12	0.04	0.07	-0.13	0.12
6	1.24	1.48	1.32	0.19	0.03	0.02	0.09	-0.14	0.12
7	1.31	1.57	1.41	0.20	0.01	0.01	0.11	-0.15	0.12
8	1.54	1.69	1.55	0.23	0.04	0.05	0.11	-0.13	0.13
9	1.63	1.76	1.62	0.25	0.03	0.04	0.11	-0.12	0.13
10	1.80	1.88	1.74	0.28	0.04	0.05	0.13	-0.13	0.14
11	1.93	1.94	1.87	0.30	0.05	0.03	0.14	-0.14	0.15
12	2.03	1.97	1.98	0.31	0.05	0.03	0.15	-0.14	0.16
13	2.15	2.11	2.07	0.34	0.05	0.01	0.15	-0.15	0.16
14	2.30	2.16	2.19	0.36	0.04	0.04	0.16	-0.16	0.17
15	2.09	2.19	2.25	0.33	0.03	-0.07	0.17	-0.15	0.33
16	2.03	2.13	2.31	0.31	0.00	-0.06	0.18	-0.16	0.38

Spending propensities

Year	$\dfrac{\Delta YPD}{\Delta XGNP}$	$\dfrac{\Delta CE}{\Delta YPD}$	$\dfrac{\Delta CE}{\Delta XGNP}$	$\dfrac{\Delta IGB}{\Delta XGNP}$	$\dfrac{\Delta HGIN}{\Delta XGNP}$	$\dfrac{\Delta IINF}{\Delta XGNP}$	$\dfrac{\Delta GSL}{\Delta XGNP}$	$\dfrac{\Delta FEX}{\Delta XGNP}$	$\dfrac{\Delta FIM}{\Delta XGNP}$
1	1.42	0.52	0.74	0.13	0.13	0.22	-0.00	-0.06	0.06
2	1.65	0.69	1.14	0.14	0.17	-0.01	0.00	-0.12	0.09
3	1.34	0.78	1.05	0.15	0.14	0.07	0.03	-0.11	0.09
4	1.19	0.79	0.95	0.14	0.15	0.07	0.04	-0.09	0.09
5	1.18	0.85	1.00	0.15	0.10	0.03	0.06	-0.10	0.09
6	1.19	0.89	1.06	0.16	0.03	0.01	0.07	-0.11	0.10
7	1.21	0.89	1.08	0.16	0.01	0.01	0.08	-0.11	0.09
8	1.00	0.91	1.01	0.15	0.03	0.30	0.07	-0.08	0.08
9	1.08	0.92	0.99	0.15	0.02	0.02	0.07	-0.07	0.08
10	1.04	0.93	0.97	0.15	0.02	0.03	0.07	-0.07	0.08
11	1.00	0.96	0.97	0.15	0.02	0.02	0.07	-0.07	0.08
12	0.97	1.00	0.97	0.15	0.02	0.01	0.07	-0.07	0.08
13	0.99	0.98	0.96	0.16	0.02	0.01	0.07	-0.07	0.07
14	0.94	1.02	0.95	0.16	0.02	0.02	0.07	-0.07	0.07
15	1.05	1.03	1.08	0.16	0.01	-0.03	0.08	-0.07	0.16
16	1.05	1.08	1.14	0.15	0.00	-0.03	0.09	-0.08	0.19

TABLE 8.7

Real multipliers and gross spending propensities, exogenous reduction in personal taxes with accommodating monetary policy.

Multipliers

Year	XGNP	YPD	CE	IGB	HGIN	IINF	GSL	FEX	FIM
1	0.84	1.19	0.61	0.10	0.13	0.17	-0.00	-0.05	0.05
2	0.82	0.94	0.80	0.12	0.20	0.05	0.01	-0.10	0.08
3	0.91	1.22	0.95	0.15	0.20	0.02	0.04	-0.10	0.09
4	1.20	1.42	1.11	0.18	0.19	0.08	0.05	-0.12	0.11
5	1.37	1.44	1.28	0.22	0.17	0.07	0.07	-0.13	0.13
6	1.30	1.47	1.35	0.23	0.19	0.00	0.09	-0.15	0.13
7	1.37	1.54	1.43	0.23	0.05	0.01	0.11	-0.16	0.13
8	1.52	1.68	1.54	0.25	0.05	0.02	0.11	-0.13	0.13
9	1.69	1.73	1.63	0.28	0.05	0.05	0.11	-0.13	0.14
10	1.80	1.82	1.73	0.30	0.04	0.04	0.13	-0.13	0.14
11	1.91	1.91	1.85	0.31	0.04	0.02	0.13	-0.14	0.15
12	2.01	1.92	1.96	0.33	0.04	0.02	0.14	-0.14	0.15
13	2.11	1.99	2.02	0.35	0.03	0.02	0.15	-0.15	0.16
14	2.24	2.01	2.15	0.37	0.04	0.03	0.16	-0.16	0.17
15	2.04	2.11	2.20	0.35	0.01	-0.06	0.16	-0.15	0.33
16	2.00	1.95	2.24	0.34	0.01	-0.03	0.17	-0.16	0.39

Spending propensities

Year	$\frac{\Delta YPD}{\Delta XGNP}$	$\frac{\Delta CE}{\Delta YPD}$	$\frac{\Delta CE}{\Delta XGNP}$	$\frac{\Delta IGB}{\Delta XGNP}$	$\frac{\Delta HGIN}{\Delta XGNP}$	$\frac{\Delta IINF}{\Delta XGNP}$	$\frac{\Delta GSL}{\Delta XGNP}$	$\frac{\Delta FEX}{\Delta XGNP}$	$\frac{\Delta FIM}{\Delta XGNP}$
1	1.42	0.51	0.73	0.12	0.16	0.19	0.00	−0.06	0.06
2	1.15	0.84	0.98	0.15	0.25	0.07	0.01	−0.12	0.10
3	1.33	0.77	1.03	0.16	0.22	0.03	0.04	−0.11	0.10
4	1.18	0.79	0.93	0.15	0.16	0.07	0.04	−0.10	0.09
5	1.06	0.89	0.94	0.16	0.12	0.05	0.05	−0.09	0.09
6	1.13	0.91	1.03	0.18	0.07	0.00	0.07	−0.12	0.10
7	1.13	0.93	1.05	0.17	0.03	0.01	0.08	−0.12	0.09
8	1.11	0.91	1.01	0.17	0.03	0.01	0.07	−0.09	0.09
9	1.13	0.94	0.99	0.17	0.03	0.03	0.06	−0.08	0.08
10	1.01	0.95	0.96	0.17	0.02	0.02	0.07	−0.07	0.08
11	1.00	0.97	0.97	0.16	0.02	0.01	0.07	−0.07	0.08
12	0.96	1.02	0.97	0.16	0.02	0.01	0.07	−0.07	0.07
13	0.95	1.06	0.96	0.17	0.02	0.01	0.07	−0.07	0.08
14	0.93	1.03	0.96	0.17	0.01	0.01	0.07	−0.07	0.08
15	1.04	1.00	1.08	0.17	0.01	−0.03	0.08	−0.07	0.16
16	1.12	1.88	0.97	0.17	0.00	−0.01	0.09	−0.08	0.20

TABLE 8.8

Real multipliers and gross spending propensities, exogenous increase in investment tax credit, variant (1).

Year					Multipliers				
	XGNP	YPD	CE	IGB	HGIN	IINF	GSL	FEX	FIM
1	2.46	1.70	0.86	0.30	0.18	0.69	0.02	0.34	-0.01
2	3.40	1.83	1.23	1.34	0.26	0.39	0.05	0.19	0.06
3	2.97	1.78	1.26	1.21	0.22	0.10	0.11	0.18	0.08
4	3.26	1.97	1.46	1.27	0.20	0.11	0.16	0.19	0.10
5	3.05	2.09	1.46	1.16	0.16	0.10	0.16	0.18	0.12
6	3.20	2.27	1.60	1.19	0.11	0.09	0.18	0.22	0.14
7	3.21	2.37	1.66	1.18	0.01	0.07	0.21	0.24	0.16
8	3.14	2.48	1.67	1.13	0.08	0.08	0.23	0.21	0.17
9	3.08	2.58	1.66	1.09	0.08	0.07	0.25	0.23	0.19
10	3.17	2.73	1.75	1.10	0.07	0.06	0.28	0.24	0.21
11	3.05	2.80	1.70	1.03	0.07	0.08	0.29	0.24	0.22
12	2.86	2.83	1.62	0.96	0.07	0.06	0.30	0.22	0.23
13	2.76	2.94	1.58	0.91	0.07	0.05	0.32	0.24	0.24
14	2.75	3.02	1.58	0.88	0.07	0.07	0.33	0.24	0.26
15	2.45	3.05	1.47	0.81	0.06	0.03	0.37	0.24	0.36
16	2.23	2.96	1.37	0.74	0.05	0.03	0.35	0.21	0.42

Spending propensities

Year	$\dfrac{\Delta YPD}{\Delta XGNP}$	$\dfrac{\Delta CE}{\Delta YPD}$	$\dfrac{\Delta CE}{\Delta XGNP}$	$\dfrac{\Delta IGB}{\Delta XGNP}$	$\dfrac{\Delta HGIN}{\Delta XGNP}$	$\dfrac{\Delta IINF}{\Delta XGNP}$	$\dfrac{\Delta GSL}{\Delta XGNP}$	$\dfrac{\Delta FEX}{\Delta XGNP}$	$\dfrac{\Delta FIM}{\Delta XGNP}$
1	0.69	0.51	0.35	0.12	0.07	0.28	0.01	0.14	0.00
2	0.54	0.67	0.36	0.39	0.08	0.11	0.01	0.06	0.02
3	0.60	0.71	0.42	0.41	0.07	0.03	0.04	0.06	0.03
4	0.60	0.74	0.45	0.39	0.06	0.03	0.05	0.06	0.03
5	0.69	0.70	0.48	0.38	0.05	0.03	0.05	0.06	0.04
6	0.71	0.71	0.50	0.37	0.03	0.03	0.06	0.07	0.04
7	0.74	0.70	0.52	0.37	0.00	0.03	0.07	0.07	0.05
8	0.79	0.67	0.53	0.36	0.03	0.02	0.07	0.07	0.05
9	0.84	0.64	0.54	0.35	0.03	0.02	0.08	0.07	0.06
10	0.86	0.64	0.55	0.35	0.02	0.02	0.09	0.08	0.07
11	0.92	0.61	0.55	0.34	0.02	0.03	0.09	0.08	0.07
12	0.99	0.57	0.57	0.33	0.02	0.02	0.10	0.08	0.08
13	1.06	0.54	0.57	0.33	0.02	0.02	0.12	0.09	0.09
14	1.10	0.52	0.58	0.32	0.02	0.03	0.12	0.09	0.09
15	1.25	0.48	0.60	0.33	0.02	0.01	0.15	0.10	0.15
16	1.32	0.47	0.60	0.33	0.02	0.01	0.16	0.09	0.19

TABLE 8.9

Real multipliers and gross spending propensities, exogenous increase in investment tax credit, variant (2).

					Multipliers				
Year	XGNP	YPD	CE	IGB	HGIN	IINF	GSL	FEX	FIM
1	-0.10	-0.05	-0.26	-0.01	-0.05	0.03	0.01	0.15	-0.04
2	0.72	-0.00[a]	-0.33	0.72	0.00	0.18	-0.01	0.13	-0.03
3	0.49	0.02	-0.31	0.64	0.02	-0.01	-0.04	0.16	-0.04
4	0.42	-0.23	-0.33	0.64	-0.04	0.00	-0.06	0.17	-0.05
5	0.40	-0.18	-0.33	0.64	-0.03	-0.01	-0.07	0.16	-0.04
6	0.53	-0.18	-0.29	0.68	0.01	0.03	-0.09	0.17	-0.03
7	0.53	-0.20	-0.30	0.69	0.01	0.01	-0.08	0.17	-0.02
8	0.39	-0.22	-0.33	0.68	0.01	-0.03	-0.07	0.14	-0.02
9	0.47	-0.22	-0.31	0.70	0.00	0.01	-0.07	0.13	-0.01
10	0.47	-0.25	-0.31	0.71	-0.01	0.01	-0.07	0.13	-0.01
11	0.44	-0.27	-0.34	0.71	-0.01	0.01	-0.06	0.13	0.00
12	0.43	-0.19	-0.34	0.71	0.00	0.01	-0.06	0.14	0.00
13	0.50	-0.19	-0.31	0.71	0.00	0.02	-0.06	0.14	0.00
14	0.51	-0.18	-0.32	0.72	0.01	0.02	-0.05	0.15	0.00
15	0.61	-0.14	-0.29	0.73	0.01	0.03	-0.05	0.14	-0.03
16	0.72	0.02	-0.24	0.74	0.04	0.03	-0.04	0.15	-0.04

Spending propensities

Year	$\dfrac{\Delta YPD}{\Delta XGNP}$	$\dfrac{\Delta CE}{\Delta YPD}$	$\dfrac{\Delta CE}{\Delta XGNP}$	$\dfrac{\Delta IGB}{\Delta XGNP}$	$\dfrac{\Delta HGIN}{\Delta XGNP}$	$\dfrac{\Delta IINF}{\Delta XGNP}$	$\dfrac{\Delta GSL}{\Delta XGNP}$	$\dfrac{\Delta FEX}{\Delta XGNP}$	$\dfrac{\Delta FIM}{\Delta XGNP}$
1	0.50	5.20	2.60	0.10	0.50	-0.30	-0.10	-1.50	0.40
2	0.00	114.81[a]	-0.46	1.00	0.00	0.25	-0.01	0.18	-0.04
3	0.04	-15.50	-0.63	1.31	0.04	-0.02	-0.08	0.33	-0.08
4	-0.55	1.43	-0.79	1.52	-0.10	0.00	-0.14	0.40	-0.12
5	-0.45	1.83	-0.82	1.60	-0.08	-0.02	-0.18	0.40	-0.10
6	-0.34	1.61	-0.55	1.28	0.02	0.06	-0.17	0.32	-0.06
7	-0.38	1.50	-0.57	1.30	0.02	0.02	-0.15	0.32	-0.04
8	-0.56	1.50	-0.85	1.74	-0.03	-0.08	-0.18	0.36	-0.05
9	-0.47	1.41	-0.66	1.49	0.00	0.02	-0.15	0.28	-0.02
10	-0.53	1.25	-0.66	1.51	-0.02	0.02	-0.15	0.28	-0.02
11	-0.61	1.26	-0.77	1.61	-0.02	0.02	-0.14	0.30	0.00
12	-0.44	1.79	-0.79	1.65	0.00	0.02	-0.14	0.33	0.00
13	-0.38	1.63	-0.62	1.42	0.00	0.04	-0.12	0.28	0.00
14	-0.35	1.78	-0.63	1.41	0.02	0.04	-0.10	0.29	0.00
15	-0.23	2.07	-0.48	1.20	0.02	0.05	-0.08	0.23	-0.05
16	-0.03	12.00	-0.33	1.03	0.06	0.04	-0.06	0.21	-0.06

[a] The unrounded reduction in *YPD* is 0.0027 in year 2.

These restraining effects diminish gradually over time, however, for two main reasons. First, the corporate profit share, which initially rises at the expense of the labor and other property incomes, owing to lags of factor prices behind product prices, gradually diminishes, reducing the drag of undistributed profits and corporate taxes on disposable income. Second, the longer-run responses of dividends and taxes to income change are gradually realized as behavioral and institutional lags are overcome.

The incremental business fixed investment ratio to *GNP* adjusts rapidly to a fairly stable value of about 0.16 with and 0.15 without an accommodating monetary policy. The ratio is stable because the diminishing flow of new investment over time, owing to the gradual adjustment of desired to actual capital stock, is offset by the gradual increase in replacement expenditures as the actual stock grows.

The incremental ratios for housing and inventory investment are small (except in the first year for *IINF*) and variable without an accommodating monetary policy. Under accommodating policy, however, residential construction is favored by the growth of disposable income and no longer retarded by monetary restraints, with the result of greater stability and higher investment during the first decade. In contrast, the behavior of inventory investment is relatively unaffected by monetary conditions.

The growth of personal income gradually increases the demand for additional real expenditure by state and local governments. After five years the marginal response to *GNP* stabilizes at about 0.08.

Finally, foreign trade dampens the expenditure multipliers. The induced rise of real imports constitutes a leakage from the income stream analogous to savings and taxes. Rudimentary income–expenditure models usually take real exports as exogenous. However, they are endogenous in our model and vary inversely with the induced change in export prices. This is because we take export demand to be exogenous in nominal units, on the basis that it is more realistic to assume a price elasticity of unity than zero for exports. Since prices are increased and real exports decreased in the present simulations, the government expenditure multiplier is reduced from the side of exports as well as imports.

It is also important to notice that the marginal propensity to import increases substantially in the last two years of the simulation following the U.S.–Canadian automobile agreement of 1965 (see Chapter 2, section 6). This explains the otherwise puzzling decline in the *GNP* multiplier in those years after many years of steady expansion. That is to say, the final decline in *GNP* is not the result of endogenous cyclical dynamics, but rather the accidental reflection of a structural change in the import function.

4.2. The Personal Tax Multipliers

An exogenous reduction of personal taxes is a principal expansionary alternative to an increase of government expenditure, so that much of the interest in the tax multipliers in tables 8.6 and 8.7 lies in their behavior relative to the expenditure multipliers already examined.

The impact multipliers for a personal tax reduction are less than unity and much smaller than for an expenditure increase. This difference is partly eliminated over time but remains substantial.

The distribution of expenditure increases between public and private outlays is quite different under the alternative policies, of course. Real federal expenditure (not shown in the tables) actually falls under the tax reduction policy (which assumes federal spending unchanged in nominal terms), whereas it is approximately 1.0 billion higher each year under the expenditure policy. Thus real private expenditure increases by more than real *GNP* under the former policy and by less under the latter. The marginal share of state and local expenditure is about the same under both policies.

Among private expenditures, the personal tax reduction decisively favors consumption over investment. The gross marginal propensity for business fixed investment is about the same as for the expenditure multiplier, but the consumption propensity is much higher under the personal tax cut. Thus after allowing for the smaller absolute effect of a tax reduction on *GNP*, the principal difference between the two policies lies in the trade-off between federal spending and private consumption, since there is little differential impact on business investment.

In the first decade $\Delta CE / \Delta YPD$ is actually lower when taxes are reduced than when government expenditures are increased, tending to restrain consumption in the former case. However,

$\Delta \, YPD/\Delta \, XGNP$ is so much larger because of the cut in personal taxes that $\Delta \, CE/\Delta \, XGNP$ is close to unity for that case.

Residential construction is favored more by the tax cut, because interest rates rise less and disposable income more than under an expenditure increase.

The marginal response of state and local spending and of foreign trade differ little from the expenditure case.

An inventory cycle is also observable in the tax multiplier, but its amplitude is smaller than in the expenditure multipliers.

4.3. The Investment Tax Credit Multipliers

This policy successfully favors business fixed investment, as it is designed to do (tables 8.8 and 8.9). Without allowance for direct price effects [variant (2)], the augmented investment share is at the expense of an absolute decline in real consumption. In comparison with the expenditure multipliers, however, the enhanced investment share under variant (1) is at the expense of federal public goods and services rather than private consumption, since $\Delta \, CE/\Delta \, XGNP$ is as large or larger in the case of the investment credit (tables 8.4 and 8.8). The two tax policies–a personal tax reduction or an increase in the investment credit–are of course directly competitive in their effects on the relative shares of investment and consumption expenditure (tables 8.6 and 8.8–8.9).

The *GNP* multipliers for the investment credit [variant (1)] substantially exceed those for a personal tax cut, although the difference between the two narrows somewhat over time. Business fixed investment responds to the tax credit with a lag, so that the large impact multiplier is due primarily to a spurt in consumption demand. The latter in turn is touched off by a rise in real disposable income stemming initially from the price reductions induced by the tax credit and reinforced by the expansion of production. As noted earlier, the price reductions may be overstated in these simulations, but the direction of the effect is clear. The price effects of the tax credit are an important real income stimulus over and above the direct impact on investment demand.

The situation is quite different under variant (2). Without a direct effect of the tax credit on prices, the fall in prices is moderated and is insufficient to offset the decline in nominal labor income from reduced wages and employment. Hence real disposable income and consumption are reduced. In the early years, consumption actually falls much further than disposable income, owing to the depressing effect of higher unemployment on expenditure for automobiles and other durables [equations (2.7) and (2.8)]. Thus without a direct pass-through of the investment credit to product prices, the stimulus to income from investment spending is largely offset by reduced labor income and consumption, so that the real *GNP* multiplier is quite small and unemployment actually increases to a permanently higher level. As we noted above, variants (1) and (2) of the investment credit simulation portray two limiting cases which probably bracket the true impacts of the credit.

5. Capacity Multipliers, 1951–66

In table 8.10 we compare the multipliers for potential output and related concepts under the alternative economic policies. The comparison is confined to the first variant of the expenditure, personal tax and monetary policy simulations, but both variants are shown for the investment credit.

Potential output varies directly with full-employment man-hours and lagged capital stock [equation (1.24)]. As seen in the previous section, all the policies induce additional net investment, but this does not begin to augment potential output until the second year, owing to the lag on capital stock in the potential production function.[3] Potential actually diminishes during the first year in most of the cases, owing to a decline in full-employment man-hours. Capital accumulation gradually overcomes the reduction in full-employment man-hours, however, so that potential does increase over time.

The increase is at widely varying rates under the different policies, however. As expected, the investment credit induces the largest

---

[3] Thus current investment is assumed not to become effective in the production process until the following year. Our annual time unit may overstate this installation and shakedown lag, but with only minor effects on the time shape of the potential multipliers.

TABLE 8.10
Multipliers–Potential, capacity and full-employment output and utilization rates.

Year	Potential output (1958 prices)					Capacity output (1958 prices)					Full-employment output (1958 prices)				
	ΔG (1)	ΔT (1)	ΔM (1)	ΔTC (1)	ΔTC (2)	ΔG (1)	ΔT (1)	ΔM (1)	ΔTC (1)	ΔTC (2)	ΔG (1)	ΔT (1)	ΔM (1)	ΔTC (1)	ΔTC (2)
1	-0.01	-0.01	-0.01	-0.19	0.03	0.01	-0.04	-0.04	-0.06	-0.01	0.10	0.00	0.05	3.23	2.36
2	0.09	0.04	0.08	-0.01	0.08	0.08	0.03	0.12	-6.25	-4.06	-0.55	-0.19	-0.38	3.89	3.34
3	0.15	0.08	0.07	0.55	0.39	0.23	0.10	0.22	-4.45	-2.83	-0.61	-0.30	-0.76	3.54	3.36
4	0.19	0.11	0.20	1.06	0.61	0.34	0.18	0.36	-3.41	-2.27	-0.67	-0.42	-0.65	3.65	3.59
5	0.27	0.17	0.17	1.41	0.75	0.48	0.30	0.45	-2.19	-1.83	-0.91	-0.60	-0.09	3.41	3.60
6	0.35	0.23	0.14	1.83	0.93	0.68	0.40	0.33	-1.43	-1.51	-1.07	-0.79	-0.16	3.33	3.82
7	0.42	0.28	0.14	2.19	1.08	0.85	0.53	0.25	-0.71	-1.34	-1.23	-0.83	-0.30	3.23	3.87
8	0.50	0.33	0.17	2.47	1.21	1.07	0.67	0.33	-0.02	-1.07	-1.30	-0.87	-0.26	3.10	3.94
9	0.56	0.38	0.14	2.70	1.32	1.20	0.79	0.31	0.55	-0.87	-1.46	-1.01	-0.19	2.97	4.11
10	0.63	0.44	0.18	3.04	1.43	1.39	0.92	0.33	1.04	-0.73	-1.55	-1.16	-0.36	2.94	4.25
11	0.71	0.51	0.17	3.19	1.49	1.65	1.07	0.40	1.55	-0.59	-1.73	-1.32	-0.18	2.73	4.22
12	0.80	0.57	0.14	3.30	1.54	1.85	1.20	0.27	1.92	-0.40	-1.96	-1.45	-0.22	2.52	4.23
13	0.87	0.64	0.14	3.47	1.62	1.96	1.34	0.22	2.27	-0.25	-2.02	-1.50	-0.17	2.47	4.33
14	0.93	0.69	0.13	3.60	1.65	2.18	1.48	0.26	2.65	-0.17	-2.10	-1.66	-0.02	2.25	4.30
15	0.98	0.77	0.11	3.65	1.66	2.27	1.66	0.22	2.91	-0.08	-2.23	-1.70	-0.01	1.96	4.22
16	1.07	0.82	0.09	3.66	1.66	2.52	1.94	0.26	3.16	0.04	-2.24	-1.53	0.09	1.84	4.06

	Potential utilization					Capacity utilization					Full-employment utilization				
Year	ΔG (1)	ΔT (1)	ΔM (1)	ΔTC (1)	ΔTC (2)	ΔG (1)	ΔT (1)	ΔM (1)	ΔTC (1)	ΔTC (2)	ΔG (1)	ΔT (1)	ΔM (1)	ΔTC (1)	ΔTC (2)
1	0.54	0.26	0.57	0.91	−0.04	0.67	0.35	0.74	1.11	0.04	0.49	0.26	0.54	−0.28	−0.84
2	0.31	0.21	0.51	1.22	0.20	0.37	0.26	0.58	4.71	2.34	0.55	0.30	0.68	−0.15	−0.94
3	0.38	0.25	0.14	0.92	0.03	0.42	0.29	0.14	3.62	1.61	0.65	0.39	0.46	−0.09	−0.98
4	0.48	0.31	−0.15	0.85	−0.06	0.51	0.34	−0.27	3.01	1.24	0.76	0.49	0.12	0.03	−1.00
5	0.45	0.32	−0.02	0.75	−0.11	0.45	0.32	−0.18	2.56	1.02	0.81	0.54	0.06	0.16	−0.95
6	0.40	0.28	0.08	0.70	−0.11	0.34	0.25	0.01	2.14	0.87	0.82	0.57	0.17	0.29	−0.91
7	0.41	0.23	0.08	0.64	−0.15	0.30	0.17	0.04	1.80	0.72	0.85	0.47	0.20	0.36	−0.88
8	0.45	0.31	−0.02	0.59	−0.20	0.30	0.22	−0.10	1.52	0.54	0.92	0.62	0.09	0.43	−0.88
9	0.43	0.31	0.14	0.57	−0.20	0.26	0.21	0.10	1.31	0.47	0.93	0.65	0.22	0.50	−0.84
10	0.44	0.33	−0.02	0.55	−0.22	0.24	0.21	−0.09	1.16	0.39	0.92	0.69	0.10	0.57	−0.80
11	0.44	0.33	−0.03	0.53	−0.24	0.18	0.18	−0.12	1.01	0.33	0.97	0.72	0.05	0.63	−0.78
12	0.45	0.33	0.00	0.51	−0.24	0.15	0.16	−0.05	0.88	0.25	1.02	0.75	0.08	0.68	−0.78
13	0.43	0.33	−0.05	0.49	−0.23	0.13	0.14	−0.09	0.77	0.22	0.99	0.74	0.02	0.70	−0.74
14	0.43	0.33	−0.03	0.49	−0.23	0.08	0.12	−0.09	0.70	0.19	0.99	0.77	−0.00	0.76	−0.70
15	0.34	0.26	−0.02	0.43	−0.20	−0.05	−0.01	−0.07	0.54	0.18	0.92	0.71	0.00	0.75	−0.70
16	0.27	0.21	0.14	0.39	−0.18	−0.19	0.14	0.12	0.42	0.17	0.88	0.65	0.13	0.74	−0.60

increases in potential, since it directly favors investment demand. Monetary policy has little effect on investment demand and potential output, whereas the expenditure and personal tax policies are in an intermediate position, with the former more powerful than the latter in this respect.

Capacity output is an increasing function of the lagged capital stock and of the ratio of the rental rate to the wage rate [equation (1.14)]. A reduction in the relative price of capital occurs under all the policies, but it is naturally much larger for the investment credit. Without direct price effects [variant (2)], the decline in the relative price of capital under the tax credit induces a long-lasting reduction of capacity output despite a pronounced growth of capital stock. In variant (1) of the tax credit case, capital-stock growth eventually outweighs the relative price effect and results in positive capacity growth beginning in the ninth year. For the remaining policies, the relative price effect is slight, and significant capacity growth accompanies capital-stock growth after the first year.[4]

The multipliers for full-employment output also vary widely under the alternative policies. Full-employment output varies directly with full-employment man-hours and inversely with the relative price of capital and labor and with lagged man-hours [equation (1.22)]. The large reduction in the factor price ratio under the investment credit swamps the effects of the reduction in full-employment man-hours so that full-employment output rises sharply under both variants of this policy. In contrast, full-employment output falls after the first year under the other policies, since the relative-price effect is unimportant in those cases.

Turning now to the utilization measures, we observe that an increase in federal expenditure or a reduction in personal taxes permanently increases the potential utilization rate. Thus these policies provide a lasting additional stimulus to production by raising

---

[4] The first-year capacity multipliers for all the policies are dominated by stochastic elements. As explained in Chapter 4, section 4, the utilization ratios for capacity and full-employment output are free of stochastic elements, but the levels of capacity and full-employment output are not. On a deterministic basis, capacity output should be unchanged in the first year in all the policy experiments, since the expected factor price ratio is a function of lagged prices and the capital stock is also lagged in the capacity function.

potential utilization as well as potential output. Monetary policy has no lasting effect on either potential or its utilization. As for the investment credit, potential utilization is increased under variant (1) and reduced under variant (2). As was noted in the previous section, the stimulus to actual output is small in the second case despite a large rise of investment demand, so that the utilization rate falls even as potential output expands.

Capacity utilization is raised at least until the last year or two by all policies except monetary expansion. The increases are especially striking for the investment credit. This is because the investment credit induces a high level of net investment, and capacity utilization is directly proportional to the capital expansion ratio (K/K_{-1}). [See equation (1.16).][5]

Finally, we find that utilization of full-employment output is raised temporarily by expansionary monetary policy and permanently by fiscal policy in the form of a personal tax reduction or an expenditure increase. Since full-employment utilization is inversely correlated with the unemployment rate,[6] this is simply another way of describing the effects of these policies on unemployment. By the same token, the permanent reduction of full-employment utilization under the investment credit, variant (2), reflects the corresponding permanent increase of unemployment observed in the previous section.

6. Summary and Conclusions

The model suggests that sustained changes in various instruments of federal policy may have substantially different impacts on the time

---

[5] Thus net investment can be expressed as a function either of the gap between desired and actual capital stock, as in equation (1.5), or of the gap between actual and capacity output [equation (1.16) inverted]. Given our cost-minimizing concept of capacity, one can say either that capacity utilization is high because net investment is high, or vice-versa. The first statement is proper when investment itself is explained by the capital-stock gap, and the second when investment is explained by the capacity utilization rate. Since we infer capacity from observed investment behavior on a capital-stock adjustment model, the first direction of influence is to be preferred in our conceptual scheme.

[6] The correlation is akin to that of Okun's law, as explained in Appendix D.

path of the U.S. economy. Conventional expansionary fiscal policies—
an increase in federal expenditures or reduction in personal taxes—
can permanently raise real output, whether or not they are accompanied by an accommodating monetary policy. The investment tax
credit can also permanently raise real output, although the increase is
rather small if the credit has no direct effect on product prices. Thus,
the monetarist view that fiscal policies unaccompanied by monetary
expansion can affect real output only for a short period is rejected in
this model.[7] On the other hand, expansionary monetary policy by
itself is found to raise real output only for two or three years, and the
long-run path of real output is largely invariant to a change in
monetary policy, consistent with the monetarist view.

Growth of real output can occur either when potential output (an
endogenous variable in our model) grows or when the utilization rate
of potential output rises. We find that both potential and its utilization
are permanently increased by the expansionary fiscal policies assumed in the simulations, except under variant (2) of the investment
credit when potential rises but utilization does not.[8] Monetary expansion, however, has no appreciable effect on the path of potential
output, since it does not directly influence business fixed capital
formation and the indirect stimulus to business investment from
increased activity in the housing and consumption sectors is short-
lived. An expenditure increase or personal tax cut can have a lasting
effect on potential because it can induce capital-stock growth by
permanently raising aggregate demand. The investment credit is an
even more powerful tool for raising potential, since it combines a
direct stimulus to capital formation with the indirect effects of rising
demand.

A policy-induced change in real output may be associated with a
variety of changes in unemployment, depending on the policy instru-

---

[7] See Anderson (1973) for a summary of the monetarist debate.

[8] It should be recalled that the average unemployment rate in the control solution
was 4.2 percent. With this degree of slack in the economy, the model implies that
output gains will occur from higher utilization as well as from higher growth of
potential itself, in all cases except for the investment credit without direct price effects.
The output gains from increased utilization would be greater, of course, if the control
solution were one of lower employment.

ment. The primary reason for this is that both labor demand and supply depend, among other things, on relative prices. Insofar as responses of relative prices differ under alternative policy changes, the unemployment responses may also differ, even though output responses are the same. For the policy experiments examined in this chapter, relative price effects are not especially important, except in the case of the investment credit. Thus, the real output changes generated by the expenditure increase, the personal tax cut, and the increase in unborrowed reserves are all inversely related in roughly similar ways to changes in the unemployment rate. The expansionary fiscal policies, which permanently increase real output, reduce the unemployment rate both in the short and long run; however, monetary expansion, which raises real output only in the short run, reduces the unemployment rate only temporarily.

The investment credit is another matter. Although like the other fiscal policies it permanently increases real output, the capital–labor substitution which it induces by lowering the relative price of capital leads to higher unemployment rates in the short run. Indeed, this perverse effect is maintained over the longer run, provided that the credit has no direct effects on product prices. If instead the credit is fully passed through to lower product prices, thus raising real income and demand, the initial increase in unemployment is eventually reversed and a permanently lower unemployment rate is established.

Finally, the trade-off between unemployment and inflation in these complete model simulations is broadly consistent with the non-monetarist view. According to the monetarist view, the unemployment rate cannot be permanently lowered from its "natural" (equilibrium) level by effective demand policies. A temporary reduction of unemployment may be achieved at the expense of a higher inflation rate, but unemployment will return to the natural rate over the long run and the inflation rate will ultimately depend on the rate of growth of the money supply. In our model the character of the trade-off, in both the short and long runs, differs according to the policy instrument used to augment effective demand. A trade-off does exist for conventional fiscal policies in the first few years, but the inflation rate diminishes rapidly and the price level actually declines after five years, although not back to the original level. Thus the long-run trade-off is between lower unemployment and a higher price level rather than a higher inflation rate. In the case of a once-for-all monetary stimulus, prices eventually revert to the original level,[9] but so also does unemployment. As for the investment credit, price deflation is bought at the expense of increased unemployment at least in the short run, but under favorable circumstances (that is, when tax credits are passed on in price reductions) both prices and unemployment are reduced in the long run.

A final caution is in order concerning these multiplier results. The sample period ended in 1966, before the recent surge of inflation. The estimated wage equation implies an unchanged expected rate of wage inflation during the post-war years (see Chapter 5, section 3), but a change in wage expectations probably occurred in the late Sixties and early Seventies. This could substantially modify the inflation dynamics of the model and the estimated trade-offs.

---

[9] This is because, in the long run, the income velocity of money is sufficiently diminished (by the reduction of interest rates which results from an expansion of unborrowed reserves in the model) to offset the induced expansion of the money stock.

CHAPTER 9

Dynamic Properties of the Model

1. Introduction

While the policy simulations discussed in the preceding chapter indicate the dynamic responses of the model to changes in selected policy instruments, they do not fully reveal the nature of the interactions within the model's structure which give rise to these responses. Section 1 of this chapter explores these interactions for the case of an increase in federal expenditures, employing a technique which was introduced in the study of large-scale econometric models by Ando and Modigliani (1969). The dynamic multipliers of federal expenditure on *GNP* and its components are built up by successively endogenizing major blocs of the model, so that the impacts of new additions to the induced components of aggregate demand and supply or of monetary factors on the magnitudes and time paths of the multipliers can be assessed.

The second purpose of this chapter is to examine the implications of our model for the stability of the U.S. economy in the pre-war period as compared with the post-war period. The question which we address is as follows: would an exogenous shock to the pre-war economy have produced larger movements in *GNP* than those resulting from an equivalent shock to the post-war economy? Of course, there is good reason to believe that the answer is yes, since many built-in stabilizers stemming from tax and transfer mechanisms in the post-war economy were not present in the pre-war economy.[1] A

---

[1] Although taxes and some transfers were endogenous for all or part of the pre-war period, their ability to cushion the economy was limited by the small size of tax revenues and transfers relative to national income.

more precise, quantitative comparison of stability properties can be made by calculating dynamic multipliers for the pre-war era and contrasting them with dynamic multipliers for the post-war era. In section 2 below, we shall investigate the relationships between pre-war and post-war multipliers associated with changes in federal expenditure.

2. Dynamic Interactions of Components of Aggregate Demand and Monetary Factors

The computer program which we use to solve our model is capable of treating any specified set of blocs as exogenous. This feature allows us to study the principal interactions within the model which give rise to the dynamic multipliers in the complete model corresponding to a particular exogenous shock. We shall examine these interactions for a sustained rise of one billion dollars in real federal expenditure over the period 1951–66.[2] Five sets of multipliers have been calculated, with each set corresponding to a different specification of endogenous and exogenous blocs, as follows:

(1) The government, foreign trade, investment, housing, wage, price, and money blocs are exogenous; all other blocs are endogenous. This case approximates the simplest textbook version of a national income model, except for additional disaggregation of income and expenditure. Consumption and income are the central endogenous variables, with income essentially determined by an elementary multiplier relationship. However, since the tax and transfer bloc is endogenous, the value of the multiplier will be reduced by tax leakages and enlarged by transfer injections. Also, recalling that two of our consumption equations (autos and other durables) embody stock-adjustment hypotheses, it is evident that we do not in fact have a pure multiplier model; acceleration influences are introduced by these two equations.

(2) For this case, we add the government and foreign trade blocs to

---

[2] Note that the multiplier results to be reported here will differ somewhat from those presented in Chapter 8, since we are now imposing a one billion dollar rise in real rather than nominal federal expenditure.

the endogenous set. This leads to the inclusion of induced changes in state and local government expenditures and imports in the multiplier results. Since government expenditures are an injection to and imports a leakage from the spending stream, the multipliers in this case might be either larger or smaller than those found in case 1.

(3) We next introduce the major acceleration factors in aggregate demand – business fixed investment, inventory investment, and residential construction – by endogenizing the investment and housing blocs, in addition to those already endogenized in case 2. This gives us a full-fledged, multiplier-accelerator interaction model of national income determination. Since we have substantially enlarged the scope of induced changes in spending, we should generally expect the multipliers in this case to exceed those in cases 1 and 2. Moreover, the acceleration character of the newly endogenized spending compo-nents increases the likelihood of cyclical patterns in the dynamic multipliers.

(4) Wages and prices are now added to the list of endogenous variables, allowing for the possibility that increases in aggregate demand may encounter supply constraints and thus be partially dissipated in rising prices rather than expansions in real output. Also, induced changes in relative product and factor prices may in this case influence consumer spending decisions and business investment and employment behavior.

(5) Finally, the money bloc is endogenized, giving us the complete model. Interest rates are now permitted to respond to induced changes in the demand for and supply of money, and their movements will feed back to influence consumer expenditures and residential construction. We should expect the introduction of these financial constraints to reduce the magnitude of the multipliers.

The multipliers for real *GNP* and its components, the *GNP* implicit deflator, and interest rates are presented in tables 9.1 and 9.2. For each variable, the multipliers corresponding to the above five cases, or to the relevant subset of them, are shown side by side, with column numbers identifying the cases.

The only induced component of aggregate demand in the first case is consumption expenditures, so that the multiplier on *GNP* each year is simply the sum of the one billion rise in real federal spending and the induced rise in consumption. We find that the multiplier on

TABLE 9.1
Real government expenditure multipliers, successive endogenization of model blocs:
Part 1.

Year	GNP (1958 prices)					Disposable personal income (1958 prices)				
	1	2	3	4	5	1	2	3	4	5
1	1.24	1.18	2.08	1.77	1.60	0.26	0.28	0.50	0.41	0.22
2	1.42	1.34	1.93	1.40	1.08	0.32	0.33	0.27	0.09	0.02
3	1.55	1.47	2.08	1.53	1.27	0.44	0.45	0.43	0.21	0.12
4	1.62	1.54	2.11	1.73	1.71	0.69	0.72	0.88	0.66	0.64
5	1.75	1.68	2.39	1.93	1.90	0.70	0.74	0.95	0.78	0.75
6	1.85	1.80	2.54	1.96	1.87	0.76	0.79	1.12	0.85	0.89
7	1.90	1.86	2.56	2.05	2.02	0.85	0.86	1.20	0.94	0.96
8	1.92	1.88	2.64	2.23	2.31	1.01	0.99	1.31	1.07	1.16
9	1.96	1.95	2.74	2.35	2.35	1.01	1.00	1.39	1.14	1.24
10	2.02	2.01	2.80	2.42	2.50	1.09	1.05	1.48	1.25	1.31
11	2.08	2.07	2.94	2.55	2.64	1.17	1.11	1.52	1.30	1.34
12	2.16	2.14	3.08	2.68	2.74	1.19	1.12	1.54	1.28	1.38
13	2.19	2.18	3.12	2.70	2.80	1.23	1.15	1.61	1.39	1.50
14	2.27	2.25	3.24	2.83	2.96	1.30	1.20	1.70	1.40	1.52
15	2.34	2.19	3.05	2.48	2.59	1.33	1.16	1.65	1.38	1.50
16	2.47	2.24	3.13	2.40	2.37	1.25	1.03	1.53	1.23	1.36

Year	Personal consumption expenditures (1958 prices)					State and local government expenditures (1958 prices)			
	1	2	3	4	5	2	3	4	5
1	0.24	0.23	0.40	0.35	0.27	0.00	0.00	0.00	0.00
2	0.42	0.40	0.62	0.40	0.28	0.01	0.02	0.01	0.01
3	0.55	0.52	0.78	0.42	0.32	0.03	0.05	0.05	0.05
4	0.62	0.58	0.80	0.56	0.53	0.05	0.05	0.09	0.07
5	0.75	0.71	0.98	0.72	0.69	0.07	0.07	0.11	0.10
6	0.85	0.82	1.12	0.80	0.76	0.09	0.11	0.15	0.14
7	0.90	0.88	1.18	0.89	0.86	0.10	0.13	0.16	0.16
8	0.92	0.90	1.24	0.99	1.03	0.10	0.14	0.17	0.17
9	0.96	0.96	1.31	1.07	1.09	0.11	0.15	0.17	0.18
10	1.02	1.01	1.38	1.15	1.18	0.12	0.16	0.18	0.19
11	1.08	1.07	1.49	1.26	1.30	0.12	0.17	0.19	0.20
12	1.16	1.15	1.61	1.35	1.40	0.13	0.18	0.20	0.20
13	1.19	1.18	1.66	1.40	1.46	0.13	0.18	0.20	0.21
14	1.27	1.25	1.77	1.49	1.57	0.13	0.18	0.20	0.22
15	1.34	1.30	1.81	1.49	1.57	0.13	0.19	0.21	0.22
16	1.47	1.39	1.92	1.50	1.54	0.13	0.19	0.21	0.22

TABLE 9.2

Real government expenditure multipliers, successive endogenization of model blocs: Part 2.

Year	Imports (1958 prices)				Non-farm inventory investment (1958 prices)			Business fixed investment (1958 prices)		
	2	3	4	5	3	4	5	3	4	5
1	0.05	0.08	0.10	0.09	0.46	0.36	0.34	0.25	0.21	0.20
2	0.07	0.10	0.13	0.12	0.12	0.01	-0.04	0.23	0.19	0.17
3	0.08	0.12	0.16	0.14	0.07	0.06	0.05	0.25	0.23	0.21
4	0.09	0.13	0.17	0.16	0.03	0.07	0.10	0.26	0.26	0.26
5	0.10	0.14	0.18	0.17	0.06	0.06	0.08	0.30	0.28	0.29
6	0.11	0.15	0.18	0.17	0.06	0.03	0.01	0.32	0.29	0.29
7	0.11	0.16	0.18	0.18	0.02	0.04	0.05	0.32	0.31	0.31
8	0.12	0.16	0.18	0.19	0.03	0.05	0.07	0.32	0.33	0.35
9	0.12	0.17	0.19	0.19	0.03	0.05	0.04	0.34	0.36	0.36
10	0.12	0.17	0.19	0.19	0.02	0.04	0.06	0.34	0.37	0.38
11	0.13	0.18	0.19	0.20	0.04	0.04	0.05	0.36	0.39	0.40
12	0.13	0.19	0.20	0.21	0.04	0.05	0.04	0.37	0.41	0.42
13	0.13	0.19	0.20	0.21	0.02	0.01	0.02	0.39	0.43	0.44
14	0.14	0.20	0.21	0.22	0.03	0.05	0.06	0.40	0.45	0.47
15	0.24	0.34	0.40	0.42	-0.03	-0.08	-0.08	0.38	0.42	0.44
16	0.28	0.39	0.47	0.46	0.00	-0.05	-0.10	0.39	0.40	0.39

Year	Residential construction (1958 prices)			GNP implicit price index (1958 prices)		Exports (1958 prices)		Short-term interest rate[a]	Long-term interest rate[b]
	3	4	5	4	5	4	5	5	5
1	0.05	0.07	0.00	0.33	0.34	-0.12	-0.12	0.03	0.00
2	0.05	0.10	-0.08	0.61	0.52	-0.18	-0.15	0.05	0.03
3	0.05	0.10	-0.07	0.71	0.61	-0.18	-0.16	0.04	0.02
4	0.10	0.12	0.09	0.60	0.58	-0.19	-0.18	0.02	0.01
5	0.12	0.13	0.11	0.59	0.58	-0.20	-0.19	0.04	0.02
6	0.09	0.08	0.05	0.53	0.50	-0.21	-0.20	0.05	0.03
7	0.07	0.05	0.03	0.49	0.47	-0.22	-0.21	0.06	0.03
8	0.07	0.05	0.07	0.46	0.47	-0.18	-0.18	0.04	0.02
9	0.08	0.05	0.06	0.43	0.43	-0.17	-0.17	0.06	0.03
10	0.06	0.05	0.06	0.39	0.40	-0.17	-0.18	0.05	0.02
11	0.06	0.05	0.06	0.39	0.40	-0.17	-0.17	0.05	0.02
12	0.06	0.05	0.06	0.42	0.42	-0.18	-0.18	0.04	0.02
13	0.05	0.05	0.06	0.40	0.40	-0.18	-0.18	0.04	0.02
14	0.05	0.04	0.05	0.41	0.41	-0.20	-0.20	0.05	0.02
15	0.04	0.03	0.04	0.37	0.37	-0.18	-0.19	0.04	0.02
16	0.02	0.01	-0.04	0.40	0.38	-0.20	-0.19	0.08	0.05

[a] Short-term interest rate is RS.

[b] Long-term interest rate is RL.

GNP rises continuously from a value of 1.24 in the initial year to 2.47 in the last year (table 9.1). The acceleration influences stemming from auto and durables purchases are not strong enough to produce absolute decreases in the *GNP* multiplier as stock adjustments are completed, but they do lead to variations in the year-to-year growth of the multiplier, with the largest increases occurring in the first two years. While the *GNP* multiplier is rising at a relatively modest rate by the end of the period, it apparently has still not converged after 16 years to a steady, long-run value.

Introduction in case 2 of induced changes in state and local expenditures and imports reduces the *GNP* multipliers in every year, although by the ninth year the reductions are rather small. The reason for this is that import leakages (table 9.2) exceed the induced rises in state and local spending (table 9.1) until the middle of the period. The dip in the *GNP* multipliers in the last two years results from structural changes in the import equation associated with the U.S.–Canadian auto agreements of 1965, a point which was noted in Chapter 8, section 4.

Case 3 exhibits substantial increases in the *GNP* multipliers in all years, as we should expect with the endogenization of the investment components of aggregate demand. The induced rise in inventory investment in the first year is especially large, accounting for about half of the increase in the *GNP* multiplier in that year (table 9.2). After the first year, however, the contribution of inventory investment wanes, and the higher *GNP* multipliers are predominantly the result of induced changes in business fixed investment, with more modest contributions arising in residential construction (table 9.2). Indeed, the decline in inventory investment in the second year is large enough to bring about a decline in the *GNP* multiplier, indicating a brief inventory cycle in the years immediately following the rise in federal spending. Aside from this initial inventory cycle, it is interesting to note that the *GNP* multipliers rise monotonically, except in the last two years when once again the aberration occurring in imports dominates the findings. The element of acceleration in business fixed investment is not sufficient to produce cycles in that series; and although both inventory investment and residential construction display cycles, the timing and magnitude of their fluctuations do not result in cyclical swings in the *GNP* multiplier after the third year.

Endogenization of wages and prices in case 4 markedly reduces the *GNP* multipliers in all years and somewhat intensifies the initial inventory cycle. Increased demand pressures in the labor and product markets raise the overall *GNP* deflator throughout the period, with the inflation rate large and positive in the first three years but negative thereafter (table 9.2). While nearly all components of aggregate demand are curtailed by the general rise in prices, it appears that consumer spending and net exports are most sensitive to this change. The rise in prices moderates increases in real income relative to case 3, and real income is a prime determinant of all components of consumer spending. On the other hand, smaller increases in real income should reduce import leakages and improve the trade balance. This effect is offset, however, by two factors. First, the rise in domestic prices relative to import prices, which are exogenous, stimulates imports. Second, we assume in these calculations that nominal exports are exogenous but that real exports are determined by the ratio of nominal exports to the endogenous domestic price level. Hence, the rise in domestic prices in this case must reduce real exports.

In addition to the general rise in prices in case 4, induced changes in relative prices also take place, beyond those relating to foreign trade.[4] Their impact is most pronounced on residential construction and state and local expenditures, both of which exhibit larger multipliers relative to case 3 in many years despite the overall reductions in the *GNP* multipliers. Business fixed investment also exhibits larger multipliers relative to case 3 after the midpoint of the simulation period, suggesting that induced changes in relative factor prices begin to favor fixed investment.

The complete model multipliers on *GNP* from case 5 are smaller than those from case 4 for approximately the first half of the period but larger for the second half. As *GNP* is increased, the demand for money rises, interest rates rise, and the difference between the short and long rate is widened (table 9.2). Increases in the long rate discourage purchases of consumer durables, moderating gains in total consumption expenditures in the first seven years; but since the long

---

[3] The rationale for this assumption was explained in section 4 of Chapter 8.

[4] We do not display these changes in relative prices in the tables.

rate stabilizes at a permanently higher level, the interest-induced stock adjustment effects on consumer expenditures eventually die out. Residential construction contracts sharply in the first three years relative to case 4, reflecting the rise in the long rate and disintermediation caused by the shift in the term structure.[5] This downturn in construction reinforces the swing in inventory investment and creates a more pronounced cycle in the early years. However, it is largely reversed in the fourth year, after which point the multipliers on construction are quite similar for cases 4 and 5.[6] As to the other components of aggregate spending, they display few noteworthy changes between cases 4 and 5. The inflation rate in the first year is nearly identical in the two cases, but the accommodating monetary policy of case 4 produces higher inflation rates in the second and third years.

In summary, these multiplier results portray a generally stable system subject to a brief inventory-construction cycle in the years immediately following an exogenous increase in federal expenditure. While the severity of the initial cycle is largely accounted for by the stock-adjustment aspect of inventory investment, the absolute reduction in residential construction occasioned by induced changes in interest rates is an important contributing factor. We also find that the magnitude of the long-run multiplier on *GNP* in the complete model is significantly influenced by the operation of supply and monetary restraints. In the absence of these restraints, the *GNP* multiplier peaks at a value which is 11 percent higher than that occurring when these restraints are introduced. Caution must be exercised in drawing broad conclusions from these particular experiments, since they are limited to a specific type of shock to the system and to a particular time period. Moreover, the dynamic responses which were examined pertain to the deterministic form of

---

[5] Recall that both the long rate and the ratio of the long rate to the short rate appear in the housing starts equation (2.41). The former variable enters the starts equation through the expected sales price, which is expressed as the rent on the existing housing stock capitalized at the long rate.

[6] Although residential construction does recover in case 5 to levels comparable to case 4, the reductions in the early years are never offset so far as the stock of housing is concerned. The induced rise in the real housing stock in case 4 is $0.9 billion by the end of the period, but it is only $0.5 billion in case 5.

the model. Whether or not a succession of fluctuating disturbances over time to the stochastic relations or to the exogenous variables of the model would generate more enduring cyclical movements is an issue that remains to be studied.

3. Pre-war and Post-war Multipliers

Although estimated from a pooled sample of pre-war and post-war observations, the model is not an invariant monolith with identical properties before and after World War II. It is true that many of the behavioral equations have identical parameters in the two eras. Even so, the log-linear form of some of the important equations with constant parameters – such as those for consumer purchases of automobiles and other durables, business fixed investment, residential construction, and man-hours – means that the marginal absolute responses may differ pre-war and post-war even though the elasticities do not. Moreover, other important equations, including those for consumer non-durables and services, inventory investment, and imports, do have different parameters in the two periods. Finally, there are a few equations, primarily in the tax and transfer bloc, in which the specification itself changes in the post-war period. Structural changes of all three types imply that substantial differences may exist in the pre-war and post-war response mechanisms. In this section we assess the quantitative importance of these changes by comparing the pre-war and post-war multipliers for an exogenous increase in federal expenditure.

Dynamic multipliers for several important variables are shown for 1926–40 and 1951–65 in tables 9.3 and 9.4. Sustained increases respectively of 0.5 and 1.0 billion dollars in nominal federal expenditures were used to generate the pre-war and post-war multipliers, in order to scale the implicit real shocks approximately to the size of the economy in the two periods. The multipliers in table 9.3 are per dollar of nominal input ($\Delta GGF\$$), whereas those in table 9.4 are normalized by the corresponding real injection ($\Delta GGF\$$)/($PGGF$). The multipliers for 1951–65 are those already discussed in Chapter 8 and are reproduced from tables 8.1, 8.2, and 8.4.

The multiplier for nominal GNP is considerably larger pre-war

TABLE 9.3
Pre-war and post-war multipliers for an exogenous increase in nominal government expenditure.

Year	GNP (current prices)		Real GNP (1958 prices)		GNP implicit price index (1958 = 100)		Unemployment rate (percent)	
	1926–40	1951–65	1926–40	1951–65	1926–40	1951–65	1926–40	1951–65
1	3.77	2.73	5.42	1.64	0.62	0.34	−0.78	−0.12
2	5.64	2.51	6.35	0.92	1.35	0.44	−1.16	−0.11
3	7.40	2.93	7.40	1.10	1.93	0.47	−1.40	−0.12
4	8.83	3.54	8.45	1.59	2.31	0.50	−1.59	−0.15
5	10.80	3.73	13.21	1.65	2.34	0.50	−2.40	−0.17
6	10.60	3.55	15.86	1.64	2.02	0.45	−3.32	−0.17
7	10.91	3.59	20.59	1.71	1.47	0.43	−4.79	−0.17
8	8.49	3.87	17.66	1.90	1.01	0.42	−5.00	−0.19
9	8.07	3.87	14.73	1.98	1.22	0.40	−4.31	−0.19
10	7.52	3.90	13.53	2.11	0.85	0.36	−3.66	−0.20
11	5.49	4.09	11.57	2.19	0.07	0.35	−3.08	−0.20
12	3.73	4.30	9.81	2.25	−0.42	0.36	−2.61	−0.20
13	2.44	4.33	7.91	2.28	−0.59	0.33	−2.19	−0.19
14	2.16	4.35	7.16	2.38	−0.48	0.33	−1.79	−0.19
15	2.23	4.24	6.45	2.13	−0.25	0.30	−1.48	−0.17

than post-war during the first decade of the simulations (table 9.3). The contrast is even greater in the multiplier for real GNP per dollar of nominal input, but this comparison is seriously distorted because of the differences in price levels in the two periods. The real input multipliers for GNP in table 9.4 are corrected for this distortion, however, and it remains true that the pre-war values substantially exceed the post-war. Similarly, the multipliers for the implicit price deflator and the unemployment rate in table 9.3 are much larger in the pre-war years and would remain so even if normalized by real federal expenditure.

The comparisons in tables 9.3 and 9.4 unfortunately reflect other influences than structural differences in the pre-war and post-war response mechanisms. In the pre-war period the massive unemployment and excess capacity of the 1930's greatly augments the multipliers for years 5–10. The multipliers for those years are therefore dominated as much by the initial conditions of economic slack as by the cumulative dynamic responses to the shock that began in the 1920's. This is not true of the 1–4 year multipliers from 1926–29, of course. On the other hand, the 1–4 year multipliers for 1951–54

TABLE 9.4

Real multipliers for an exogenous increase in nominal government expenditure, pre-war and post-war periods.[a]

Year	XGNP	YPD	CE	IGB	HGIN	IINF	GSL	FEX	FIM
A. Pre-war (1926–40)									
1	3.22	2.15	1.40	0.61	0.01	0.46	0.00	0.13	0.12
2	3.64	2.61	1.83	0.66	-0.01	0.30	0.07	-0.26	0.12
3	3.87	3.13	2.18	0.75	-0.01	0.23	0.26	-0.39	0.14
4	4.33	3.59	2.48	0.83	0.06	0.20	0.39	-0.48	0.16
5	6.40	5.19	3.45	1.26	0.47	0.44	0.45	0.44	0.23
6	6.81	5.63	3.70	1.40	0.41	0.37	0.49	-0.31	0.25
7	7.67	6.25	4.16	1.51	0.39	0.43	0.56	-0.23	0.28
8	5.95	4.82	3.23	1.19	0.29	0.07	0.61	-0.19	0.22
9	5.63	4.87	3.20	0.89	0.31	0.11	0.74	0.19	0.20
10	5.61	4.78	3.18	0.75	0.40	-0.14	0.73	-0.10	0.20
11	5.00	4.20	2.80	0.54	0.36	-0.20	0.69	-0.01	0.18
12	4.21	3.49	2.32	0.36	0.23	-0.22	0.60	0.06	0.16
13	3.22	2.66	1.74	0.22	0.10	-0.22	0.54	0.08	0.12
14	2.81	2.30	1.50	0.15	0.01	-0.16	0.35	0.07	0.10
15	2.55	2.05	1.36	0.15	-0.08	-0.13	0.28	0.05	0.09
B. Post-war (1951–65)									
1	1.59	0.31	0.29	0.19	0.00	0.32	-0.00	-0.12	0.09
2	1.06	0.14	0.32	0.16	-0.07	-0.09	0.01	0.16	0.12
3	1.39	0.29	0.39	0.20	0.04	0.06	0.08	0.16	0.14
4	1.83	0.63	0.58	0.26	0.10	0.14	0.08	0.18	0.16
5	1.87	0.75	0.70	0.28	0.09	0.06	0.10	-0.19	0.17
6	1.83	0.82	0.75	0.28	0.07	0.01	0.14	-0.20	0.17
7	1.96	0.88	0.84	0.30	-0.01	0.04	0.16	-0.21	0.18
8	2.26	1.12	1.03	0.34	0.05	0.04	0.17	-0.19	0.19
9	2.32	1.16	1.07	0.35	0.04	0.05	0.17	-0.18	0.19
10	2.44	1.32	1.17	0.36	0.05	0.04	0.18	-0.18	0.19
11	2.62	1.42	1.30	0.38	0.07	0.03	0.20	-0.18	0.20
12	2.81	1.45	1.47	0.41	0.04	0.02	0.22	-0.19	0.21
13	2.86	1.58	1.53	0.43	0.07	0.01	0.23	-0.19	0.21
14	3.00	1.70	1.66	0.44	0.07	0.03	0.23	-0.21	0.22
15	2.70	1.58	1.67	0.41	0.05	-0.05	0.24	-0.19	0.43

[a] As explained in the text, although the expenditure shock was in nominal dollars, the multipliers in this table are normalized by the real value of the injection.

refer to the Korean War, when unemployment was smaller than in the 1920's.[7]

In order better to isolate the response mechanism from other

[7] As explained in Chapter 4 and Appendix C, our new estimates of unemployment rates during the 1920's are much higher than those previously published by Lebergott (1964) and exceed the average level for 1951–54.

influences on the pre-war and post-war comparisons, we decided to construct a hypothetical high-employment control solution for the early thirties. This was done by assigning hypothetical values to some of the exogenous variables during 1930–35, as shown in table 9.5. The most important changes in exogenous inputs concerned nominal exports, standardized households, and unborrowed reserves. Export proceeds and standardized households were assumed to grow in 1930–35 at the same rate as in the late 1920's, instead of declining or decelerating as they actually did. Unborrowed reserves were adjusted to reduce upward pressures on interest rates in the early Thirties. Farm exports and some exogenous categories of residential construction were smoothed and raised somewhat on the average. Finally, the inventory valuation adjustment was smoothed to remove the fluctuations associated with the actual price gyrations of the early Thirties.

In combination, these arbitrary adjustments to exogenous inputs produced a hypothetical high-employment path during 1930–35, as illustrated by the six endogenous variables in the lower section of table 9.5. It will be seen that a cyclical fluctuation has not been eliminated in the hypothetical data, but it has been moderated into something resembling a post-war recession.

It should be stressed that this simulation was designed only to yield a reasonable high-employment path to serve as a baseline for the comparison of pre-war and post-war multipliers. It is not intended to "explain" the causes of the Great Depression or to show how it might have been prevented. That is an interesting application of the model which will be pursued elsewhere but cannot be undertaken herein. Meanwhile, we may briefly observe that export demand may not have been controllable by U.S. policy alone, and the same is true of the growth of standardized households, given the restrictive immigration legislation of 1924. Monetary policy was controllable, however. In later work it will be interesting to search for feasible policies that would have prevented the depression, given the actual paths of the non-controllable exogenous variables, and also to investigate the importance of individual non-controllable variables.

The high-employment solution for 1926–35 provides the basis for a multiplier calculation free of distorting effects of massive unemployment during the early Thirties. The average predicted unemployment rate is still high as compared with the early Fifties, however. In order to standardize the initial conditions for unemployment as much as possible for the comparative analysis, we have calculated the multipliers for the period 1953–. During those years, the unemployment rate for the control solution is 6.7 percent as compared with 5.0 percent in the pre-war high-employment solution. It was provided a comparison of dynamic ten-year multipliers under approximately equal initial total labor force utilization, thereby highlighting structural changes between the periods.

Let us begin with the traditional Keynesian consumption multiplier. If all other expenditures were exogenous, the value of the multiplier would depend only on the marginal propensity to consume out of GNP, according to the formula $m = 1/(1 - \Delta CE/\Delta XGNP)$. The values for $\Delta CE/\Delta XGNP$ imply impact pre-war and post-war multipliers respectively of 1.8. In the ten-year multiplier (the values of the post-war multipliers for the ninth and tenth years are excluded from the comparison because of the structural change in the import function in those years.) Thus the change in $\Delta CE/\Delta XGNP$ is in the stabilizing direction.

TABLE 9.5
Comparison of exogenous inputs and selected endogenous outputs for the control (C) and high-employment (H) solutions, 1926–35.

A. Exogenous inputs

Year	RESU C	RESU H	PEXS C	PEXS H	IVA$ C	IVA$ H	HOUSE^a C	HOUSE^a H	HHS C	HHS H	XF C	XF H
1926	1.6		6.4		1.7		2.9		21.4		16.3	
1927	2.0		6.5		0.8		2.8		22.0		17.0	
1928	1.4		6.8		0.1		2.6		22.5		16.4	
1929	1.6		7.0		0.6		2.3		23.0		17.0	
1930	2.1	2.4	5.4	7.5	4.0	0	2.0	2.5	23.5	23.5	16.1	17.2
1931	1.3	1.9	3.6	7.9	3.0	0	1.2	2.5	24.0	24.2	18.5	17.5
1932	2.2	2.5	2.5	8.4	-1.3	0	0.9	2.5	24.3	24.8	18.0	17.7
1933	2.5	2.4	2.4	8.9	-2.7	0	1.0	2.5	24.7	25.4	17.5	17.9
1934	4.0	3.1	3.0	9.5	-0.7	0	1.6	2.5	25.1	26.1	14.6	18.2
1935	5.7	3.2	3.3	10.0	-0.3	0	1.7	2.5	25.6	26.7	16.5	18.4

B. Endogenous outputs

Year	XGNP$ C	XGNP$ H	XGNP C	XGNP H	PXGNP$ C	PXGNP$ H	UI C	UI H	CE C	CE H	IGPD C	IGPD H
1926	87.6		179.8		48.7		5.6		122.0		35.5	
1927	90.9		190.6		47.7		5.5		129.1		38.1	
1928	94.1		197.6		47.6		5.5		134.8		37.8	
1929	97.2		203.7		47.7		5.6		140.1		37.2	
1930	89.5	107.4	190.9	219.1	46.9	49.0	8.3	4.7	137.1	150.2	27.6	41.1
1931	75.6	114.8	171.1	227.5	44.2	50.5	12.7	3.9	127.5	156.4	18.2	41.7
1932	62.9	123.7	151.0	235.4	41.7	52.5	18.0	3.1	118.0	163.3	9.3	41.7
1933	54.6	111.5	136.8	215.5	39.9	51.7	21.9	4.9	109.3	151.7	2.9	28.5
1934	64.0	119.7	154.7	220.2	41.4	54.4	21.6	6.1	118.2	155.2	9.3	25.9
1935	79.8	131.6	182.5	240.8	43.7	54.6	18.4	5.1	131.9	164.0	24.6	37.0

^a Sum of HGIF, HGAA, HGNH, HGBC, HGUS.

rate is still high as compared with the early Fifties, however. In order to standardize the initial conditions for unemployment as much as possible for the comparative analysis, we have calculated the post-war multipliers for the period 1957–66. During those years, the average unemployment rate for the control solution is 5.1 percent, as compared with 5.0 percent in the pre-war high-employment solution. Thus these two solutions provide the basis for a comparison of dynamic ten-year multipliers under approximately equal initial conditions of labor force utilization, thereby highlighting structural differences between the periods.

The pre-war and post-war multipliers were calculated for sustained shocks respectively of 0.4 and 1.0 billion dollars in real government expenditure (table 9.6). According to these results, the economy was inherently less stable in the pre-war years. The dynamic response to an exogenous shock was larger and more cyclical than after World War II. The impact multiplier for real *GNP* was 1.9 post-war and the peak value, reached in the eighth year, was 2.5. In contrast, the pre-war multiplier rose from 3.2 in the first year to a peak of 5.1 in the fifth year and then declined again to 3.2 in the eighth year.

The factors behind the greater stability of the post-war economy may be better understood with the assistance of the gross spending propensities in the lower half of table 9.6. The reader is reminded that these ratios, like those in Chapter 8, are not pure measures of demand responses to income change, since the numerators are affected by other influences – especially changes in unemployment, relative prices and interest rates – on spending decisions. Neverthe-less, they may be interpreted in much the usual way with the understanding that they are not ceterus paribus income multipliers.

Let us begin with the traditional Keynesian consumption multiplier. If all other expenditures were exogenous, the value of the multiplier would depend only on the marginal propensity to consume with respect to *GNP*, according to the formula $m = 1/(1 - \Delta CE/\Delta XGNP)$. The values for $\Delta CE/\Delta XGNP$ imply impact multipliers in the pre-war and post-war periods respectively of 1.8 and 1.3, and eight-year multipliers of 2.3 and 1.9. (The values of the post-war multipliers for the ninth and tenth years are excluded from the comparison because of the structural change in the import function in those years.) Thus the change in $\Delta CE/\Delta XGNP$ is in the stabilizing direction.

According to our model, however, the response of real consumption to real disposable personal income alone is higher now than before World War II, a change of behavior in the destabilizing direction. Suppose there were no income leakages from business saving or taxes and no transfer payments, so that $YPD = GNP$, and that all expenditures except consumption were exogenous. The multiplier would then depend only on $\Delta CE/\Delta YPD$. According to our estimates, the first and eighth-year multipliers pre-war would be 2.9 and 3.2, and the post-war values would be 3.8 and 20.0!

It is worthy of note that the post-war rise in $\Delta CE/\Delta YPD$ is not indicative of an enhanced response to changes in disposable income itself. This may be seen from table 9.7, which shows the income-specific short-run marginal propensities as calculated from the income coefficients of the consumption functions of the model. Although the marginal spending propensities for durables are slightly larger post-war, those for non-durables and services are sharply lower. The net result is a decline in the overall marginal propensity to consume from 0.59 to 0.46. Nevertheless, it is clear from the gross spending propensities in table 9.6, that changes in the expenditure responses to other variables in the consumption functions were in a destabilizing direction, so that total consumption changed more per dollar of income changes in the post-war years than pre-war.

Fortunately, the growth in importance of built-in stabilizers has greatly augmented the stability of the post-war economy. Induced changes in corporate saving served to moderate the change in personal income per dollar change in GNP even in the pre-war economy, of course, and this private stabilizer, in combination with induced changes in tax revenues, meant that real disposable income increased only two-thirds as much as real GNP during the first year of response to an exogenous disturbance. The stabilizing power of the tax-transfer system is much greater now, however, owing to the growth in size of the federal tax base and the development of unemployment insurance. The first-year marginal response of real disposable personal income to real GNP is nowadays about one-third, or half as much as in the 1920's.

It is the added power of the tax-transfer stabilizers which is responsible for the sharp reduction in the consumption multiplier in the post-war economy. For example, the first-year value of $\Delta CE/\Delta XGNP$ in 1957, which is the product of $\Delta YPD/\Delta XGNP$

TABLE 9.6

Real multipliers and gross spending propensities, exogenous increase in real government expenditure under high-employment conditions, pre-war and post-war periods.

					Multipliers				
Year	XGNP	YPD	CE	IGB	HGIN	IINF	GSL	FEX	FIM
A. Pre-war									
1	3.23	2.14	1.40	0.61	-0.00	0.45	-0.00	-0.12	0.12
2	3.52	2.66	1.87	0.68	0.00	0.29	0.07	-0.27	0.13
3	4.01	3.24	2.26	0.77	0.01	0.23	0.28	-0.41	0.14
4	4.43	3.69	2.56	0.84	0.10	0.18	0.41	-0.50	0.16
5	5.09	4.13	2.98	0.93	0.22	0.21	0.50	-0.57	0.18
6	4.66	3.79	2.81	0.85	0.16	0.05	0.56	-0.61	0.17
7	4.83	3.62	2.93	0.86	0.23	0.05	0.61	-0.67	0.12
8	3.24	2.65	1.84	0.56	0.16	0.19	0.60	-0.60	0.12
9	3.54	2.82	1.89	0.55	0.17	-0.07	0.55	-0.43	0.13
10	3.48	2.44	1.79	0.55	0.18	-0.04	0.48	-0.30	0.13
B. Post-war									
1	1.88	0.58	0.43	0.24	0.01	0.41	-0.00	-0.12	0.09
2	1.62	0.64	0.54	0.24	0.01	0.05	0.02	-0.12	0.12
3	1.77	0.76	0.63	0.26	0.04	0.06	0.08	-0.13	0.13
4	1.96	0.92	0.75	0.29	0.04	0.06	0.11	-0.14	0.15
5	2.10	0.98	0.86	0.31	0.05	0.05	0.13	-0.15	0.16
6	2.23	1.07	0.98	0.33	0.06	0.04	0.14	-0.15	0.16
7	2.34	1.20	1.06	0.35	0.07	0.03	0.16	-0.16	0.17
8	2.50	1.24	1.18	0.38	0.07	0.06	0.17	-0.18	0.18
9	2.25	1.26	1.22	0.35	0.07	-0.05	0.18	-0.16	0.36
10	2.17	1.20	1.25	0.33	0.05	-0.06	0.18	-0.17	0.41

Spending propensities

Year	$\dfrac{\Delta YPD}{\Delta XGNP}$	$\dfrac{\Delta CE}{\Delta YPD}$	$\dfrac{\Delta CE}{\Delta XGNP}$	$\dfrac{\Delta IGB}{\Delta XGNP}$	$\dfrac{\Delta HGIN}{\Delta XGNP}$	$\dfrac{\Delta IINF}{\Delta XGNP}$	$\dfrac{\Delta GSL}{\Delta XGNP}$	$\dfrac{\Delta FEX}{\Delta XGNP}$	$\dfrac{\Delta FIM}{\Delta XGNP}$
A. Pre-war									
1	0.66	0.65	0.43	0.19	−0.00	0.14	−0.00	−0.04	0.04
2	0.76	0.70	0.53	0.19	0.00	0.08	0.02	−0.08	0.04
3	0.81	0.70	0.56	0.19	0.00	0.06	0.07	−0.10	0.04
4	0.83	0.69	0.58	0.19	0.02	0.04	0.09	−0.11	0.04
5	0.81	0.72	0.59	0.18	0.04	0.04	0.10	−0.11	0.04
6	0.81	0.74	0.60	0.18	0.03	0.01	0.12	−0.13	0.04
7	0.75	0.81	0.61	0.48	0.05	0.01	0.13	−0.14	0.04
8	0.82	0.69	0.57	0.17	0.05	0.06	0.19	−0.19	0.04
9	0.80	0.67	0.53	0.16	0.05	0.02	0.16	−0.12	0.04
10	0.70	0.73	0.51	0.14	0.05	0.01	0.14	−0.09	0.04
B. Post-war									
1	0.31	0.74	0.23	0.13	0.01	0.22	−0.00	−0.06	0.05
2	0.40	0.84	0.33	0.15	0.01	0.03	0.01	−0.07	0.07
3	0.43	0.83	0.36	0.15	0.00	0.03	0.05	−0.07	0.07
4	0.47	0.82	0.38	0.15	0.02	0.03	0.06	−0.07	0.08
5	0.47	0.88	0.41	0.15	0.02	0.02	0.06	−0.07	0.08
6	0.48	0.92	0.44	0.15	0.03	0.02	0.06	−0.07	0.07
7	0.51	0.88	0.45	0.15	0.03	0.02	0.07	−0.07	0.07
8	0.50	0.95	0.47	0.15	0.03	0.02	0.07	−0.07	0.07
9	0.56	0.97	0.54	0.16	0.03	0.03	0.08	−0.07	0.16
10	0.55	1.04	0.58	0.15	0.02	0.03	0.08	−0.08	0.19

TABLE 9.7

Impact income elasticities and propensities, consumer expenditures, 1926 and 1957[a].

	Elasticities[f]		Marginal propensities[a]	
Variable	1926	1957	1926	1957
Consumer non-durables (CND)	0.63	0.48	0.29[b]	0.21[b]
Consumer services (CS)	0.45	0.21	0.16[c]	0.07[c]
Automobiles (CA)	1.28	1.51	0.07[d]	0.09[d]
Other durables (COD)	1.14	1.14	0.07[e]	0.09[e]
Total consumer expenditures (CE)			0.59	0.46

 [a] Elasticities (η) with respect to real disposable personal income. Marginal propensities are of the form ($\Delta C/\Delta Y$) and are income-specific.
 [b] From equations (2.3) and (2.4).
 [c] From equations (2.5) and (2.6).
 [d] Calculated from $\Delta CA/\Delta Y = \Delta CAK/\Delta Y = (\eta_{CAK})(CAK/Y)$, with η_{CAK} (= 0.45) from equation (2.7), and using 1926 and 1957 values of CAK and Y.
 [e] Calculated from $\Delta COD/\Delta Y = \Delta CODK/\Delta Y = (\eta_{CODK})(CODK/Y)$, with η_{CODK} (= 0.24) from equation (2.8), and using 1926 and 1957 values of COD and Y.
 [f] Calculated from the formula $\eta_i = (\Delta C_i/\Delta Y)(Y/C_i)$, where C_i is the ith expenditure component and the values of C_i and Y are for 1926 and 1957.

and $\Delta CE/\Delta YPD$, is estimated as $(0.31)(0.74) = 0.23$, implying a consumption multiplier of 1.3. As already noted, the corresponding multiplier in 1926 was 1.8. Had $\Delta YPD/\Delta XGNP$ stayed at its pre-war level but $\Delta CE/\Delta YPD$ changed as it actually did, the post-war (1957) multiplier would have been about 2.0 instead of 1.3. On the other hand, the pre-war value of $\Delta CE/\Delta YPD$ in combination with the post-war ratio of $\Delta YPD/\Delta XGNP$, would mean a multiplier of 1.25, or little different from its estimated actual value of 1.3. It is apparent from table 9.6 that the tax-transfer stabilizers have also reduced the longer-run multipliers by substantial, though varying, margins throughout the simulation interval.

 Other stabilizing changes include the reduction in the marginal responses of business fixed investment and state and local expenditures to a change in GNP. With regard to the foreign sector, both a positive import propensity and a negative export propensity reduce the multiplier. The combined post-war change in the two propensities implies a reduction in the multipliers for years 1 and 2 and an increase for years 6–8. After the U.S.–Canadian automobile agreement of 1965 the marked increase in the import propensity meant an additional structural reduction in the multiplier for years 9 and 10.

In conclusion, a comparison of dynamic multipliers for the pre-war and post-war eras implies a marked reduction in the instability of the post-war economy. Structural changes have reduced the impact multiplier for an exogenous expenditure change from about 3 in the pre-war economy to 2 post-war. The pre-war multipliers exhibit a major cycle with a peak of 5.1 in the fifth year and a trough of 3.2 in the eighth. In contrast, the post-war sequence includes a mild inventory contraction in the second year and then a monotonic rise to an eighth year value of 2.5. Were it not for the structural change in the import function in 1965, the post-war multipliers in table 9.6 would doubtless continue to rise through the tenth year and beyond, as they did in the simulations beginning in 1951 and reported in tables 9.1 and 9.4. There are minor differences among the three post-war sequences examined in this chapter, owing to differences in initial conditions and whether the shock was in real or nominal terms, but all of them lead to the same conclusion regarding the absence of an endogenous mechanism for either a single major cycle or a series of self-sustaining minor cycles in the post-war period.

These findings concerning the post-war period are broadly consistent with those for post-war quarterly econometric models of the U.S. economy [see Hickman (1972)]. Our pre-war multipliers suggest, however, that the economy was considerably less stable before the development of automatic stabilizers. Unfortunately, the multiplier sequence in table 9.6 is too short to ascertain whether additional cyclical fluctuations would persist after the completion of the first major cycle in the eighth year. A firm conclusion on this point would require a longer simulation horizon, perhaps based on a hypothetical control solution along a steady growth path from the mid-Twenties to the mid-Forties. Meanwhile, we may provisionally accept the finding of greater dynamic instability in the pre-war era while leaving open the question of the degree of damping inherent in the response mechanism at that time.

CHAPTER 10

Constant or Increasing Returns to Scale?

1. Introduction

As we noted in Chapter 3, joint estimation of the labor and investment demand equations did not lead to a clear-cut choice between
constant returns and increasing returns in the underlying production
function. The imposition of constant returns yielded a superior fit for
the investment function, whereas free estimation of returns to scale
resulted in increasing returns and a superior fit for the labor demand
function. In light of this ambiguity, we have included both sets of
factor demand equations in the coded form of the model, with an
option to use either set. Since our price equations and utilization
measures also embody parameters from the underlying production
function, they too appear in the coded model in both constant- and
increasing-returns versions.

The simulation and multiplier analyses presented in Chapters 7–9
were all based on the constant-returns technology. We selected
constant returns as our standard framework for this book, because
error statistics for sample-period dynamic simulations of the complete model generally favor constant over increasing returns. In
section 2 below, we shall examine these error statistics. The third
section of this chapter compares dynamic multipliers resulting from
an increase in real federal expenditure for the two versions of the
model.

2. Comparison of Errors in Dynamic Simulations

Table 10.1 presents error measures for the constant- and increasing-
returns versions of the model from dynamic simulations covering

TABLE 10.1
Prediction errors for dynamic solutions, constant returns (CR) and increasing returns (IR).

| | RMSE/Mean[a] | | | | | |
| | 1926–40 | | 1951–66 | | 1967–72 | |
Variable	CR	IR	CR	IR	CR	IR
GNP	5.3	8.4	2.0	2.0	3.1	4.1
Real GNP	3.5	3.8	2.1	2.2	2.3	2.5
Real consumption	2.7	3.0	1.6	1.7	1.7	1.7
Real business fixed investment	13.4	15.9	8.2	8.0	4.6	4.8
Real residential construction	16.1	16.1	12.6	13.2	15.1	16.8
Real inventory investment	735.0	752.5	67.2	68.4	81.5	79.5
Real state and local purchases	2.3	2.9	1.9	1.7	3.7	3.9
Real exports	7.8	10.5	3.3	3.7	4.0	5.0
Real imports	7.7	7.6	3.4	3.6	4.9	5.5
Implicit price deflator (1958 = 100)[b]	3.5	4.8	2.3	2.4	3.9	5.0
Civilian labor force	2.3	1.8	0.7	0.7	2.7	2.9
Employment	2.7	2.2	1.6	1.6	2.0	2.5
Unemployment rate	8.2	10.6	22.2	21.2	22.2	18.7
Wage rate	3.5	4.4	2.3	2.3	6.3	6.9
Labor income	4.5	6.7	2.3	2.2	6.1	7.4
Personal income	3.9	7.0	1.2	1.4	6.4	7.2
Corporate profits before tax	44.1	53.1	13.0	11.0	41.8	36.5
Commercial paper rate (percent)	32.1	34.5	9.1	9.8	36.1	41.0
Corporate bond rate (percent)	10.8	11.5	6.0	6.2	37.7	40.2
Money stock (M1)	4.2	6.1	1.7	1.9	11.4	11.7
Money stock (M2)	4.3	6.5	2.3	2.4	7.7	8.6

[a] Root-mean-square-error as a percent of the mean of the variable.
[b] Prediction of PXGNP1 (see section 4 of Chapter 5).

three intervals: 1926–40, 1951–66, and 1967–72. For each interval, the first-year solutions make use of initial conditions at the beginning of the interval, and solutions in subsequent years are based on the time paths of lagged endogenous variables generated by the model. The error statistic, as in Chapter 7, is the root-mean-square-prediction-error as a percentage of the mean of the variable, and these measures are tabulated for the same 21 variables discussed in Chapter 7. Indeed, the columns of table 10.1 pertaining to constant returns are simply transcribed from table 7.1.

Constant returns produces moderately smaller errors in real GNP for all three periods, and its superiority over increasing returns in predictions of nominal *GNP* is substantial for the first and third periods. The more accurate estimates of nominal *GNP* are largely traceable to improvements in price predictions under constant returns. It may be recalled that the basic price equation in the model (1.29) differs in a fundamental way according to whether constant or increasing returns is assumed. In the former case, normal average total cost [see (1.27)] does not depend on the level of output, whereas in the latter case it does. Hence, output does not enter the price equation under constant returns, but it does enter with a negative coefficient under increasing returns. As a consequence, errors in output predictions influence price predictions under increasing returns but not under constant returns. While this might partially account for the better price performance of constant returns, its importance cannot be isolated within the highly interactive structure. Certainly the smaller errors in wage predictions under constant returns are another contributing factor.

Regarding the remaining variables, we find each one predicted with roughly equal or greater accuracy in the constant-returns case for 1926–40, except for employment and labor force. The single-equation superiority of the increasing-returns labor demand function carries over to the complete model for this period. However, the improvement in employment predictions under increasing returns is not sufficient to overcome the poorer estimates of business fixed investment insofar as the overall predictions are concerned; the critical position of investment spending as a direct determinant of aggregate demand appears to accord greater weight to accuracy in the investment function.

The detailed results for 1951–66 are virtually identical in the two cases and merit no special comment. The post-sample errors for 1967–72 are smaller under constant returns for all but three variables – inventory investment, the unemployment rate, and corporate profits. Again, given the complexity of interactions within the model in the determination of these variables, it is difficult, if not impossible, to pinpoint sources of the improvements arising in the increasing-returns case.

On balance, the complete-model errors clearly indicate constant returns to be the better of the two alternatives. There is a possibility, of course, that future experiments with the model may turn up

TABLE 10.2

Real government expenditure multipliers, constant returns (CR) and increasing returns (IR).

Year	XGNP$		XGNP		PXGNP		U1		GBSF$		CE	
	CR	IR	CR	IR	CR	IR	CR	IR	CR	IR	CR	IR
1	2.65	2.57	1.60	1.74	0.34	0.28	−0.12	−0.12	0.07	0.05	0.27	0.37
2	3.06	2.99	1.08	1.17	0.52	0.47	−0.12	−0.11	0.02	0.03	0.28	0.35
3	3.70	3.39	1.27	1.38	0.61	0.50	−0.13	−0.12	0.10	0.05	0.32	0.38
4	4.00	3.55	1.71	1.86	0.58	0.45	−0.16	−0.16	0.14	0.06	0.53	0.59
5	4.28	3.69	1.90	2.00	0.58	0.42	−0.19	−0.17	0.25	0.11	0.69	0.74
6	3.98	3.39	1.87	2.03	0.50	0.34	−0.19	−0.17	0.13	0.01	0.76	0.83
7	4.05	3.43	2.02	2.17	0.47	0.30	−0.20	−0.18	0.12	0.00	0.86	0.94
8	4.46	3.74	2.31	2.50	0.47	0.29	−0.22	−0.20	0.21	0.07	1.03	1.12
9	4.40	3.70	2.35	2.56	0.43	0.25	−0.23	−0.20	0.17	0.04	1.09	1.19
10	4.41	3.72	2.50	2.70	0.40	0.21	−0.24	−0.21	0.18	0.04	1.18	1.31
11	4.72	3.97	2.64	2.89	0.40	0.20	−0.24	−0.21	0.24	0.10	1.30	1.45
12	5.10	4.26	2.74	3.03	0.42	0.21	−0.24	−0.22	0.30	0.14	1.40	1.56
13	5.19	4.31	2.80	3.07	0.40	0.19	−0.24	−0.22	0.31	0.14	1.46	1.61
14	5.52	4.55	2.96	3.23	0.41	0.18	−0.24	−0.22	0.34	0.14	1.57	1.74
15	5.21	4.30	2.59	2.96	0.37	0.15	−0.22	−0.19	0.16	−0.02	1.57	1.77
16	5.31	4.38	2.37	2.93	0.38	0.17	−0.19	−0.18	0.13	−0.01	1.54	1.78

	IGB		HGIN		IINF		GSL		FEX		FIM	
Year	CR	IR	CR	IR	CR	IR	CR	IR	CR	IR	CR	IR
1	0.20	0.18	0.00	0.02	0.34	0.36	0.00	0.00	−0.12	−0.10	0.09	0.09
2	0.17	0.18	−0.08	−0.06	−0.04	−0.04	0.01	0.02	−0.15	−0.15	0.12	0.12
3	0.21	0.19	−0.07	−0.05	0.05	0.05	0.05	0.07	−0.16	−0.14	0.14	0.13
4	0.26	0.25	0.09	0.10	0.10	0.14	0.07	0.08	−0.18	−0.14	0.16	0.16
5	0.29	0.28	0.11	0.12	0.08	0.07	0.10	0.10	−0.19	−0.15	0.17	0.17
6	0.29	0.29	0.05	0.05	0.01	0.03	0.14	0.14	−0.20	−0.14	0.17	0.17
7	0.31	0.30	0.03	0.04	0.05	0.05	0.16	0.16	−0.21	−0.14	0.18	0.17
8	0.35	0.34	0.07	0.08	0.07	0.09	0.17	0.17	−0.18	−0.12	0.19	0.18
9	0.36	0.36	0.06	0.06	0.04	0.05	0.18	0.18	−0.17	−0.10	0.19	0.18
10	0.38	0.37	0.06	0.07	0.06	0.04	0.19	0.19	−0.18	−0.10	0.20	0.19
11	0.40	0.39	0.06	0.07	0.05	0.06	0.20	0.20	−0.17	−0.09	0.21	0.19
12	0.42	0.42	0.06	0.07	0.04	0.06	0.21	0.21	−0.18	−0.09	0.21	0.20
13	0.44	0.45	0.06	0.06	0.02	0.03	0.22	0.22	−0.18	−0.09	0.22	0.21
14	0.47	0.47	0.05	0.06	0.06	0.05	0.22	0.22	−0.20	−0.09	0.42	0.22
15	0.44	0.44	0.04	0.06	−0.08	−0.07	0.22	0.23	−0.19	−0.08	0.46	0.38
16	0.39	0.45	−0.04	−0.02	−0.10	0.01	0.22	0.23	−0.19	−0.07		0.44

evidence supporting increasing returns, and in any event the differences between the two were negligible in the post-war simulation covering 1951–66. For these reasons, it seems worthwhile to examine the dynamic responses of the model to an exogenous shock under each alternative, in order to gain an appreciation of possible differences in policy implications of the two systems. This is the topic to which we now turn.

3. Comparison of Dynamic Multipliers

Table 10.2 presents dynamic multipliers for the period 1951–66 based on a sustained rise of one billion dollars in real federal expenditure. The multipliers pertaining to the constant- and increasing-returns versions of the model are shown side by side for *GNP* and its major expenditure components, as well as for other related variables.[1] The accompanying table 10.3 gives the multipliers on potential, capacity, and full-employment output and their utilization rates in a corresponding format.

We find that constant returns yields consistently larger multipliers on nominal *GNP* but smaller ones on real *GNP*. The initial exogenous increase in real demand gives rise to larger gains in real output and smaller increases in prices under increasing returns; and although these opposite influences of increasing returns are not completely offsetting insofar as nominal *GNP* is concerned, together they lead to smaller changes in nominal *GNP* as compared with constant returns. At first thought, one might suspect that these overall differences between the two cases result from the moderating effects on capacity and labor utilization of scale economies under increasing returns. A glance at the utilization rates in table 10.3 indicates that the reverse is true, however. In the first year, both capacity and full-employment utilization rise more sharply under increasing returns. Hence, it appears that the smaller initial price increases under increasing returns are due to the moderating effects of scale economies on average total cost rather than on utilization rates. After the first year,

---

[1] The multipliers on most of these variables for the constant-returns version of the model were shown above in tables 9.1 and 9.2 (case 5 in those tables).

TABLE 10.3

Real government expenditure multipliers, constant returns (CR) and increasing returns (IR) – Potential, capacity, and full-employment output and utilization rates.

Year	Potential output (1958 prices)		Capacity output (1958 prices)		Full-employment output (1958 prices)	
	CR	IR	CR	IR	CR	IR
1	− 0.01	− 0.03	− 0.06	0.00	0.02	0.10
2	0.07	0.05	− 0.04	− 0.13	− 0.54	− 0.31
3	0.14	0.10	0.06	0.14	− 0.56	− 0.28
4	0.20	0.14	0.26	0.28	− 0.61	− 0.40
5	0.29	0.22	0.46	0.45	− 0.87	− 0.56
6	0.37	0.28	0.69	0.69	− 1.05	− 0.67
7	0.43	0.33	0.88	0.90	− 1.20	− 0.73
8	0.50	0.38	1.06	1.07	− 1.29	− 0.80
9	0.58	0.45	1.24	1.21	− 1.49	− 0.95
10	0.64	0.51	1.39	1.45	− 1.70	− 1.00
11	0.71	0.56	1.52	1.65	− 1.89	− 1.09
12	0.77	0.60	1.64	1.75	− 2.01	− 1.23
13	0.85	0.66	1.75	1.80	− 2.06	− 1.32
14	0.91	0.71	1.88	1.99	− 2.25	− 1.43
15	0.98	0.79	2.01	2.16	− 2.29	− 1.37
16	1.02	0.78	2.24	2.27	− 2.00	− 1.43

Year	Potential utilization		Capacity utilization		Full-employment utilization	
	CR	IR	CR	IR	CR	IR
1	0.54	0.59	0.72	0.76	0.52	0.54
2	0.32	0.36	0.44	0.54	0.55	0.49
3	0.35	0.39	0.45	0.47	0.60	0.53
4	0.45	0.51	0.50	0.55	0.71	0.68
5	0.46	0.50	0.47	0.52	0.81	0.74
6	0.41	0.48	0.35	0.41	0.82	0.74
7	0.42	0.48	0.31	0.35	0.86	0.77
8	0.47	0.54	0.32	0.38	0.92	0.83
9	0.44	0.52	0.26	0.34	0.93	0.84
10	0.45	0.52	0.25	0.28	0.96	0.84
11	0.45	0.53	0.23	0.25	0.99	0.87
12	0.44	0.54	0.20	0.24	1.01	0.91
13	0.42	0.51	0.17	0.22	0.98	0.89
14	0.43	0.52	0.16	0.19	1.01	0.90
15	0.32	0.43	0.01	0.04	0.91	0.80
16	0.26	0.41	− 0.13	0.02	0.81	0.80

full-employment utilization is consistently lower under increasing returns than constant returns, and this factor contributes further to smaller increases in prices in the increasing-returns case by relieving the upward pressure on wages.[2] On the other hand, capacity utilization remains permanently higher under increasing returns.

Inspection of the expenditure items composing real *GNP* reveals that in the early years the larger multipliers on real *GNP* under increasing returns are almost wholly due to larger increases in consumer spending. Since the rate of deflation after the third year is more rapid and pronounced under increasing returns, real exports decline more modestly in this case. Thus, in the later years the larger multipliers on real *GNP* under increasing returns are accounted for both by larger induced increases in consumption and smaller induced declines in real exports.

Accumulation of business fixed capital responds in about the same way in both cases, but because the capital elasticity in the production function for potential output is larger under constant returns than under increasing returns (0.32 as compared to 0.28), growth in potential is greater in the former case.[3] This observation, in conjunction with the greater gains in real output under increasing returns, explains why potential utilization is consistently higher in the case of increasing returns.

Finally, it is interesting to note the different impact on the federal budget surplus in the two cases. Under both constant and increasing returns the budget surplus is initially enlarged despite the rise in federal spending. Tax receipts are, of course, sensitive to changes in nominal *GNP*, and the induced increases in nominal *GNP* are great enough to generate receipts which more than offset higher expenditures. However, the smaller gains in nominal *GNP* associated with increasing returns, especially after the third year, produce much smaller increases in the budget surplus. Indeed, the greater deflation

---

[2] The multipliers on wages are not shown in the tables, but they do in fact follow the pattern suggested here. The induced rise in the wage rate is larger in the first year under increasing returns, but it is smaller thereafter.

[3] The multipliers on full-employment man-hours, the other major determinant of potential, are negative in both cases but smaller in absolute value under constant returns. This also contributes to higher growth of potential under constant returns.

exhibited in the increasing-returns case eventually leads to absolute declines in the budget surplus by the end of the period.[4]

In summary, the constant- and increasing-returns versions of the model produce notably different dynamic multipliers over the 1951–66 period, even though there is little to choose between them on the basis of prediction errors during this interval. Unlike other macro-econometric models of the U.S. economy, ours is capable of highlighting the implications of alternative hypotheses regarding returns to scale, and these are the first results of this type to appear in the literature. The present evidence clearly favors constant returns, however, and we will retain this assumption until such time as further experience with applications of the model may provide a basis for choosing otherwise.

---

[4] As we have noted several times above, multipliers in the last two years of this particular period are distorted by a structural shift in import propensities resulting from the U.S.–Canadian auto agreements of 1965. This aberration influences both sets of multipliers under discussion here and therefore does not complicate the comparison of the two. However, the absolute decline in the budget surplus under increasing returns in the last two years is no doubt due in part to this special feature of the period.

CHAPTER 11

Summary and Concluding Observations

1. Introduction

This book was designed to describe the major structural features and dynamic properties of the Hickman–Coen model. The narrative flow has therefore emphasized the model as a whole and its interactive processes. This approach, while suitable for the main purpose at hand, tends to obscure some significant independent by-products of the research. The first part of this chapter calls attention to those by-products, of which some are included in the appendices of this book and others are published elsewhere. The second section summarizes our findings on policy multipliers and dynamic properties of the model. The final section discusses potential applications and improvements of the model in future research.

2. Contributions on Specific Topics

These contributions are by-products of our decision to build an annual model for medium-term analysis and to estimate it over a longer sample period than has been usual for large-scale models. On the conceptual side, the principal self-contained contributions are (1) the system of interrelated factor demand, production, and resource utilization functions, (2) the long-run housing model, (3) the model of the monetary sector, and (4) the reformulation of the wage equation to incorporate a measure of the excess demand for labor independent of the unemployment rate. On the empirical side, we may note the development of (1) consistent time series on principal components of the U.S. national income accounts for 1922–28, (2) new measures of potential output and related concepts for 1924–40 and 1949–72, (3) new data on the housing sector since 1922, and (4) new estimates of labor force and unemployment for 1922–40.

The conceptual system of factor demand functions is described in section 3 of Chapter 1, and the estimated equations are discussed in Chapter 2, section 3, and in Chapter 3, section 2. Additional details may be found in Coen and Hickman (1970). The extension of the system to incorporate endogenous measures of capacity and labor utilization in the short-run production function is treated in section 4 of Chapter 1, and to measures of potential and full-employment output in section 5 of Chapter 1. In Appendix D we present our annual estimates of all four concepts of aggregate measures of utilization for 1924–40 and 1949–72, and we compare the estimates of capacity and potential utilization with similar measures of other investigators. To our knowledge, the system of factor demand and production functions has not been estimated empirically on the micro-economic level, although it would be directly applicable to firm or industry data. Macro-economic versions of the system have been estimated by Dramais and Waelbroeck (1975) for eight European countries, however, for incorporation in their DESMOS model of the European Economic Community.

The long-run housing model is summarized in section 4 of Chapter 2. A more detailed derivation is given in Hickman, Hinz and Willig (1973). This model predicts household formation endogenously and explicitly models the interaction between the housing market and the construction industry. Whereas our business investment function is a demand-oriented stock-adjustment hypothesis, the residential construction equation is modelled as a supply-oriented production relation. The demand function for business investment incorporates the implicit rental rate on capital as an argument, but the rental rate on residential capital is an explicit price determined in the market for the services of the existing housing stock. Thus the structure of the housing model is reminiscent of the general Foley–Sidrouski[1] invest-

---

[1] See Foley and Sidrouski (1971). An earlier statement of the theory is given by Witte (1963). One problem in applying this general theory to non-residential investment is the absence of active second-hand markets for business plant and equipment.

ment theory, which stresses the relation between the price of existing assets and the supply price of new capital goods production, although it is formulated as a disequilibrium model and was developed independently of their work. The housing model was used in a simulation study of the determinants of residential construction during the Great Depression and of the hypothesis of an endogenous long building cycle in a paper by Hickman (1974). The data for the housing model, which include new annual estimates of housing stock and vacancies since the early 1920's, are presented in Appendices E and F.

The monetary sector combines an earlier term-structure model of interest rates due to Nelson (1972) with a new model for the demand and supply of money developed by John Scadding with the collaboration of Jae-ik Kim. In contrast with the usual partial adjustment approach to the demand for money, Scadding allows for a transitory component in the measured velocity of money. His major contribution is on the supply side, however, in that he provides in explicit theory of the portfolio behavior of the individual banking firm and its relation to the portfolio behavior of the banking system as a whole. These micro-economic foundations of the banking model are fully developed in Scadding (1974).

The wage equation of the model is taken from Hurd's (1974) study. Its principal novelty lies in the derivation of the excess demand for labor from the labor demand function of the model rather than from the observed unemployment rate in the labor market. Since the excess demand for labor is independently specified, the unemployment rate no longer does double duty as an indicator both of excess labor demand and of the probability of acceptance of wage offers by workers.

The equation for labor force participation incorporates the long-run influence of real wages on labor supply as well as the usual deterrent effects of unemployment on participation rates in the short run. The equation was fitted to post-war data and then extrapolated backwards to the pre-war period as described in Coen (1973a). The resulting new time series for labor force and unemployment in the 1920's and 1930's are presented and discussed in Appendix C.

Finally, Appendix A contains our national income and product estimates for 1922–28, and Appendix B discusses the concept and measurement of labor income in the model. The new estimates of items in the national income accounts consist primarily of backward extrapolations of the official estimates for 1929 and rely heavily on earlier work by Kuznets, Kendrick and Goldsmith. Full references are cited in Appendix A.

3. Policy Multipliers and Dynamic Properties of the Model

Our findings under this heading are set forth in Chapters 8–10. They will be briefly summarized in this section at considerable risk of over-simplification, and the reader is referred to the original chapters and their summary sections for a broader and deeper discussion of the model's dynamic properties.

The policy simulations in Chapter 8 support elements of both the monetarist and non-monetarist views of fiscal and monetary policy, but favor the latter more than the former. The monetarist view that the growth path of real output cannot be lastingly affected by monetary policy is broadly confirmed by the model. Thus the predicted path of potential *GNP* is largely invariant to monetary policy because the latter has no direct effect on business fixed capital formation and the indirect stimulus to business investment from the housing and consumer durable goods sectors is short-lived. On the other hand, the monetarist hypothesis that fiscal policy unaccompanied by monetary expansion can affect real *GNP* only briefly is rejected in our model. Our simulations show that conventional expansionary fiscal policies in the form either of expenditure increases or personal tax cuts can have a lasting affect on the growth paths of capital stock and potential output, and that the investment tax credit provides an even more powerful tool for raising potential.

According to the monetarists, the price level can be permanently affected by a once-for-all change in the stock of nominal money even though output cannot. Our simulations indicate that in the long run (after 10 years), money is neutral with regard to the price level as well as to output, however, again contradicting the monetarist viewpoint.

With regard to the trade-off between unemployment and inflation, the complete model simulations are broadly consistent with the non-monetarist view rather than the natural rate hypothesis favored by monetarist economists. A short-run trade-off is found between unemployment and inflation in the case of conventional fiscal policies, but the inflation rate diminishes rapidly and turns negative after five years. Thus in the case of an increase in federal expenditure or a cut in personal taxes, the long-run trade-off is between lower unemployment and a higher price level rather than a higher inflation rate. A monetary stimulus in the form of a once-for-all increase in unborrowed reserves also reduces the unemployment rate and raises the inflation rate in the short run, but in the long run both unemployment and the price level revert to their original paths. Finally, introduction of an investment tax credit–an expansionary policy insofar as real output is concerned–increases the unemployment rate in the short run, due to capital–labor substitution, and reduces the price level. The long-run consequences of the investment credit depend critically on whether product prices are reduced directly by the decline in production costs resulting from the credit. If tax credits are passed on in price reductions, then both the price level and the unemployment rate are reduced in the long run; if not, a permanent decline in the price level is accompanied by a permanent rise in the unemployment rate.

All of these policy simulations are based on the time interval 1951–66 and incorporate a wage-expectations parameter revealed by the fitted wage equation for this period (see Chapter 5, section 3). A shift in the wage-expectations parameter, as may well have occurred after 1966, could substantially alter the inflation dynamics and trade-offs observed in the simulations.

Two important aspects of the dynamic properties of the model were investigated in Chapter 9. First, interactions among the various sectors of the model in the period 1951–66 were explored by studying the effects of new additions to the induced components of aggregate demand and supply or of monetary factors on the magnitudes and time paths of the dynamic multipliers as major sectors were successively endogenized. When supply and monetary restraints are ignored and the investment components of aggregate demand are treated as exogenous, the model produces a monotonic, though diminishing rise in real *GNP* over time in response to a sustained increase in federal expenditure. Endogenization of investment spending, which introduces multiplier–accelerator interactions, leads to a brief inventory cycle in real *GNP* in the first three years, but thereafter *GNP* again rises steadily. Finally, inclusion of supply and monetary restraints increases the severity of the short-run cycle, largely due to the depressing influence of higher interest rates on residential construction; and although there is once again no evidence of longer-term major cycles, the supply and monetary factors are found to reduce the long-run multiplier of federal expenditure on real *GNP* by about 10 percent.

Second, dynamic multipliers before and after World War II were compared in order to assess the quantitative importance of stabilizing structural changes in the post-war economy. These changes include, but are not restricted to, the enhanced importance of built-in fiscal stabilizers. The calculated multipliers do indeed imply a marked reduction of instability after World War II. Structural changes have reduced the impact multiplier for federal expenditures from about 3 in the pre-war economy to 2 post-war. Moreover, the pre-war multipliers exhibit a major cycle, whereas only a minor inventory cycle can be discerned post-war. Thus our post-war results are broadly consistent with those for other econometric models of the post-war structure, but our pre-war multipliers imply that the economy was considerably less stable before the development of automatic fiscal stabilizers.

In Chapter 10 we investigated the properties of the model on alternative assumptions of constant or increasing returns to scale in the underlying production function. Since the parameters of the production function appear in the factor demand, resource utilization and price equations, the assumption on returns to scale can have a pervasive influence on the behavior of the model. The prediction errors in dynamic simulations for the two alternatives were studied in section 2 of Chapter 10. The assumption of constant returns produced moderately smaller errors in real *GNP* and a substantial improvement in price predictions. Examination of errors in other important variables substantiated the superiority of the constant returns assumption, and hence it was adopted as the standard framework for this book.

A comparison of the post-war dynamic multipliers under constant and increasing returns was undertaken in section 3 of Chapter 10 and produced notably different results for the two versions of the model.

Constant returns yielded consistently larger multipliers on nominal *GNP* and the implicit *GNP* deflator but smaller ones on real *GNP*. It is difficult to trace these differences to specific equations or blocs in an interdependent model such as ours, but some proximate factors are discussed in Chapter 10, section 3.

4. Potential Applications and Improvements

In this concluding section we will briefly discuss some possible applications and improvements of the model. Some of the improvements would strengthen the model for medium-term applications, whereas others would be needed if the forecasting horizon were to be lengthened beyond 5 or 10 years.

One interesting topic to be pursued with the existing structure is an analysis of the causes and consequences of the Great Depression of the 1930's. Simulations are planned to isolate the influence of individual exogenous variables on the depression and to investigate feasible policies or combinations which might have prevented the collapse. In a similar vein, it was shown in Chapter 9 that structural changes have augmented the stability of the post-war economy. We plan to subject the pre-war model to exogenous deflationary shocks approximating actual post-war magnitudes and study the responses. Conversely, shocks such as occurred in the 1930's can be imposed on the post-war model to assess the extent to which the Great Depression was the consequence of an unstable structure which no longer exists. Although we have stressed that the growth orientation and annual unit of the model reduce its effectiveness for cyclical analysis, the fluctuations in the 1930's are sufficiently large and prolonged to be meaningfully analyzed with its aid.

A second application would be to construct alternative full-employment solutions for the post-war period, with each solution corresponding to a different mix of policy variables. Comparison of the growth and inflation rates and income distributions for the different policy combinations should illuminate some of the welfare consequences of alternative full-employment policies.

Ex-ante projections and policy analyses could constitute a third application of the model in an area of contemporary interest. This would require adjustments to the constant terms of the equations to correct for systematic biases in the post-sample predictions, as discussed in Chapter 7. Such corrections would put the model on track in recent years and provide a firmer base for ex-ante projections. Before undertaking extensive extrapolations, however, it would be preferable to take account of structural change since 1966 by re-estimating the model through a recent year. The extended sample would sharpen the parameter estimates and also facilitate tests on structural breaks during the post-war period. In particular, it is widely believed that inflationary expectations have changed since the Vietnam War began, and a separate expectations parameter could be estimated in the wage equation for the recent period, albeit with few degrees of freedom. The coefficients of the model could also be improved in the re-estimation by wider use of simultaneous equation techniques than in the present version.

New specifications would also be desirable to capture recent structural changes affecting foreign trade and the international transmission of inflationary pressures. Import quantities and prices should be disaggregated into the four commodity groups used in Project LINK: food and agricultural production, raw materials, fuel and lubricants, and manufactured products.[2] Given the OPEC cartel and the increasing world demands for raw materials, it is important to allow separately for the effects of the various external price changes on the balance of trade. Moreover, in this changed world environment the explanatory power of the domestic price equations would be substantially improved by the inclusion of import prices of materials and fuels as new arguments.

A final class of improvements or extensions would serve to lengthen the projection horizon of the model to, say, 25 years or more. Population and its age composition are exogenous in the present version, although household formation and labor force participation are not. For projections exceeding 15 years it would be highly desirable, though possibly visionary, to endogenize birth and

---

[2] For a description of Project LINK, which incorporates national econometric models into a linked world model, see Ball (1973). Although less essential, a similar disaggregation of exports would also be desirable.

death rates, so that full account could be taken of long-run economic–demographic interactions.

The other major amplification for long-run analysis would be the incorporation of fuel and materials inputs into the production process. The value-added framework presently employed in our aggregate production function could be extended to a gross output basis with fuels and materials as added inputs. Another possibility would be to combine input–output with the macro-model, along the lines of recent work by Preston (1972, 1975), Hudson and Jorgenson (1974), and Almon (1975). In any event, the model should allow for the possibility of price-induced resource-substitution in response to energy and materials shortages if it is to be applied to the very long run.

National Income and Product Estimates, 1922-28

1. Introduction

Since the official government series on national income and product were available in sufficient detail for our purposes only for years since 1929, it was necessary to derive consistent estimates for 1922–28 and to link them to the official series in 1929. For the most part, the new estimates for 1922–28 are simply backward extrapolations of the official estimates as published in citation [10] below.

The sources of data used for extrapolation were [1] Simon Kuznets, unpublished technical tables underlying series in: *Capital in the American Economy*, Princeton, 1961. [2] John W. Kendrick, *Productivity Trends in the United States*, Princeton, 1961. [3] U.S. Department of Commerce, Office of Business Economics, *1966 Capital Stock Study*. [4] U.S. Department of Commerce, Business and Defense Services Administration, *Construction Statistics, 1915–1964*. [5] Harold Barger, *Outlay and Income in the United States, 1921–38*, National Bureau of Economic Research, 1942. [6] U.S. Department of Commerce, Bureau of the Census, *Historical Statistics of the United States*, 1960. [7] Simon Kuznets, *National Income and Its Composition, 1919–1938*, National Bureau of Economic Research, 1941. [8] *Basic Facts on Employment and Production*, Report to the Committee on Banking and Currency, Senate Committee Print no. 4, 79th Congress, 1st Session. [9] Raymond Goldsmith, *A Study of Saving in the United States*, Princeton, 1955. [10] U.S. Department of Commerce, Office of Business Economics, *The National Income and Product Accounts of the United States, 1929–1965*.

2. Gross National Product (tables A.1 and A.2)

2.1. Personal Consumption Expenditures

Total consumption in current dollars was estimated from the income side as the difference between independent estimates of disposable personal income (net of interest paid by consumers and personal transfer payments to foreigners) and personal saving (see below, table A.5). A breakdown of the total by purchase activity was then obtained as follows. First, each purchase category was extrapolated separately. Second, the components were summed to yield an estimate of total consumption from the product side, and each component was expressed as a percent of the total. Third, the resulting percentage distribution was then used to allocate the initial control estimate of total consumption among its components.

The extrapolators for durables and non-durables were from [1, table T-6, columns 5–7]. The extrapolator for services was obtained as the sum of Barger's series on purchased services in [5, table 22], and Kendrick's estimates of unpaid services of financial intermediaries in [2, table A-IIb].

Total consumption in 1958 dollars was estimated by summing the deflated series for the separate components. The price deflators for consumer durables, non-durables, and services were those implicit in Kuznets' estimates of purchases in current and 1929 dollars in [1, tables T-6 and T-7, columns 5–8] converted to the base 1958 = 100.

2.2. Non-residential Fixed Investment

These are direct estimates rather than extrapolations. The data for non-residential structures are from [3, table 3 (current dollars) and table 4 (1958 dollars)]. The corresponding estimates for producers' durable equipment are from [3, tables 1 and 2].

2.3. Residential Structures

The extrapolators are from [4, table 2 (current dollars) and table 3 (constant dollars)]. Non-farm residential construction was extrapolated by the series for residential non-farm buildings and farm residential construction by that for farm operator buildings.

TABLE A.1

Gross national product, 1922–28 (millions of current dollars).

	1922	1923	1924	1925	1926	1927	1928
1. Gross National Product	71,557	86,053	84,358	92,144	96,446	94,107	97,173
2. Personal consumption expenditures	54,418	63,114	64,002	67,513	71,182	70,037	73,485
3. Durable goods	5,494	7,283	7,238	8,182	8,580	8,050	8,476
4. Non-durable goods	27,534	31,392	31,278	33,047	35,224	34,430	36,030
5. Services	21,390	24,439	25,486	26,284	27,378	27,557	28,979
6. Gross private domestic investment	10,190	15,911	12,304	16,288	17,141	15,133	14,127
7. Fixed investment	9,660	12,919	13,240	14,536	15,618	14,726	14,506
8. Non-residential	6,015	8,163	7,807	8,619	9,617	9,156	9,347
9. Structures	2,754	3,464	3,591	3,986	4,584	4,631	4,572
10. Producers' durable equipment	3,261	4,699	4,216	4,633	5,033	4,525	4,775
11. Residential structures	3,645	4,756	5,433	5,917	6,001	5,570	5,159
12. Non-farm	3,503	4,587	5,275	5,749	5,838	5,379	4,973
13. Farm	142	169	158	168	163	191	186
14. Change in business inventories	530	2,992	−936	1,752	1,523	407	−379
15. Net exports of goods and services	997	842	1,351	1,087	826	1,073	1,377
16. Exports	4,954	5,494	5,911	6,348	6,381	6,456	6,842
17. Imports	3,957	4,652	4,560	5,261	5,555	5,383	5,465
18. Government purchases of goods and services	5,952	6,186	6,701	7,256	7,297	7,864	8,184
19. Addendum: Income originating in general gov't.	3,100	3,200	3,400	3,500	3,700	3,900	4,100
20. Addendum: Private gross national product	68,457	82,853	80,958	88,644	92,746	90,207	93,073
21. Addendum: Housing rent	9,919	10,668	11,490	11,520	11,392	11,408	11,369
22. Addendum: Private gross non-residential product	58,538	72,185	69,468	77,124	81,354	78,799	81,704

TABLE A.2
Gross national product, 1922–28 (billions of 1958 dollars).

	1922	1923	1924	1925	1926	1927	1928
1. Gross National Product	144.5	169.9	168.6	182.3	190.6	190.3	193.7
2. Personal consumption expenditures	100.0	113.6	116.7	120.1	126.2	127.6	132.8
3. Durable goods	9.2	12.5	12.9	14.4	16.1	15.0	15.8
4. Non-durable goods	52.2	57.5	59.0	59.8	62.3	64.1	65.5
5. Services	38.6	43.6	44.8	45.9	47.8	48.5	51.5
6. Gross private domestic investment	27.5	39.0	32.5	41.4	43.4	39.8	37.2
7. Fixed investment	27.0	33.2	34.6	38.1	41.0	39.0	38.1
8. Non-residential	16.1	20.5	19.8	21.9	24.7	23.7	24.0
9. Structures	8.4	9.6	10.0	11.2	12.9	13.3	13.0
10. Producers' durable equipment	7.7	10.9	9.8	10.7	11.8	10.4	11.0
11. Residential structures	10.9	12.7	14.8	16.2	16.3	15.3	14.1
12. Non-farm	10.5	12.3	14.4	15.8	15.9	14.8	13.6
13. Farm	0.4	0.4	0.4	0.4	0.4	0.5	0.5
14. Change in business inventories	0.5	5.8	-2.1	3.3	2.4	0.8	-0.9
15. Net exports of goods and services	0.5	0.8	1.5	1.7	1.9	2.4	2.4
16. Exports	7.7	8.0	8.7	9.3	10.1	11.0	11.4
17. Imports	7.2	7.2	7.2	7.6	8.2	8.6	9.0
18. Government purchases of goods and services	16.5	16.5	17.9	19.1	19.1	20.5	21.3
19. Addendum: Income originating in general gov't.	10.3	10.5	10.9	11.3	11.6	12.0	12.3
20. Addendum: Private gross national product	134.2	159.4	157.7	171.0	179.0	178.3	181.4
21. Addendum: Housing rent	11.5	12.1	12.6	12.5	12.5	12.7	13.0
22. Addendum: Private gross non-residential product	122.7	147.3	145.1	158.5	166.5	165.6	168.4

2.4. Change in Business Inventories

The current dollar estimates are taken directly from [2, table A-IIb]. The extrapolator for the constant dollar series is from [2, table A-IIa].

2.5. Net Exports

The data for exports and imports in current dollars are direct estimates taken from [6, series U-168 and U-175]. The implicit price deflators for exports and imports were extrapolated by indexes of unit value given in [6, series U-22 and U-34].

2.6. Government Purchases of Goods and Services

The current dollar estimates are taken directly from [2, table A-IIb]. The extrapolator for the constant dollar series is from [2, table A-IIa]. The current and constant dollar estimates of income originating in general government are from [10, table 1.20].

2.7. Private Gross National Product

Gross national product less income originating in general government.

2.8. Housing Rent

This item is the sum of farm and non-farm components and comprises actual space rent on tenant-occupied homes and imputed rent on owner-occupied homes as carried in the consumer expenditure component of the *GNP* accounts. The current dollar series from 1929 forward are from [10, table 2.5, lines 22–25]. The three non-farm components on lines 22, 23 and 25 of [10, table 2.5] were extrapolated separately by the corresponding series from [5, table 22] and were summed to derive the non-farm total. The extrapolator for the farm component on line 24 of [10, table 2.5] was also taken from [5, table 22]. Both the farm and non-farm components were deflated by the rent component of the Bureau of Labor Statistics Consumer Price Index on the base 1958 = 100 to yield the constant-dollar estimates.

2.9. Private Gross Non-residential Product

Private gross national product less housing rent.

3. National Income (table A.3)

3.1. Compensation of Employees

Extrapolator from [8, table E.2].

3.2. Proprietors' Income

The series on the inventory valuation adjustment in line 5 of table A.3 is from [9, vol. 1, table P-19]. The extrapolator for proprietors' income in line 3 is the sum of the inventory valuation adjustment as measured in [8, table E.2] and the unadjusted series on proprietors' income from the same source. The final estimates of income of unincorporated enterprises were obtained by subtraction of line 5 from line 3.

3.3. Rental Income of Persons

The extrapolator is from [7, table 22].

3.4. Corporate Profits and Inventory Valuation Adjustment

Dividends were extrapolated by the series in [7, table 54]. The extrapolators for undistributed profits and profits tax liability are from [9, vol. III, table N-5]. Profits before tax were obtained as the sum of the components. The inventory valuation adjustment is taken directly from [9, table P-19].

3.5. Net Interest

The extrapolator was obtained as the difference between the estimates of total interest and government interest in [7, table 55].

TABLE A.3
National income, 1922–28 (millions of current dollars).

	1922	1923	1924	1925	1926	1927	1928
1. National Income	61,059	72,569	72,264	77,486	81,674	79,408	81,928
2. Compensation of employees	36,182	42,534	42,438	44,073	46,960	47,345	48,211
3. Proprietors' income	11,056	13,147	13,348	14,964	15,193	14,278	14,418
4. Income of unincorporated enterprises	11,300	13,189	13,307	15,053	14,774	14,091	14,404
5. Non-corporate inventory valuation adjustment	−244	−42	41	−89	419	187	14
6. Rental income of persons	5,425	5,757	6,200	6,089	5,646	5,646	5,425
7. Corporate profits and inventory valuation adjustment	5,522	8,017	6,926	8,791	10,174	8,152	9,507
8. Profits before tax	6,155	8,131	6,810	9,052	8,898	7,555	9,461
9. Profits tax liability	878	1,039	988	1,297	1,373	1,283	1,307
10. Profits after tax	5,277	7,092	5,822	7,755	7,525	6,272	8,154
11. Dividends	2,809	3,551	3,493	4,049	4,377	4,664	5,068
12. Undistributed profits	2,468	3,541	2,329	3,706	3,148	1,608	3,086
13. Corporate inventory valuation adjustment	−633	−114	116	−261	1,276	597	46
14. Net interest	2,874	3,114	3,352	3,569	3,701	3,987	4,367

4. Relation of Gross National Product, National Income and Personal Income (table A.4)

4.1. Gross National Product

From table A.1.

4.2. Capital Consumption Allowances

The extrapolator is from [9, vol. III, table N-5, column 2].

4.3. Indirect Business Tax and Non-tax Liability

Taken directly from [9, vol. III, table N-5].

4.4. Business Transfer Payments

Held constant at 1929 level for 1922–28.

4.5. Statistical Discrepancy

Line 1 less the sum of lines 2, 4, 5 and 8. This is not a pure statistical discrepancy, since the consumption total included in *GNP* was estimated from the income side (see tables A.1 and A.5).

4.6. Subsidies Less Current Surplus of Government Enterprises

Assumed to be zero throughout the period.

4.7. National Income

From table A.3.

4.8. Corporate Profits and IVA

From table A.3.

TABLE A.4

Relation of gross national product, national income, and personal income, 1922–28 (millions of current dollars).

	1922	1923	1924	1925	1926	1927	1928
1. Gross National Product	71,557	86,053	84,358	92,144	96,446	94,107	97,173
2. Less: Capital consumption allowances	5,321	5,609	5,906	6,242	6,625	7,005	7,426
3. Equals: Net National Product	66,236	80,444	78,452	85,902	89,821	87,102	89,747
4. Less: Indirect tax liability	4,817	5,134	5,461	5,818	6,219	6,543	6,916
5. Business transfer payments	587	587	587	587	587	587	587
6. Statistical discrepancy	−227	2,154	140	2,011	1,341	564	316
7. Plus: Subsidies less current surplus of government enterprises	0	0	0	0	0	0	0
8. Equals: National Income	61,059	72,569	72,264	77,486	81,674	79,408	81,928
9. Less: Corporate profits and IVA	5,522	8,017	6,926	8,791	10,174	8,152	9,507
10. Contributions for social insurance	117	130	141	150	165	186	212
11. Plus: Government transfer payments	509	505	498	532	586	627	654
12. Interest paid by government	1,091	1,018	916	916	876	848	815
13. Interest paid by consumers	531	584	585	757	794	804	1,247
14. Dividends	2,809	3,551	3,493	4,049	4,377	4,664	5,068
15. Business transfer payments	587	587	587	587	587	587	587
16. Equals: Personal Income	60,947	70,667	71,276	75,386	78,555	78,600	80,580

4.9. Contributions for Social Insurance, Government Transfer Payments, and Net Interest Paid by Government

Taken directly from [9, vol. III, table N-5].

4.10. Dividends

From table A.3.

4.11. Interest Paid by Consumers

Separate estimates were prepared for interest on personal debt and on brokers' loans. The first item was estimated from a linear regression of interest on personal debt as measured in the national income and product accounts on the sum of installment credit on automobiles and non-installment single-payment consumer loans, as given in Federal Reserve Board, *Money and Banking Supplement*, 1965, p. 33. The regression was fitted for 1929–40 and extrapolated for 1922–28. Several attempts were made to adjust the independent variable for changes in interest rates paid, but the unadjusted volume of credit proved to be a better explanatory variable in the regression. Interest on brokers' loans was also estimated from a regression fit to data for 1929–40. The independent variable was the product of the interest rate on new stock exchange call loans and the volume of sales on the New York Stock Exchange. The data were obtained from [6, series X-307 and X-373]. Interest paid by consumers was obtained as the sum of the extrapolators for interest on personal debt and on brokers' loans. The series may have a large margin of error. Personal income is a much larger total, however, so any error introduced into the latter by an error in the former will be small.

5. Personal Income and its Disposition (table A.5)

5.1. Personal Income

From table A.4.

TABLE A.5

Personal income and its disposition, 1922–28 (millions of current dollars).

	1922	1923	1924	1925	1926	1927	1928
1. Personal Income	60,947	70,667	71,276	75,386	78,555	78,600	80,580
2. Less: Personal tax and non-tax payments	1,694	1,887	1,785	1,931	2,065	2,170	2,308
3. Equals: Disposable Personal Income	59,253	68,780	69,491	73,455	76,490	76,430	78,272
4. Less: Personal outlays	55,263	64,026	64,926	68,643	72,337	71,196	75,078
5. Personal consumption expenditure	54,418	63,114	64,002	67,513	71,182	70,037	73,485
6. Interest paid by consumers	531	584	585	757	794	804	1,247
7. Personal transfer payments to foreigners	314	328	339	373	361	355	346
8. Equals: Personal Saving	3,990	4,754	4,565	4,812	4,153	5,234	3,194

5.2. Personal Tax and Non-tax Payments

Taken directly from [9, vol. III, table N-1, column 4 minus column 5].

5.3. Personal Consumption Expenditures

Calculated as a residual from independent estimates of disposable personal income (net of interest paid by consumers and personal transfer payments to foreigners) and personal savings. This procedure was adopted because better estimates of personal saving were obtained by the direct method described below than would have been implicit in the difference between disposable personal income (net of interest paid by consumers and personal transfer payments to foreigners) and an independent extrapolation of consumption expenditure from the product side.

5.4. Interest Paid by Consumers

From table A.4. It should be noted that the residual estimate of personal consumption expenditures is independent of this item, since disposable personal income would change in identical amount to any change in the estimate of interest paid by consumers.

5.5. Personal Transfer Payments to Foreigners

Taken directly from [6, series U-183].

5.6. Personal Saving

Estimated from a linear regression of personal saving in the national income accounts on a "roughly comparable" saving series given in [9, vol. II, table B-11, column 2]. The regression was fitted for 1929–40 and extrapolated for 1922–28.

6. Implicit Price Deflators (table A.6)

Each deflator is the ratio of the corresponding series on current and constant dollar expenditures shown in tables A.1 and A.2. The

TABLE A.6

Implicit price deflators for gross national product, 1922–28 (index numbers, 1958 = 100).

	1922	1923	1924	1925	1926	1927	1928
1. Gross National Product	49.5	50.6	50.0	50.6	50.6	49.4	50.2
2. Personal consumption expenditures	54.4	55.6	54.8	56.2	56.4	54.9	55.3
3. Durable goods	59.7	58.3	56.1	56.8	53.3	53.7	53.6
4. Non-durable goods	52.8	54.6	53.0	55.3	56.5	53.7	54.9
5. Services	55.4	56.0	56.9	57.3	57.3	56.8	56.4
6. Fixed investment	35.8	38.9	38.3	38.2	38.1	37.8	38.1
7. Non-residential	37.4	39.8	39.4	39.4	38.9	38.6	39.0
8. Structures	32.8	36.1	35.9	35.6	35.5	34.8	35.2
9. Producers' durable equipment	42.4	43.1	43.0	43.3	42.7	43.5	43.4
10. Residential	33.4	37.4	36.7	36.5	36.8	36.4	36.6
11. Non-farm	33.4	37.3	36.6	36.4	36.7	36.3	36.6
12. Farm	35.5	42.2	39.5	42.0	40.8	38.2	37.2
13. Exports	64.3	68.7	67.9	68.3	63.2	58.7	60.0
14. Imports	55.0	64.6	63.3	69.2	67.7	62.6	60.7
15. Government purchases of goods and services	36.1	37.5	37.4	38.0	38.2	38.4	38.4
16. Addendum: Private gross national product	51.0	52.0	51.3	51.8	51.8	50.6	51.3
17. Addendum: Private gross non-residential product	47.7	49.0	47.9	48.7	48.9	47.6	48.5

deflator for fixed investment in non-residential structures is variant 2 from [3], rather than the variant 1 which is given in the official *GNP* accounts. Correspondingly, all price deflators dependent on the non-residential structures component may differ from their counterparts in the official accounts.

Explanatory Notes on Labor Income and its Measurement

1. Measurement of Private Labor Income

Private labor income as defined in this model is the sum of private employee compensation (exclusive of that paid by sole proprietors and partnerships) and the imputed labor share originating in proprietorships and partnerships. The derivation of the estimates from 1929 to date will be described first. (The references are to tables in: [1] *The National Income and Product Accounts of the United States, 1929–65,* U.S. Department of Commerce, Office of Business Economics.)

Private employee compensation exclusive of that paid by sole proprietors and partnerships is equal to total employee compensation [1, table 1.10, line 2], less income originating in general government [1, table 1.13, line 30] and employee compensation originating in proprietorships and partnerships [1, table 1.13, line 12].

Imputed labor income originating in proprietorships and partnerships was estimated as follows. The basic assumption is that the division of income originating in proprietorships and parterships between labor and non-labor shares is the same as the distribution of labor and non-labor income in the corporate sector. Thus the estimate of imputed labor income originating in proprietorships and partnerships was calculated for each year by multiplying total income originating in proprietorships and partnerships [1, table 1.13, line 11] by the ratio of corporate employee compensation [1, table 1.13, line 4] to total income originating in corporate business [1, table 1.13, line 3].

It was not possible to use the same method for allocating proprietors' income during 1922–28, lacking estimates of income originating in proprietorships and partnerships. It was necessary instead to use an approximation method devised by [2] Edward F. Denison, *The Sources of Economic Growth in the United States*, Committee for Economic Development, 1962, Appendix B. Estimates of the share of corporate property income (profits plus interest) in total income originating in corporations were computed for 1922–28 from data given in [3] Harlow D. Osborne and Joseph B. Epstein, "Corporate Profits Since World War II", *Survey of Current Business*, January 1956, Appendix. The property share of proprietors' income (*not* of income originating in proprietorships) was then calculated from the data for 1929 and extrapolated for 1922–28 by the corporate property income shares from Osborne and Epstein. Next the extrapolated property income shares were applied to the estimates of proprietors' income for 1922–28 from table A.3 above to obtain a preliminary estimate of the imputed property share of proprietors' income and, hence, a residual preliminary estimate of imputed labor income. A second estimate of imputed labor income was then obtained by extrapolating the 1929 imputed labor share of proprietors' income by the corporate labor share implicit in the Osborne and Epstein data for 1922–28, and applying the extrapolated labor shares to the estimates of proprietors' income during 1922–28 from table A.3. The two estimates of imputed labor income in total proprietors' income were then averaged for each year to yield the final estimates for 1922–28. The final step was to add the estimates of proprietors' imputed labor income to those of private employee compensation (compensation of employees from table A.3 minus income originating in general government from table A.1) to derive private labor income for 1922–28.

2. Measurement of Private Wage Rate

The basic wage variable in the model is W, the private money wage rate. It is an implicit wage obtained as the ratio of private labor income to private man-hours. It differs from an index of straight-time earnings because it includes compensation for overtime. It also differs by including the implicit wage of self-employed proprietors and partners. Our measures of employment, unemployment and labor force include self-employed proprietors, and the corresponding wage rate in the identity for private labor income,

$$YL\$ = (W)(MH) = (W)(EP)(AH),$$

should reflect the imputed wage of these persons for consistency, as it does in our measures.

New Estimates of Labor Force and Unemployment, 1922-40

As we noted in Chapter 4, annual labor force and unemployment statistics were not collected by the federal government before 1940, and the series used in the model are our own estimates. The labor force estimates were prepared by "backcasting" participation rates for 1922-40 from our post-war participation equation and multiplying the predicted participation rate in each year by the non-institutional, working-age population in that year. Unemployment was then calculated by subtracting employment from the estimated labor force.

Since labor force enumerations are available from decennial censuses in the pre-war period, a partial check on the validity of our procedure was possible. In particular, we could examine how accurately we were able to predict observed participation rates in 1930 and 1940. Our backcasts gave underestimates of participation rates in both years, although the errors were quite similar (0.0305 in 1930 and 0.0328 in 1940). This suggested that the slope coefficients in the post-war participation equation were reasonably accurate indicators of responses of participation in the pre-war period to changing labor market conditions, but that an upward adjustment of the constant term was necessary. Hence, we added to the post-war constant term the average of the 1930 and 1940 errors, so that our labor force predictions in those years are nearly identical to the decennial census estimates, as adjusted by Lebergott (1964).[1]

---

[1] Lebergott adjusted the decennial census figures prior to 1940, which measured "gainful workers", to make them consistent with the labor force concept used thereafter, as well as with the sampling procedures used by the Census Bureau in its *Current Population Surveys* beginning in 1940.

The tendency of our post-war participation relation to underpredict participation in the pre-war period might result in part from two noteworthy changes in the structure of the population between the pre-war and post-war periods, neither of which are captured by the variables included in the participation relation. First, individuals 65 years old and over, a group with a relatively low participation rate, comprised 5.4 percent of the population in 1930 and 9.2 percent in 1960. Second, 24.5 percent of the population in 1930 lived on farms as compared to only 7.5 percent in 1960. If participation rates of the farm population exceed those of the non-farm population, which seems likely although evidence is not available to substantiate this, then this structural change would also suggest higher aggregate participation in the pre-war period. Beyond these two factors, it is possible that workers' expectations of a higher normal level of unemployment in the pre-war period contributed to a higher rate of participation, for as Coen (1973a) has shown, the constant term in the participation equation depends positively on the unemployment rate which workers view as normal. While such structural differences between the pre-war and post-war periods might account for the higher pre-war constant in the participation relation, it is rather striking that, according to our findings, they had little influence on the slope coefficients in the relation.

Our new estimates of the labor force and unemployment rate for 1922–40 are presented in table C.1 (the columns labelled "H–C"), where they are compared with the widely used series constructed by Lebergott (1964). Unlike our estimates, which allow for the impact of changing labor market conditions on participation, Lebergott's estimates are based on a simple linear interpolation of participation rates between decennial censuses. Thus, his labor-force series is dominated by the trend in population and displays almost no cyclical movements; it might more reasonably be viewed as a series on potential labor force than on actual, or measured, labor force. For this reason, our series diverges most sharply from Lebergott's in the early 1930's, when substantial slack in the labor market so discouraged job searchers that the labor force shrank absolutely, according to our estimates. The relatively steady labor-force growth characteristic of Lebergott's series gives a peak unemployment rate of 25.2 percent in 1933, whereas our series implies a lower peak at 21.3 percent occurring in 1934 rather than 1933.

TABLE C.1

Estimates of civilian labor force and unemployment rate, 1922–40.

Year	Civilian labor force (millions of persons)		Unemployment rate (percent)	
	H–C	Lebergott[a]	H–C	Lebergott[a]
1922	42.675	42.496	7.3	6.7
1923	44.373	43.444	4.5	2.4
1924	44.725	44.235	6.0	5.0
1925	45.962	44.934	4.9	2.7
1926	46.722	45.629	4.1	1.8
1927	47.220	46.375	5.0	3.3
1928	47.737	47.105	5.5	4.2
1929	48.873	47.757	5.5	3.2
1930	48.622	48.523	9.1	8.9
1931	47.500	49.325	13.0	16.3
1932	46.842	50.098	18.8	24.1
1933	47.440	50.882	19.8	25.2
1934	51.227	51.650	21.3	22.0
1935	51.754	52.283	19.5	20.3
1936	52.759	53.019	16.6	17.0
1937	53.599	53.768	14.1	14.3
1938	53.676	54.532	17.8	19.1
1939	54.475	55.218	16.0	17.2
1940	55.526	55.640	14.4	14.6

[a] From Lebergott (1964, table A-3).

We further note that Lebergott's estimates for the 1920's are strongly influenced by the relatively low participation rate recorded in the 1930 census at the onset of the Great Depression. The labor market was much tighter throughout the 1920's than in 1930, however, so that when participation rates in the 1920's are permitted to reflect market conditions in those years, as in our series, consistently larger estimates of the labor force result. As compared with Lebergott's estimates of unusually low unemployment rates in the mid-1920's, our higher estimates are more in line with commonly observed peacetime unemployment rates in the U.S., and they also seem more consistent with the remarkable stability of wages and prices during the 1922–29 period.

For further details and discussion of these estimates, see Coen (1971b, 1973a, 1973b) and Lebergott (1973).

Estimates of the Utilization Rates

1. *Four Measures of Resource Utilization*

We present in table D.1 estimates of our four utilization measures for 1924–40 and 1949–72, assuming constant returns to scale of production. No measures have been computed for 1941–48, owing to the abnormal disturbances associated with World War II and its aftermath. Our output measure is gross private non-residential product in 1958 dollars, which is equal to real *GNP* minus real output originating in general government and real housing rent. Thus our potential utilization series covers somewhat less of the economy than most other measures, whereas the capacity series has a broader industrial base than is typical. The utilization concepts are discussed in sections 4 and 5 of Chapter 1, and further details are given in section 4 of Chapter 4. The last column of table D.1 displays the conventional unemployment rate–unemployment as a percentage of the civilian labor force–which serves as a useful point of reference in examining the utilization rates. The estimates for unemployment in 1924–40 are themselves new and are discussed in Appendix C.

In discussing the estimates, we shall focus initially on the relationships among our own measures, before comparing them to other available indexes of resource utilization.

The most important feature of table D.1 is the substantial divergence which appears at times between the utilization rates of potential and full-employment output. The output which would lead employers to fully employ the labor force at given relative factor prices may at times be substantially different from the output that would be produced at full employment if labor and capital were used

TABLE D.1
Estimates of H–C model utilization rates, 1924–40 and 1949–72 (percentages).[a]

Year	Capacity[b] utilization	Labor[b] utilization	Full-employment output utilization	Potential output utilization	Unemployment rate
1924	90.7	93.8	92.0	88.2	6.0
1925	96.3	98.7	96.2	93.0	4.9
1926	103.8	97.3	99.5	94.7	4.1
1927	97.3	94.4	95.8	90.8	5.0
1928	96.3	95.4	94.2	89.3	5.5
1929	101.8	96.3	94.4	90.8	5.5
1930	86.2	90.1	81.9	77.7	8.9
1931	68.4	88.3	68.6	69.3	13.0
1932	57.5	85.9	53.5	56.6	18.8
1933	57.2	91.4	48.3	55.0	19.8
1934	61.8	92.1	42.2	58.8	21.3
1935	68.8	99.1	46.0	65.3	19.5
1936	81.9	100.3	51.3	74.2	16.6
1937	92.7	102.6	60.2	77.8	14.1
1938	75.4	87.4	49.0	70.4	17.8
1939	80.7	100.0	54.1	76.2	16.0
1940	92.8	99.6	58.8	81.5	14.6
1949	106.1	96.3	92.5	94.8	5.9
1950	110.3	99.5	95.2	101.4	5.3
1951	110.3	99.7	102.3	105.6	3.3
1952	101.2	98.4	103.4	104.5	3.0
1953	103.4	99.5	104.4	105.8	2.9
1954	97.0	95.4	94.2	99.3	5.5
1955	103.8	101.6	98.9	104.1	4.4
1956	107.1	99.7	100.0	101.7	4.1
1957	102.1	98.4	99.4	99.9	4.3
1958	87.5	95.9	89.4	93.3	6.8
1959	91.0	100.8	94.7	97.9	5.5
1960	94.7	99.5	94.4	96.5	5.5
1961	89.9	96.7	90.0	94.4	6.7
1962	95.7	99.5	94.0	99.2	5.5
1963	97.2	99.2	93.6	99.4	5.7
1964	104.7	100.1	95.6	101.5	5.2
1965	115.3	100.7	98.1	103.7	4.5
1966	121.8	99.8	100.0	106.0	3.8
1967	111.2	98.7	99.5	103.4	3.8
1968	108.7	99.6	100.5	103.7	3.6
1969	109.4	99.7	101.2	101.6	3.5
1970	100.2	97.9	92.8	94.6	4.9
1971	95.5	98.0	91.6	94.9	5.9
1972	101.8	101.1	93.3	97.1	5.6

[a] Constant returns to scale assumed.
[b] Normalized utilization rates (see section 5 of Chapter 1).

at normal intensity. In the past, this distinction has not been made, and instead the concept of potential output has done double duty.

In our system the full-employment utilization rate is the correct indicator to answer the question: how much higher (or lower) would output have to be this year in order for the unemployment rate to reach 4 percent? As can be seen from the table, the full-employment utilization rate exceeds 100 percent only in those years when the unemployment rate is at or below 4 percent. What is not revealed by the full-employment utilization rate is the relative shortage (or surplus) of capital stock that would be associated with an output sufficient to fully employ the labor force.[1] Thus 1966–69 were all full-employment years, with an average full-employment utilization rate of 100 percent, but the average potential utilization rate was 104 percent, indicating a substantial accompanying shortage of plant and equipment. The potential utilization rate was also well above 100 percent in several other years–1950, 1955, 1964 and 1965–when the full-employment rate was below 100 percent. Thus the full-employment rate can be a seriously biased measure of the current utilization of *all* productive resources, including capital as well as labor. Since we shall show below that the most widely used measures of "potential" utilization are actually equivalent to our full-employment concept, it follows that these measures display the same bias.

Turning now to our measures of capacity and labor utilization, we note that the former fluctuates markedly over time, whereas the latter seldom strays far from 100 percent. The quickness with which firms adjust man-hour inputs to the desired levels means that the labor utilization rate is usually close to its normal level–the lowest rate even at the depths of the Great Depression was only 86 percent.

Capacity utilization presents a far different picture. The long distributed lag of net investment on output and prices results in frequent and large deviations of capacity from its optimal level for current production conditions. The nadir was reached in 1932–33, when the capacity utilization rate was 57 percent, whereas the

---

[1] Potential output may also differ from full-employment output because labor utilization deviates from normal, but such deviations are usually unimportant, as may be seen from column 2.

greatest overutilization occurred in 1966 with a rate of 122 percent. Capacity utilization was within 2 percent of normal in only four post-war years – 1952, 1957, 1970 and 1972 – and in three of those years, full-employment utilization was well below normal. Thus the simultaneous achievement of full employment of labor and optimal employment of capital has persistently eluded the economy.

The situation was even worse in the pre-war period. The depressed state of the economy during the 1930's requires no comment, but it is worth stressing that our new utilization measures indicate a considerably less rosy picture of the 1920's than is commonly painted. This is principally because our own new unemployment estimates are rather high during 1924–29 and lead to a low rate of utilization of full-employment output. However, our new estimates of capacity utilization are also low during the 1920's. With both the labor force and capital stock underutilized in most years, it is not surprising that potential utilization averaged merely 91 percent in 1924–29. Our finding that utilization rates of full employment and potential output were below 100 percent during the 1924–29 period provides at least a partial explanation of the remarkably stable price level during those years.

2. Alternative Measures of Capacity Utilization

Table D.2 compares our new estimates of capacity utilization with three other indexes covering all or most of the post-war period. Ours is the most comprehensive of the group, since it excludes only the production of housing services and the output of government employees from real *GNP*. The Wharton School index covers manufacturing, mining and utilities, services, and construction, whereas the Federal Reserve and McGraw–Hill measures are for manufacturing alone.

The series are shown in their original units in the first four columns of the table. Our measure of capacity utilization often exceeds 100 percent, whereas the others never reach that level. This is basically because we measure optimal long-run capacity, which is often considerably lower than current output, whereas the other series refer to one or another concept of peak short-run capacity which can

TABLE D.2
Alternative measures of capacity utilization, 1949–70.[a]

	Original levels (percent)				Relative (1954 = 100)			
Year	H–C	Wharton	FRB	McGraw–Hill	H–C	Wharton	FRB	McGraw–Hill
1949	106.1	83.9	82.7		109.4	97.9	98.3	
1950	110.3	90.8	91.9		113.7	106.0	109.3	
1951	110.3	92.8	95.1		113.7	108.3	113.1	
1952	101.2	90.6	92.8		104.3	105.7	110.3	
1953	103.4	93.1	95.5		106.6	108.6	113.6	
1954	97.0	85.7	84.1	84	100.0	100.0	100.0	100
1955	103.8	92.3	90.0	92	107.0	107.7	107.0	110
1956	107.1	92.0	88.2	86	110.4	107.4	104.9	102
1957	102.1	89.2	84.5	78	105.3	104.1	100.5	93
1958	87.5	81.1	75.1	80	90.2	94.6	89.3	95
1959	91.0	86.0	81.4	85	93.8	100.4	96.8	101
1960	94.7	84.5	80.1	77	97.6	98.6	95.2	92
1961	89.9	82.1	77.6	83	92.7	95.8	92.3	99
1962	95.7	84.4	81.4	88	98.7	98.5	96.8	99
1963	97.2	85.6	83.0	85	100.2	99.9	98.7	101
1964	104.7	88.3	85.5	88	107.9	103.0	101.7	105
1965	115.3	91.4	89.0	90	118.9	106.7	105.8	107
1966	121.8	95.8	91.9	88	125.6	111.8	109.3	105
1967	111.2	92.7	87.9	86	114.6	108.2	104.5	102
1968	108.7	94.4	87.7	85	112.1	110.2	104.3	101
1969	109.4	95.4	86.5	83	112.8	113.2	102.9	99
1970	100.2	89.9	78.3	78	103.3	104.9	93.1	93

[a] *Sources*: H–C model: Table D.1. Wharton: Economic Research Unit, Wharton School of Finance and Commerce, University of Pennsylvania. FRB: *Federal Reserve Bulletin*. McGraw–Hill: Department of Economics, McGraw–Hill Publishing Co. Estimates are for December of each year.

never be exceeded. In order to abstract from differences in level, the four series are expressed as relatives with 1954 = 100 in the last four columns of table D.2, and it is to these relatives that the following comments refer.

In general, the new index exhibits wider cyclical fluctuations than the others. It appears that the other available indexes make inadequate allowance for the post-war shortage of capital stock, since they show capacity utilization to be about the same in 1949–51 as in 1952–54, whereas our series stands considerably higher in the earlier interval than in the later one. The disparities are even greater in 1964–70, especially with regard to the McGraw–Hill and FRB indexes. The new index also rises far above that of the Wharton School during 1964–67, although it is fairly close to the latter in 1968–70.

Examination of the underlying capacity series itself, as distinguished from the utilization index shown in table D.2, indicates that the sharp rise in our utilization index between 1963 and 1966 was due to a fall in capacity of 4 percent accompanied by a rise in output of 20 percent. Capital stock growth and technical progress continued to augment capacity during those years, but a fall in the rental price of capital relative to the money wage rate increased the optimal capital–labor ratio and reduced the optimal capacity output of the given capital stock. This relative price change probably did not reduce the technical or engineering capacity of the capital stock and hence would not be reflected in capacity measures which abstract from cost considerations, such as the other series included in table D.2.

3. Alternative Measures of Potential Utilization

Our new estimates of the rate of utilization of potential output are compared with other available measures in table D.3. The only comparable series for the pre-war economy is due to Knowles (1960). In comparison to his estimates, ours indicate substantially less intensive use of productive resources in the 1920's, and a deeper contraction and weaker recovery during the 1930's. As noted earlier, the underutilization of potential indicated by our figures for the 1920's is partly attributable to our new high unemployment estimates for the 1920's and partly to our low estimated rates of capacity utilization.

The number of potential series covering part or all of the post-war period is considerably larger. Of the two series available only for the first part of the period, Knowles' is similar to ours until 1954 and moderately lower in 1955–59, whereas Kuh's (1966) is markedly lower than ours until 1956 and moderately lower thereafter. Both the series of the Council of Economic Advisors (CEA), available for 1952–70, and the series we have constructed for 1949–70 on the basis of "Okun's Law" lie almost consistently below ours. If our estimates are accepted, then, it may be concluded that apart from the Knowles measures during the Korean War, other existing series on potential utilization are biased substantially downward. This is principally because they fail to allow for overutilization of plant and equipment during periods of economic expansion. Indeed, only Knowles has estimated potential from an aggregate production function incorporating capital stock, and his attempt to correct for cyclical variations in resource intensity by including the ratio of actual to potential man-hours is analogous to a correction for full-employment utilization [see our equation (1.23)] instead of capacity utilization.

Another major point to emerge from an inspection of table D.3 is the similarity of our series for *full-employment* utilization (column 6) to the Okun's Law measure of *potential* utilization (column 5). Okun's Law asserts the following relationship between the "potential" utilization rate and the unemployment rate [Okun (1962, p. 100)]:

$$A/P = 1/\{1 + 0.032(U - 4)\}, \tag{D.1}$$

where A and P are, respectively, actual and "potential" output, and U is the actual unemployment rate in percent.

Now, our measure of full-employment utilization is similarly linked to the ratio of actual employment to the estimated level of employment which would prevail if the unemployment rate were 4 percent. It is true that our explanatory variable is the ratio of actual man-hours to potential man-hours at full employment [equation (1.23)], but the allowance for induced changes in average hours is dominated by the allowance for induced changes in the number of persons employed, so that the man-hour ratio moves similarly to the employment ratio alone. The average relationship between the utilization rate of full-employment output and the labor–unemployment rate is sufficiently tight for the period 1949–70 to provide our analogy to Okun's Law,

$$X/X^f = e^{0.036(4-U)} \approx 1 + 0.036(4 - U). \tag{D.2}$$

A comparison of columns 5, 6 and 7 of table D.3 shows that formula

TABLE D.3

Alternative measures of potential and full-employment utilization, 1924–40 and 1949–70 (percentages).[a]

Year	Potential utilization					Full-employment utilization, H–C model	
	H–C (1)	Knowles (2)	Kuh (3)	CEA (4)	Okun's Law (5)	Actual (6)	Predicted (7)
1924	88.2	99.7				92.0	92.3
1925	93.0	104.5				96.2	96.5
1926	94.7	105.7				99.5	99.6
1927	90.8	101.2				95.8	96.1
1928	89.3	98.1				94.2	94.2
1929	90.8	101.8				94.4	94.2
1930	77.7	86.5				81.9	82.2
1931	69.3	79.5				68.6	69.8
1932	56.6	67.7				53.5	55.3
1933	55.0	65.6				48.3	45.4
1934	58.8	71.0				42.2	42.1
1935	65.3	76.6				46.0	46.1
1936	74.2	84.9				51.3	53.3
1937	77.8	87.5				60.2	60.4
1938	70.4	80.9				49.0	50.2
1939	76.2	85.0				54.1	54.9
1940	81.5	89.9				58.8	58.9
1949	94.8	96.6	85.7		94.3	92.5	93.4
1950	101.4	101.3	95.3		96.0	95.2	95.4
1951	105.6	104.7	99.0		102.0	102.3	102.6
1952	104.5	103.9	98.0	99.8	103.3	103.4	103.7
1953	105.8	104.1	98.1	100.7	103.6	104.4	104.0
1954	99.3	98.3	92.7	95.9	95.4	94.2	94.7
1955	104.1	101.7	99.9	99.7	98.7	98.9	98.6
1956	101.7	99.1	99.5	98.1	99.7	100.0	99.6
1957	99.9	96.5	97.3	96.1	99.0	99.4	98.9
1958	93.3	91.2	90.7	91.7	91.8	89.4	90.4
1959	97.9	93.1	96.8	94.2	95.4	94.7	94.7
1960	96.5		95.1	93.3	95.4	94.4	94.7
1961	94.4		91.2	91.8	92.0	90.0	90.7
1962	99.2		95.4	94.5	95.4	94.0	94.7
1963	99.4			95.5	94.8	93.6	94.1
1964	101.5			96.8	96.3	95.6	95.8
1965	103.7			99.2	98.4	98.1	98.2
1966	106.0			101.7	100.6	100.0	100.7
1967	103.4			100.3	100.6	99.5	100.7
1968	103.7			101.0	101.3	100.5	101.5
1969	101.6			99.6	101.6	101.2	101.8
1970	94.6			94.9	97.2	92.8	94.4

[a] *Sources*: See next page.

(D.2) yields predictions of the full-employment utilization rate which are similar to our direct measure of that rate and also to the Okun's Law estimate of his concept of the potential utilization rate.[2]

We may conclude, then, that the measure of resource utilization pioneered by Okun is more appropriately related to the concept of full-employment output than to potential output as we have argued the latter should be defined. The same may be said of the CEA measure, which is a variant of Okun's approach. As Okun showed in his 1962 article, a potential trend line passing through actual *GNP* in mid-1955 and growing at 3.5 percent per year yielded percentage gaps between actual and potential output which were highly correlated with the unemployment rate. This is still the method used by the CEA for establishing potential, with the assumed growth rate increased from 3.5 percent in 1952–62 to 3.75 percent for 1963–65, 4 percent for 1966–69, and 4.3 percent thereafter. Thus both Okun's Law and the CEA series on potential utilization are linked to the fluctuations of the unemployment rate around the "full-employment" level of 4 percent, the one directly and the other indirectly. This explains the similarity of the CEA and Okun's Law measures of "potential" utilization in table D.3. Both series are similar to our measure of full-employment utilization rather than to utilization of potential output as viewed from the side of production possibilities instead of labor demand.

---

[2] The linear approximation of e^x is good for small values of x. Either version of equation (D.2) produces similar estimates for 1949–70, but the linear approximation is inadequate for the 1930's because of the high unemployment rates during those years.

---

[a] *Sources*: Cols. 1 and 6: from table D.1. Col. 7 is predicted from the labor–unemployment rate using the formula $(X/X^f) = e^{k(4-U)}$ where k has a value of 0.040 during 1924–33, 0.050 during 1934–40, and 0.036 during 1949–70. See text and footnote 2 for further discussion. Col. 2: from Knowles (1960, table 2, p. 37). Col. 3: Computed from data supplied by Kuh which underlie his results reported in Kuh (1966). These figures pertain to the private business sector and are based on his best fitting labor-force equation. The estimate for 1949 is for the last three quarters of the year. Col. 4: The estimates for 1966–70 are as published in *Business Conditions Digest*, U.S. Bureau of the Census. The figures for earlier years were calculated by the present authors using the assumptions described in the footnote to Chart E1, *ibid.*, August 1971. Col. 5: Calculated from the formula given by Okun (1962, p. 100) and reproduced in the present text as equation (D.1).

4. Summary

We may summarize our principal empirical findings as follows. First, our conceptual distinctions regarding resource utilization are more than mere theoretical niceties, in the sense that they lead to actual measures which differ substantially from other series on utilization of plant capacity and potential output. Second, our measure of potential utilization since World War II exceeded 100 percent in many years in which the full-employment utilization rate was at or below 100 percent, so that the latter can be a seriously biased indicator of the current utilization of labor *and* capital resources. Third, since other widely used measures of "potential" utilization are actually equivalent to our full-employment concept, these measures exhibit the same bias. Fourth, the labor utilization rate seldom departs substantially from 100 percent, since firms rapidly adjust man-hour inputs to the desired level. Fifth, capacity utilization fluctuates over a wide range because of the slow adjustment of capital stocks to desired levels. Sixth, the simultaneous achievement of full employment of labor and optimal employment of capital – a situation in which the capacity and labor utilization rates are at their normal levels and the full-employment rate is 100 percent, so that the potential rate is also 100 percent – has persistently eluded the economy, although not by much in 1957. Seventh, our measures indicate that there was more slack in the economy during 1924–29 than is commonly recognized, with substantial underutilization of both labor and capital.

Sources and Methods for Data on Household Formation, Housing Starts and Housing Stocks *

1. Introduction

This appendix cites the basic sources of the underlying data and sets forth the formulae and assumptions used to construct the time series observations on the variables used in the housing model. The resulting series are shown for 1922–1972 in tables E.1 and E.2. Specific citations are given through 1969, and the later figures are from later editions of the same publications. The references are listed at the end of the appendix.

2. Investment (table E.1)

Current dollar series:

$HGIND(t)$ = gross private investment in new, non-farm dwelling units (1889–1928 [1, table B-3], 1929–69 [2]);

$HGP(t)$ = gross public investment in new residential structures (1934–62 [3, table 2], 1963–66 [4, table A-1], 1967–69 [5, table A-1], level adjustment to agree with [4]);

$HGAA(t)$ = gross expenditure on non-farm additions and alterations (1889–1928 [1, tables D-2 and B-4], 1929–69 [2]).

---

* This appendix was written by Mary Hinz, who developed the estimates in collaboration with Robert Willig.

Constant (1958) dollar series:

The above series are deflated by $PHGIN(t)$ = deflator for non-farm residential structures investment (1929–69 [2], 1889–1929 [1, table B-10, column 1], level adjusted to agree with [2]).

3. Non-farm Residential Wealth – Value Stock (table E.1)

This time series is created by cumulating annual net real investment in non-farm dwelling units from an 1889 benchmark. An annual 2 percent rate of depreciation-obsolescence is assumed.

Let $HKN(t)$ be the net stock of non-farm residential structures on December 31, t, in billions of 1958 dollars. Then

$$HKN(1889) = \$8.6/PHGIN(1889),$$

where the current-dollar stock figure for 1889 is from [1, table D-1], and

$$HKN(t) = 0.98\ HKN(t-1) + HGIND(t) + HGP(t) + HGAA(t),$$

for $1890 \le t$, where the investment figures are in constant dollars.

4. Housing Starts and Completions (table E.2)

The starts series are official Department of Commerce data from [9, table A-1] for 1921–62 and from [10, tables 2 and 4] for 1963–69. Completions are derived from starts on the assumption of constant technological lags. Defining

$HS(t)$ = non-farm housing starts during year t;
$HC(t)$ = non-farm housing completions during year t;
$HSPR(t)$ = private non-farm housing starts during year t;
$HSPU(t)$ = public non-farm housing starts during year t;
$HCPR(t)$ = private non-farm housing completions during year t;
$HCPU(t)$ = public non-farm housing completions during year t;

TABLE E.1

Residential construction and housing stock, 1922–40 and 1949–72 (billions of 1958 dollars).

Year	HGIND	HGP	HGAA	HKN[a]
1922	8.9	0.0	0.6	159.2
1923	10.6	0.0	0.6	167.2
1924	12.5	0.0	0.6	177.0
1925	13.5	0.0	0.7	187.6
1926	13.4	0.0	0.7	198.0
1927	12.5	0.0	0.8	207.3
1928	11.5	0.0	0.9	215.5
1929	8.0	0.0	0.9	220.1
1930	4.3	0.0	0.8	220.8
1931	3.9	0.0	0.5	220.8
1932	1.7	0.0	0.4	218.5
1933	1.1	0.0	0.5	215.7
1934	1.3	0.0	0.7	213.3
1935	2.4	0.0	0.8	212.4
1936	3.8	0.2	0.9	213.1
1937	4.3	0.3	0.9	214.4
1938	4.5	0.1	0.8	215.6
1939	6.3	0.2	0.9	218.7
1940	6.8	0.5	0.9	222.6
1949	12.8	0.5	2.8	260.5
1950	18.9	0.4	2.9	277.5
1951	15.0	0.7	2.8	290.4
1952	14.2	0.7	3.0	302.5
1953	14.6	0.6	3.2	314.9
1954	16.5	0.4	3.3	328.8
1955	19.6	0.3	3.5	345.7
1956	16.6	0.3	3.7	359.3
1957	14.7	0.5	3.8	371.1
1958	15.4	0.8	3.7	383.7
1959	18.6	0.9	4.1	399.7
1960	15.7	0.7	4.2	412.3
1961	15.4	0.8	4.2	424.5
1962	17.5	0.9	4.2	438.5
1963	18.4	0.4	4.1	452.6
1964	18.0	0.4	4.0	466.0
1965	17.8	0.4	3.9	478.7
1966	15.3	0.5	3.9	488.8
1967	14.5	0.5	4.0	498.1
1968	17.3	0.5	3.9	509.8
1969	17.7	0.8	3.9	522.0
1970	16.2	0.8	4.2	532.8
1971	22.7	0.8	4.4	550.0
1972	27.5	0.6	4.4	571.8

[a] End of year.

we have

$$HS(t) \quad = HSPR(t) + HSPU(t);$$
$$HC(t) \quad = HCPR(t) + HCPU(t);$$
$$HCPR(t) = \tfrac{1}{2}[HSPR(t-1)] + \tfrac{1}{2}[HSPR(t)];$$
$$HCPU(t) = HSPU(t-1).$$

Completions for the first quarter of any year, which are used in estimating dwelling units (see section 6 below), are given by

$$HCPR(I, t) = HSPR(III, t-1) = 0.273 \; HSPR(t-1);$$

$$HCPU(I, t) = HSPU(I, t-1) \quad = 0.200 \; HSPU(t-1),$$

where Roman numerals refer to quarters and the coefficients express the mean quarterly (1959–68) starts patterns [9, tables A-11 and 10].

5. Households (table E.2)

These series are based on data for 1919–50 from [11] and for 1950–69 from [12]. Data labelled April 1 in [12] are treated as March 1 figures. The non-farm households series (HH) used in the model is conceptually based on the 1950 Census definitions of farm and household and, hence, the 1960–69 observations, measured according to the 1960 Census definitions, were adjusted to the level of the 1950 Census definitions as follows. Let:

$$HHT(t) \quad = \text{total households (1950 definition) on July 1, } t;$$
$$HHT(t + \tfrac{1}{2}) = \text{total households (1950 definition) on}$$
$$\text{December 31, } t;$$
$$HHT(t - \tfrac{1}{3}) = \text{total households (1950 definition) on March 1, } t.$$

HHF and HH denote farm and non-farm households, respectively, and the subscript 60 denotes "measured on the 1960 Census definitions".

TABLE E.2

Housing starts and completions, stock of dwelling units, and number of households, 1922–40 and 1949–72 (millions of units).

Year	HSPR	HSPU	HC	HU	HH
1922	0.7160	0.0	0.5825	19.818	18.780
1923	0.8710	0.0	0.7935	20.612	19.492
1924	0.8930	0.0	0.8820	21.496	20.182
1925	0.9370	0.0	0.9150	22.413	20.745
1926	0.8490	0.0	0.8930	23.307	21.325
1927	0.8100	0.0	0.8295	24.138	21.941
1928	0.7530	0.0	0.7815	24.921	22.416
1929	0.5090	0.0	0.6310	25.553	22.851
1930	0.3300	0.0	0.4195	26.092	23.268
1931	0.2540	0.0	0.2920	26.508	23.476
1932	0.1340	0.0	0.1940	26.889	23.541
1933	0.0930	0.0	0.1135	27.192	23.653
1934	0.1260	0.0	0.1095	27.461	24.118
1935	0.2157	0.0053	0.1709	27.757	24.665
1936	0.3042	0.0148	0.2653	28.103	25.253
1937	0.3324	0.0036	0.3331	28.510	25.917
1938	0.3993	0.0067	0.3695	29.000	26.518
1939	0.4584	0.0566	0.4355	29.527	27.249
1940	0.5296	0.0730	0.5506	30.153	28.001
1949	1.4300	0.0360	1.4050	39.309	36.218
1950	1.9080	0.0440	1.7050	40.665	37.698
1951	1.4200	0.0710	1.7080	42.024	38.901
1952	1.4460	0.0580	1.5040	43.228	39.904
1953	1.4020	0.0360	1.4820	44.412	40.848
1954	1.5320	0.0190	1.5030	45.607	41.742
1955	1.6270	0.0190	1.5985	46.875	42.631
1956	1.3250	0.0240	1.4950	48.079	43.664
1957	1.1750	0.0490	1.2740	49.072	44.695
1958	1.3140	0.0680	1.2935	50.559	45.527
1959	1.4946	0.0367	1.4723	52.014	46.545
1960	1.2301	0.0439	1.3991	53.482	47.757
1961	1.2848	0.0520	1.3013	54.740	48.906
1962	1.4390	0.0297	1.4139	55.943	48.960
1963	1.5829	0.0318	1.5407	57.041	50.911
1964	1.5023	0.0321	1.5744	58.539	51.982
1965	1.4506	0.0369	1.5086	59.745	53.105
1966	1.1415	0.0309	1.3330	60.652	54.173
1967	1.2684	0.0303	1.2359	61.847	55.468
1968	1.4836	0.0378	1.4063	63.193	56.954
1969	1.4491	0.0328	1.5042	64.542	58.331
1970	1.4163	0.0354	1.4655	66.920	60.136
1971	2.0322	0.0323	1.7596	69.259	62.582
1972	2.3366	0.0219	2.2167	71.080	64.443

For 1960–69,

$$HHT(t - \tfrac{1}{3}) = \frac{HHT(1960 - \tfrac{1}{3})}{HHT_{60}(1960 - \tfrac{1}{3})} [HHT_{60}(t - \tfrac{1}{3})]$$
$$= 0.99602 \ HHT_{60}(t - \tfrac{1}{3});$$

$$HHF(t - \tfrac{1}{3}) = \frac{HHF(1960 - \tfrac{1}{3})}{HHF_{60}(1960 - \tfrac{1}{3})} [HHF_{60}(t - \tfrac{1}{3})]$$
$$= 1.26448 \ HHF_{60}(t - \tfrac{1}{3});$$

$$HH(t - \tfrac{1}{3}) = HHT(t - \tfrac{1}{3}) - HHF(t - \tfrac{1}{3}).$$

6. Stock of Non-farm Dwelling Units (table E.2)

This stock series (HU) is dated December 31. For the periods 1919–29, 1929–40, and 1948–55 it was created by interpolating by private completions between the benchmarks listed and footnoted below. From 1955 on, the non-farm stock of dwelling units was inferred from available aggregate occupancy rate data.

6.1. Benchmarks

Dwelling units	Date	Source
18,604,000	12/31/19	Computed from assumed non-farm vacancy rate of 6 percent and number of non-farm households
25,692,000	4/1/30	[13]
29,683,000	4/1/40	1940 Census of Housing
39,625,000	4/1/50	1950 Census of Housing
46,875,000	12/31/55	Computed from observed aggregate vacancy rate (see 1955–69 below)

The 6.0 percent vacancy rate for 12/31/19 (actually 1/1/20, the date of the 1920 Census) was derived using evidence from several sources:

(1) Naigles [13, p. 880] presents data on non-farm families and non-farm dwelling units from the 1930 Census which yield a non-farm vacancy rate of 9 percent. It seems reasonable to use this as an upper limit in estimating the 1920 vacancy rate, given the building boom that occurred during the 1920's.

(2) Wickens [14, p. 55] gives estimates of 1920 vacancy rates of "about 1 percent" for Philadelphia, "probably less than 1 percent" for New York and 3.6 percent for St. Louis. The 3.6 percent rate for St. Louis is believed to be higher than the average for the country as a whole because St. Louis had a higher than average proportion of 2- or 3-or-more family dwellings. Using 3.6 percent as the benchmark rate produces a series of vacancy rates which declines to zero in the early 1920's; thus the single-city data must be too low to use even as a lower limit to the national estimate.

(3) The 6.0 percent rate which was finally chosen yields a low vacancy rate of 3.4 percent at the beginning of 1923; this is lower than any rate subsequently reported. In 1950, following a depression and a war, the non-farm vacancy rate was 6.4 percent. Using 6.0 percent as the estimate for 1920 is to assume that the situation in 1920 was just slightly worse than in 1950.

(4) Estimates of conversions and demolitions during the 1920's presented by Chawner [15, p. 14] can be used to calculate a stock of dwelling units of 18,716,000 (0.6 percent larger than the 1920 benchmark) and a vacancy rate of 6.6 percent. It was felt that the small percentage difference in the stock resulting from use of the 6.0 percent vacancy rate would have an insignificant effect on the estimates of the stock for 1921–29.

6.2. 1919–29 Stock

The series during this period is interpolated by private completions between the 12/31/19 and 12/31/29 benchmarks, because the portion of the change in the stock of housing units not accounted for by completions is very small (0.17 percent). The 4/1/30 benchmark was simultaneously related to 12/31/29 by the same interpolation scheme. Let

$HU(t)$ $\quad$ = stock of non-farm dwelling units on December 31, t;

$HU(t - \frac{3}{4})$ = stock of non-farm dwelling units on April 1, t;

$$TC = \sum_{i=1920}^{1929} HCPR(i).$$

Then

$$HU(t) = HU(1919) + \sum_{i=1920}^{t} HCPR(i) \left(\frac{HU(1929) - HU(1919)}{TC} \right);$$

where $HU(1929) = X$ is the solution to

$$HU(1930 - \tfrac{3}{4}) - X = HCPR(I, 1930) \left(\frac{X - HU(1919)}{TC} \right).$$

6.3. 1929–40 Stock

During this depression decade there are assumed to be 861,000 [13, table 2] substandard additions, i.e., caves, shacks, warehouses, etc., added to the stock by acts of occupancy rather than by construction. This includes 345,000 units which were "created" by doubling-up of families in units classified structurally as single-dwelling units [13, p. 870]. According to the 1950 Census definitions, these would not have been counted as separate households or housing units; but they have been included here in order to permit use of the 1930 "family" count as "household" data.

The substandard additions are distributed over the period by the annual negative deviations of real per-capita personal disposable income [16, column A-42] from its 1930–45 average. It is assumed that a close negative correlation exists between changes in disposable income and substandard additions. The period 1930–45 is used because there are negative deviations from the mean for 1930–39 and positive deviations thereafter. Using this method, the substandard additions can be thought of as having been added to the housing stock in 1930–39 and then removed in 1940–45.

With a method analogous to that used in subsection 6.2 above, the April 1, 1940 benchmark is moved to December 31, 1939, and the stock is interpolated by the sum of substandard additions, public completions, and private completions adjusted to fit the simultaneously computed benchmark. $HU(1940)$ is extrapolated by the same method. Let

$$TCPR = \sum_{i=1930}^{1939} HCPR(i);$$

$$TCPU = \sum_{i=1930}^{1939} HCPU(i);$$

$HSA(t) = $ substandard additions during year t.

For $1930 \le t \le 1940$,

$$HU(t) = HU(t-1) + HCPU(t) + HSA(t) + \alpha\, HCPR(t);$$

where

$$\alpha = \frac{HU(1939) - HU(1929) - TCPU - 861{,}000}{TCPR},$$

and $HU(1939) = X$ is the solution to

$$HU(1940 - \tfrac{3}{4}) - X = HCPU(I, 1940) + HCPR(I, 1940)$$
$$\times \left(\frac{[X - HU(1929) - TCPU - 861{,}000]}{TCPR} \right).$$

6.4. 1948–55 Stock

During this period, too, private completions are adjusted by interpolation between a fixed benchmark and a simultaneously redated one. $HU(1948)$ is extrapolated backwards by the same adjustment scheme. Let

$$TCPR = \sum_{i=1950}^{1954} HCPR(i);$$

$$TCPU = \sum_{i=1950}^{1954} HCPU(i).$$

For $1949 \le t \le 1955$,

$$HU(t) = HU(t-1) + HCPU(t) + HCPR(t)$$
$$\times \left(\frac{HU(1955) - HU(1949) - TCPU}{TCPR} \right);$$

where $HU(1949) = X$ is the solution to

$$HU(1950 - \tfrac{3}{4}) - X = HCPU(I, 1950) + HCPR(I, 1950)$$
$$\times \left(\frac{HU(1955) - X - TCPU}{TCPR} \right).$$

6.5. 1955–69 Stock

For this period, observed quarterly aggregate occupancy rates were published by the Census Bureau [17]. Fourth-quarter and first-quarter rates were averaged to estimate a December 31 series. In the 1960 Census, no vacant units were included in the count of farm housing units, so no vacancy rate could be calculated. Assuming that the ratio of the farm vacancy rate for 1960 to that for 1950 is the same as the ratio of the non-farm vacancy rates for 1960 and 1950, we obtain an estimated farm vacancy rate of 0.15 for 1960. Hence, an 85 percent farm occupancy rate for December 31, 1960 was used, a constant ratio of farm to non-farm occupancy rates over the period was assumed, and the non-farm stock was computed on that basis. Let

$HOT(t + \tfrac{1}{2})$ = aggregate occupancy rate on December 31, t;
$HOF(t + \tfrac{1}{2})$ = farm occupancy rate on December 31, t;
$HO(t + \tfrac{1}{2})$ = non-farm occupancy rate on December 31, t;
$HUT(t)$ = total stock of dwelling units on December 31, t;
$HUF(t)$ = farm stock (1950 definition) of dwelling units on December 31, t.

Then, by assumption,

$$HOF(1960 + \tfrac{1}{2}) = 0.85,$$

and

$$\frac{HHT(1960 + \tfrac{1}{2})}{HOT(1960 + \tfrac{1}{2})} = HUT(1960)$$

$$= HU(1960) + HUF(1960)$$

$$= \frac{HH(1960 + \frac{1}{2})}{HO(1960 + \frac{1}{2})} + \frac{HHF(1960 + \frac{1}{2})}{HOF(1960 + \frac{1}{2})},$$

which is solved for $HO(1960 + \frac{1}{2})$.

For $1955 \le t \le 1969$, we assume that

$$\frac{HOF(t + \frac{1}{2})}{HO(t + \frac{1}{2})} = \frac{HOF(1960 + \frac{1}{2})}{HO(1960 + \frac{1}{2})} = \frac{0.85}{0.9036} = Z,$$

and

$$\frac{HHT(t + \frac{1}{2})}{HOT(t + \frac{1}{2})} = \frac{HH(t + \frac{1}{2})}{HO(t + \frac{1}{2})} + \frac{HHF(t + \frac{1}{2})}{[HO(t + \frac{1}{2})]Z},$$

which is solved for $HO(t + \frac{1}{2})$ and yields

$$HU(t) = \frac{HH(t + \frac{1}{2})}{HO(t + \frac{1}{2})}.$$

7. Sources

[1] Leo Grebler, David B. Blank and Louis Winnick, *Capital Formation in Residential Real Estate: Trends and Prospects*, Princeton University Press, 1956.
[2] U.S. Department of Commerce, *Survey of Current Business*, July issues 1967–1970; and "The National Income and Product Accounts of the United States, 1929–1965", Supplement to *Survey of Current Business*, 1966.
[3] U.S. Department of Commerce, "Construction Statistics, 1915–1964", Supplement to *Construction Review*, Jan. 1966.
[4] U.S. Department of Commerce, *Construction Review*, 13, no. 2, Feb. 1967.
[5] U.S. Department of Commerce, *Construction Review*, 17, no. 7, July 1971.
[6] U.S. Bureau of the Census, *Statistical Abstract of the United States: 1963*, Washington, 1963.

[7] Office of the President, *Economic Report of the President, February 1970.*

[8] Harold Barger, *Outlay and Income in the United States, 1921–38,* National Bureau of Economic Research, New York, 1942.

[9] U.S. Bureau of the Census, *Housing Construction Statistics, 1889–1964,* Washington, 1966.

[10] U.S. Bureau of the Census, Construction Reports, Series C20: *Housing Starts,* nos. 46–70/6, April 1963–July 1970.

[11] U.S. Bureau of the Census, Current Population Reports, Series P-20: *Population Characteristics,* no. 92, March 1959.

[12] U.S. Bureau of the Census, Current Population Reports, Series P-20: *Population Characteristics,* no. 176, Nov. 1968; no. 191, Oct. 1969; no. 200, May 1970.

[13] M. H. Naigles, "Housing and the Increase in Population", *Monthly Labor Review,* 54, no. 4, April 1942, pp. 869–880.

[14] David L. Wickens, *Residential Real Estate,* National Bureau of Economic Research, New York, 1941.

[15] Lowell J. Chawner, *Residential Building,* National Resource Committee, Housing Monograph Series, no. 1, Washington, 1939.

[16] U.S. Bureau of the Census, *Long-Term Economic Growth, 1860–1965,* Washington, 1966.

[17] U.S. Bureau of the Census, Current Housing Reports, Series H-111: *Housing Vacancies,* nos. 1–64, Sept. 1955–May 1971.

Derivation of the Standardized Household Variable *

1. Introduction

The standardized household variable represents the total number of non-farm households there would have been in each year 1922–72 if 1940 headship rates had prevailed throughout the period. A headship rate is the ratio of household heads to the total number of people in an age class. Thus, the total number of standardized households is the sum over all age groups of the product of the headship rate and the non-farm population.

1940 was used as the base year because it is the mid-point of the regression sample period (1924–40, 1949–66) and because headship rates for five-year age groups in the non-farm population had been calculated from 1940 Census data by Burnham O. Campbell [1, p. 408]. The normalized household variable was to be dated July 1, so it was necessary to adjust Campbell's headship rates from April 1 to July 1.

It was also necessary to estimate the non-farm population annually by five-year age groups. This was done by estimating farm population and subtracting it from total population, rather than estimating non-farm population directly, in order to reduce the magnitude of errors of estimation.

A description of the specific methods used in estimating the normalized household variable is presented in this appendix. Specific

---

* This appendix was written by Mary Hinz, with advice from Warren Sanderson.

citations, listed at the end of the appendix, are given through 1969. The later figures are extrapolations based on (1) the ratio of non-farm population to total population and (2) the number of standardized households in the total population.

The following subscripts have been used:

i denotes age group; $i = 1, 2, \ldots, 16, 17'$, for five-year age groups 5–9, 10–14, ..., 80–84, 85 and over. The suffix ['] denotes an open-ended age group.

I denotes total for all ages, *not* all age groups beginning with 5–9.

T denotes decade; $T = 1, 2, \ldots, 5$, for decades beginning in 1920, 1930, ..., 1960.

t denotes July 1, year of decade; $t = 1, 2, \ldots, 11$, for years ending in 0, 1, ..., 0. Note that 11-year "decades" have been used, so that year T, 11 is the same as year $(T + 1)$, 1.

An example of the use of these subscripts is $FP_{i,T,t} = FP_{3,4,5}$, which denotes farm population for age group 15–19 in 1954.

2. Farm Population (FP)

2.1. Census Years

2.1.1. 1920–1950

Rural farm population data from the Census were used as benchmarks for 1920, 1930, 1940 and 1950. These were adjusted from Census dates (January 1, 1920; April 1, other years) to July 1 by interpolation, assuming a constant rate of change between Census dates. The April 1960 benchmark described below was used in adjusting the 1950 data. Sources for the Census data are: 1920, 1930 [2, table 16, pp. 587–590]; 1940 [3, table 38]; 1950 [4, table 158].

2.1.2. 1960

1960 Census data were not used directly as a benchmark because of the size of the discrepancy between the Census and the April 1960 Current Population Survey (CPS); the Census count was 0.86 of the CPS estimate. The CPS estimate of total farm population based on the 1950 Census definition of farm [5, table 1] was multiplied by 0.95, on the assumption that the Census should have been somewhat closer to the CPS in 1960 than it was in 1950, when the Census was 0.92 of CPS. This total was then distributed among age groups, using data from the CPS and the Census and the method described in subsection 2.2.2 below for 1961–70. The estimates were adjusted to July 1 by interpolating between 1960 and 1961, assuming a constant rate of change.

2.2. Intercensal Years

2.2.1. 1921–1959

Cohorts coinciding with each five-year age group in a Census year and with the age group ten years older at the next Census were defined, and annual changes in their size due to death and migration were estimated. It was assumed that deaths occurred only among people remaining on the farm, not among those who migrated. Using decade survival rates made up from life tables, the number of survivors in the cohort in each year was calculated. Then total migration over the decade was calculated as the difference between the expected number of survivors and the Census count for the cohort at the end of the decade. Migration was assumed to occur at the same rate per year over all age groups, and total migration was distributed in each year according to a series on annual movement of the farm population published by the Department of Agriculture. The size of the cohort in each year was calculated as the number of expected survivors minus the number of migrants.

The cohorts correspond to the fixed five-year age groups only for years ending in 0 or 5. For example, the cohort that began as age group 15–19 in 1940 was aged 20–24 in 1945 and 25–29 in 1950. For all other years it was necessary to assume that there was an even distribution of ages within cohorts, divide the cohorts into fifths, and recombine them into the fixed five-year age groups.

Because of the ten-year change in the ages included in the cohorts over a decade, it was necessary to work with two extra age groups at each end of the age range. Hence data were needed for age groups

5–9, 10–14, 80–84, and 85 and over, even though the final estimates of farm population covered only age groups 15–19 through 75 and over.

(a) *Cohort size = $COH_{j,T,t}$*

For years $(t = 2, 3, \ldots, 10)$ in each decade, the size of a cohort $(j = 1, 2, \ldots, 15')$ equal to farm population in age group i in the Census year beginning the decade $(t = 1)$ and to farm population in age group $(i + 2)$ in the Census year ending the decade $(t = 11)$ was estimated as follows:

For cohorts $(j = 1, 2, \ldots, 14)$,

$$COH_{j,T,1} = FP_{i,T,1}, \qquad\qquad\qquad i = j;$$

$$COH_{j,T,11} = FP_{i+2,T,11}, \qquad\qquad\qquad i = j;$$

$$COH_{j,T,t} = [FP_{i,T,t} \cdot SR_{i,T}^{(t-1)/10}] - CUMIG_{j,T,t}, \qquad t = 2, 3, \ldots, 10,$$
$$\qquad\qquad\qquad\qquad\qquad\qquad\qquad\qquad\qquad\qquad i = j.$$

For the open-ended cohort $(j = 15')$,

$$COH_{15',T,1} = FP_{15,T,1} + FP_{16,T,1} + FP_{17',T,1};$$

$$COH_{15',T,11} = FP_{17',T,11};$$

$$COH_{15',T,t} = [FP_{15,T,1} \cdot SR_{15,T}^{(t-1)/10}]$$
$$+ [FP_{16,T,1} \cdot SR_{16,T}^{(t-1)/10}]$$
$$+ [FP_{17',T,1} \cdot SR_{17,T}^{(t-1)/10}]$$
$$- CUMIG_{15',T,t}, \qquad\qquad\qquad t = 2, 3, \ldots, 10.$$

(b) *Mean decade cohort survival rate = $SR_{i,T}$*

Life table values $(q_{i,x,y})$ for three-year periods centered on Census years $(y = 1, 2, \ldots, 5,$ for 1919–21, 1929–31, $\ldots,$ 1959–61; sources given below) were used to estimate decade survival rates for single years of age $(S_{i,x,y})$,

$$S_{i,x,y} = (1 - q_{i,x,y})(1 - q_{i,x+1,y}) \ldots (1 - q_{i,x+9,y}), \qquad \begin{aligned} i &= 1, 2, \ldots, 17, \\ x &= 1, 2, \ldots, 5, \\ y &= 1, 2, \ldots, 5; \end{aligned}$$

where q = proportion of persons alive at beginning of age interval (one year) dying during interval, y denotes three-year period centered on Census year, and x denotes year of age within age group.

These were combined into decade cohort survival rates ($DECSR_{i,y}$) by assuming an even distribution of ages within five-year groups,

$$DECSR_{i,y} = \frac{S_{i,1,y} + S_{i,2,y} + \cdots + S_{i,5,y}}{5}, \qquad \begin{aligned} i &= 1, 2, \ldots, 17, \\ y &= 1, 2, \ldots, 5. \end{aligned}$$

Note that age group 17 was treated as if it were a closed group, ages 85–89, in order to simplify calculation of the survival rates. During the period for which estimates were made, people aged 90 and over were about 25 percent of those aged 85 and over (e.g., 25.6 percent in 1920, 24.9 percent in 1960) and only about 4 percent of those aged 75 and over (e.g., 3.7 percent in 1920, 4.0 percent in 1960).

Decade cohort survival rates centered on the Census year beginning a decade and on the Census year ending it were averaged to give a mean decade cohort survival rate,

$$SR_{i,T} = \frac{DECSR_{i,y} + DECSR_{i,y+1}}{2}.$$

(c) *Sources of life table values*

Rates for total U.S. population are available only for 1959–61 [6, table 1], 1949–51 [7, table 1] and 1939–41 [8, table 1]. Race- and sex-specific rates are available for the continental U.S. for 1929–31 [9, tables I-A through I-D], and for registration states of 1920 for 1929–31 and 1919–21 [9, tables II-A through II-D, and IV-A through IV-D].

For 1929–31, rates for total U.S. population were generated by weighting the specific rates for the continental U.S. according to the proportion of population in each race–sex classification. Sources for population, July 1, 1930: ages 5 through 75 and over [10, pp. 62–63; non-white series used as Negro], ages 74 through 100 and over [2, table 21]. Census data were used to estimate ages 74 through 99: the ratio of persons each age to the total 75 or over from the Census was applied to the total 75 and over from [10]. Totals for white males and white females are sums of "native white–native parentage", "native white–foreign parentage", and "foreign-born white" for each sex. Negro series for 75 through 99 were tied to non-white series for 5 through 74.

The same method was used to generate life tables for total population for 1919–21. Tables for 1919–21 are for registration states of 1920; q's were adjusted to a continental U.S. basis by multiplying individual rates for 1919–21 by the ratio of each continental U.S. rate for 1929–31 to the corresponding rate for registration states for 1929–31. Sources for population, July 1, 1920: ages 5 to 75 and over [10, pp. 82–83], ages 74–99 [11, table 9, pp. 162–165].

(d) *Cumulative migration* $= CUMIG_{j,T,t}$

(1) *Decade cohort migrants* $= TM_{j,T}$

For cohorts $(j = 1, 2, \ldots, 14)$,

$$TM_{j,T} = (FP_{i,T,1})(SR_{i,T}) - FP_{i+2,T,11}.$$

For cohort $(j = 15')$,

$$TM_{15',T} = (FP_{15,T,1})(SR_{15,T}) + (FP_{16,T,1})(SR_{16,T}) + (FP_{17',T,1})(SR_{17',T}) - FP_{17',T,11}.$$

(2) *Cumulative migration rate* $= MIG_{T,t}$

The Department of Agriculture series showing the change in farm population due to migration (1920–50 [12, series C-76], unrevised data used for 1941–50 to maintain consistency with Census data; 1951–59 [13, series C-76]) was dated April and had to be adjusted to July 1. Between years where net migration was in the same direction, it was assumed that there had been a constant rate of change in the level of migration. Between years where the direction of migration changed, straight line interpolation was used. The adjusted net migration series was then used to calculate the proportion of total decade migration that had occurred by July 1 each year,

$$MIG_{T,t} = \left(\sum_{k=2}^{t} M_{T,k} \right) \Big/ DM_T, \qquad t = 2, 3, \ldots, 11;$$

where $M_{T,k} = M_{T,t} = $ net migrants in year ending July $1,t,T$, and $DM_T = \Sigma_{t=2}^{11} M_{T,t} = $ total decade migration.

(3) $CUMIG_{j,T,t}$

When the number of decade cohort migrants was positive (away from the farm) or zero ($TM_{j,T} \geq 0$), the product of decade cohort migrants and the cumulative migration rate for the year was used to calculate cumulative migration,

$$CUMIG_{j,T,t} = TM_{j,T} \cdot MIG_{T,t}.$$

A different method was required when the number of decade cohort migrants was negative (toward the farm)($TM_{j,T} < 0$):

For the second year of the decade ($t = 2$), cumulative migration was calculated as the product of total decade migration and a ratio of (1) the difference between the maximum value of $M_{T,t}$ for the decade and net migrants for the second year, to (2) ten times the maximum value of $M_{T,t}$ minus total decade migration,

$$CUMIG_{j,T,2} = TM_{j,T} \cdot \frac{MAXM_T - M_{T,2}}{10(MAXM_T) - DM_T},$$

where $MAXM_T = $ maximum value of $M_{T,t}$ in decade T.

Cumulative migration for years ($t = 3, 4, \ldots, 11$) was calculated by estimating migration for each year in the same way as for year 2 and adding it to cumulative migration for the preceding year,

$$CUMIG_{j,T,t} = CUMIG_{j,T,t-1} + TM_{j,T} \cdot \frac{MAXM_T - M_{T,t}}{10(MAXM_T) - DM_T},$$

$$t = 3, 4, \ldots, 11.$$

(e) *Farm population* $= FP_{i,T,t}$

Farm population was estimated by dividing the cohorts into fifths and recombining them to form five-year age groups.

For age groups ($i = 3, 4, \ldots, 14$) and ($j = i$),

$$FP_{i,T,t} = (0.2)(t - 1)(COH_{j-1,T,t}) + [1.0 - (0.2)(t - 1)](COH_{j,T,t})$$
$$t = 2, 3, \ldots, 6;$$

$$FP_{i,T,t} = (0.2)(t - 6)(COH_{j-2,T,t}) + [1.0 - (0.2)(t - 6)](COH_{j-1,T,t}),$$
$$t = 7, 8, \ldots, 10.$$

For age group ($i = 15'$),

$$FP_{15',T,t} = (0.2)(t - 1)(COH_{14,T,t}) + COH_{15',T,t}, \qquad t = 2, 3, \ldots, 6;$$

$$FP_{15',T,t} = (0.2)(t - 6)(COH_{13,T,t}) + COH_{14,T,t} + COH_{15',T,t},$$
$$t = 7, 8, \ldots, 10.$$

2.2.2. 1961–1969

It was not possible to use the method described above for 1961–69 because neither 1970 Census data, life table values for 1969–71 nor migration data for the decade were available. CPS data were used to estimate total farm population; and Census and CPS data were combined in order to distribute total farm population among age groups.

(a) *Total farm population*

CPS estimates of total farm population based on the 1960 Census definition of farm [15, table A] were adjusted to the 1950 Census definition and these were deflated to 0.95 of their value (see subsection 2.1.2 above for explanation of this procedure),

$$TFP_{I,5,t} = \frac{0.95(TFP50_{I,5,1})}{TFP60_{I,5,1}} \cdot TFP60_{I,5,t}, \qquad t = 2, 3, \ldots, 11;$$

where *TFP50* denotes total farm population, 1950 Census definition, and *TFP60* denotes total farm population, 1960 Census definition.

(b) *Distribution among age groups*

CPS data on the percent distribution of farm population in five-, ten-, or twenty-year age groups [15, table 2; 16, table 1] were combined with 1960 Census data [4, table 158] to estimate percent of total in five-year age groups ($i = 3, 4, \ldots, 15'$) as shown below. The procedure was complicated by the fact that data were not available for the same age groups in all years.

CPS60 denotes 1960 CPS data, and Census denotes 1960 Census data,

$$\%(15\text{–}19) = \frac{\%(15\text{–}19)Census}{\%(14\text{–}19)CPS60} \cdot \%(14\text{–}19)CPS_{5,t} \, ;$$

$\%(20\text{–}24)$ is from [15, table 2; 16, table 1]. $\%(35\text{–}44)$ for 1961–65 was derived from $\%(25\text{–}44)$ by assuming a constant rate of change in the ratio $\%(35\text{–}44)CPS/\%(25\text{–}44)CPS$ between 1960 and 1968, interpolating this ratio and applying it to $\%(25\text{–}44)CPS_{5,t}$. (1968 CPS data were used in these calculations because they were the most recent available at the time.) The residual $[(25\text{–}44) - (35\text{–}44)]$ was used as $\%(25\text{–}34)$ for 1961–65; $\%(25\text{–}34)$ for 1960 and 1966–70 was published in [15, table 2; 16, table 1].

$$\%(25\text{–}29) = \frac{\%(25\text{–}29)CPS60}{\%(25\text{–}34)CPS60} \cdot \%(25\text{–}34)CPS_{5,t} \, ;$$

$$\%(30\text{–}34) = \%(25\text{–}34)_{5,t} - \%(25\text{–}29)_{5,t} \, ;$$

$$\%(35\text{–}39) = \frac{\%(35\text{–}39)Census}{\%(35\text{–}44)Census} \cdot \%(35\text{–}44)_{5,t} \, ;$$

$$\%(40\text{–}44) = \%(35\text{–}44)_{5,t} - \%(35\text{–}39)_{5,t}.$$

An analogous method was used to estimate percent of total farm population in age groups 45–49, 50–54, ..., 70–74, and 75 and over, except that Census data were used where CPS data were not given in sufficient detail. Additional age groups 5–9, 10–14, 75–79, 80–84, and 85 and over were derived for 1960 and 1961 for use in interpolating the 1960 data to July 1.

The present distribution series, based on April-centered averages, were applied to $TFP_{1,5,t}$; the resulting estimates of $FP_{i,T,t}$ were treated as April 1 data and adjusted to July 1 by interpolating between single years, assuming a constant rate of change.

3. Non-farm Population (NF)

Non-farm population for 1922–69 was generated by subtracting farm population from U.S. population,

$$NF_{i,T,t} = N_{i,T,t} - FP_{i,T,t}, \qquad \begin{aligned} i &= 3, 4, \ldots, 15', \\ T &= 1, 2, \ldots, 5, \\ t &= 1, 2, \ldots, 10; \end{aligned}$$

where $N_{i,T,t}$ = U.S. population (1922–59 [10], 1960–64 [17], 1965 [18], 1966 [19], 1967–69 [20]).

4. Headship Rates (HSR)

Headship rates were calculated for 13 age groups, 15–19 through 75 and over. Headship rates are not significant for age groups below 15–19, and they do not vary sufficiently for age groups over 70–74 to make it worthwhile to break down the rates for the small proportion of the population 75 and over.

Headship rates for April 1, 1940 were adjusted to July 1, 1940 so that the product of the headship rate and the 1940 non-farm population for each age group would sum to the total number of non-farm households (HH) for July 1, 1940,

$$HSR_i = 0.997 \, (HHA_i / NFA_i),$$

where

> HHA_i = non-farm households, April 1, 1940 [21, table 11; sum of four classes covering urban and rural non-farm households with male and female heads];
> NFA_i = non-farm population, April 1, 1940
> = (U.S. population, April 1, 1940)–(farm population, April 1, 1940)[2, table 38];

$HH40$ = non-farm households, July 1, 1940;

$$0.997 = \frac{28.001}{28.083} = HH40 \bigg/ \sum_{i=3}^{15'} \left(\frac{HHA_i}{NFA_i} \cdot NF_{i,3,1} \right).$$

5. Standardized Household Variable (HHS)

The standardized household variable was calculated by summing the product of the headship rate and the non-farm population over all age groups,

$$HHS_{T,t} = \sum_{i=3}^{15'} [(HSR_i)(NF_{i,T,t})].$$

The resulting series is shown in table F.1.

TABLE F.1
Number of standardized households,
1922–40 and 1949–72 (millions).

Year	HHS	Year	HHS
1922	19.180	1949	34.737
1923	19.761	1950	35.860
1924	20.370	1951	36.594
1925	20.883	1952	37.269
1926	21.405	1953	38.020
1927	21.956	1954	38.684
1928	22.464	1955	39.302
1929	22.957	1956	39.942
1930	23.532	1957	40.623
1931	23.954	1958	41.198
1932	24.329	1959	41.815
1933	24.689	1960	42.483
1934	25.140	1961	43.151
1935	25.594	1962	43.810
1936	26.023	1963	44.500
1937	26.462	1964	45.102
1938	26.931	1965	45.720
1939	27.415	1966	46.373
1940	28.005	1967	47.213
		1968	37.937
		1969	48.627
		1970	49.284
		1971	50.021
		1972	50.755

6. Sources

[1] Burnham O. Campbell, "The Housing Life Cycle and Long Swings in Residential Construction: A Statistical and Theoretical Analysis", unpublished Ph.D. dissertation, Stanford University, 1961.

[2] U.S. Bureau of the Census, *Fifteenth Census of the United States, 1930: Population*, vol. II.

[3] U.S. Bureau of the Census, *U.S. Census of Population: 1950*, vol. I, *Characteristics of the Population*, part I, U.S. Summary.

[4] U.S. Bureau of the Census, *U.S. Census of Population: 1960*, vol. I, *Characteristics of the Population*, part I, U.S. Summary.

[5] U.S. Bureau of the Census, Current Population Reports, Series P-27: *Farm Population*, no. 29, April 1961.

[6] U.S. Department of Health, Education and Welfare, *Life Tables: 1959–61*, vol. I, no. 1, Public Health Service Publication no. 1252, Dec. 1964.

[7] U.S. Department of Health, Education and Welfare, *Vital Statistics – Special Reports*, vol. 41, no. 1, "United States Life Tables 1949–51", Nov. 1954.

[8] U.S. Bureau of the Census, *Sixteenth Census of the United States; 1940*, "United States Life Tables and Actuarial Tables, 1939–1941", by Thomas N. W. Greville, 1946.

[9] U.S. Bureau of the Census, "United States Life Tables, 1929 to 1931, 1920 to 1929, 1919 to 1921, 1909 to 1911, 1901 to 1910, 1900 to 1902", prepared by Joseph A. Hill, 1936.

[10] U.S. Bureau of the Census, Current Population Reports, Series P-25: *Population Estimates*, no. 311, July 1965.

[11] U.S. Bureau of the Census, *Fourteenth Census of the United States Taken in the Year 1920*, vol. II, *Population 1920*.

[12] U.S. Bureau of the Census, *Historical Statistics of the United States, Colonial Times to 1957*, Washington, 1960.

[13] U.S. Bureau of the Census, *Historical Statistics of the United States, Colonial Times to 1957; Continuation to 1962 and Revisions*, Washington, 1965.

[14] U.S. Bureau of the Census, Current Population Reports, Series P-27: *Farm Population*, no. 42, Aug. 1971.

[15] U.S. Bureau of the Census, Current Population Reports, Series

P-27: *Farm Population*, no. 31, March 1962; nos. 33–37, June 1962–April 1967, no. 39, May 1969.

[16] U.S. Bureau of the Census, Current Population Reports, Series P-27: *Farm Population*, nos. 4–42, July 1969–Aug. 1970.

[17] U.S. Bureau of the Census, Current Population Reports, Series P-25: *Population Estimates*, no. 314, Aug. 1965.

[18] U.S. Bureau of the Census, Current Population Reports, Series P-25: *Population Estimates*, no. 321, Nov. 1965.

[19] U.S. Bureau of the Census, Current Population Reports, Series P-25: *Population Estimates*, no. 352, Nov. 1966.

[20] U.S. Bureau of the Census, Current Population Reports, Series P-25: *Population Estimates*, no. 441, March 1970.

[21] U.S. Bureau of the Census, *Sixteenth Census of the United States, 1940: Reports on Population*, vol. II, *Characteristics by Age*, part I, U.S. Summary.

References

Almon, C., 1975, 1973–1985 in figures (Lexington Books, Lexington, Mass.).

Amemiya, T., 1974, The nonlinear two stage least squares estimators, Journal of Econometrics, July.

Anderson, L.C., 1973, The state of the monetarist debate, Federal Reserve Bank of St. Louis Review, Sept.

Ando, A. and F. Modigliani, 1969, Econometric analysis of stabilization policies, American Economic Review, May.

Ball, R. J., 1973, The international linkage of national economic models (North-Holland, Amsterdam).

Bowen, W. G. and T. A. Finegan, 1969, The economics of labor force participation (Princeton University Press, Princeton, N.J.).

Brainard, W. C. and J. Tobin, 1968, Pitfalls in financial model building, American Economic Review, May.

Brittain, J. A., 1966, Corporate dividend policy (Brookings Institution, Washington, D.C.).

Brown, T. M., 1952, Habit persistence and lags in consumer behavior, Econometrica, July.

Campbell, B. O., 1961, The housing cycle and long swings, Ph.D. dissertation (Stanford University, Stanford, Calif.).

Campbell, B. O., 1963, Long swings in residential construction: The postwar experience, American Economic Review, May.

Christ, C. F., 1967, A short-run aggregate-demand model of the interdependence and effects of monetary and fiscal policies with Keynesian and classical interest elasticities, American Economic Review, May.

Coen, R. M., 1971a, The effect of cash flow on the speed of adjustment, in: G. Fromm, ed., Tax incentives and capital spending (Brookings Institution, Washington, D.C.).

Coen, R. M., 1971b, Aggregate labor supply in the United States economy, Research Memorandum no. 117 (Center for Research in Economic Growth, Stanford University, Stanford, Calif.).

Coen, R.M., 1973a, Labor force and unemployment in the 1920's and 1930's: A re-examination based on postwar experience, Review of Economics and Statistics, Feb.

Coen, R. M., 1973b, Labor force and unemployment in the 1920's and 1930's: A reply, Review of Economics and Statistics, Nov.

Coen, R. M. and B. G. Hickman, 1970, Constrained joint estimation of factor demand and production functions, Review of Economics and Statistics, Aug.

Dernburg, R. and K. Strand, 1966, Hidden unemployment 1953–62: A quantitative analysis by age and sex, American Economic Review, March.

Dramais, A. and J. Waelbroeck, 1975, A model of policy coordination for the EEC countries, in: A. Ando et al., eds., Conference on International Aspects of Stabilization Policies (Federal Reserve Bank of Boston, Boston, Mass.)

Durand, D., 1942, Basic yields of corporate bonds, 1900–1942, Technical Paper no. 3 (National Bureau of Economic Research, New York).

Foley, D. and M. Sidrauski, 1971, Monetary and fiscal policy in a growing economy (Macmillan, London).

Friedman, M., 1957, A theory of the consumption function (Princeton University Press, Princeton, N.J.).

Fromm, G. and L. R. Klein, 1975, The NBER/NSF model comparison seminar: An analysis of results, processed.

Fromm, G. and P. Taubman, 1968, Policy simulations with an econometric model (Brookings Institution, Washington, D.C.).

Goldsmith, R., 1955, A study of saving in the United States (Princeton University Press, Princeton, N.J.).

Hall, R. E. and D. W. Jorgenson, 1971, Application of the theory of optimum capital accumulation, in: G. Fromm, ed., Tax incentives and capital spending (Brookings Institution, Washington, D.C.).

Hansen, B., 1970, Excess demand, unemployment, vacancies and wages, Quarterly Journal of Economics, Feb.

Hickman, B. G., 1964, On a new method of capacity estimation, Journal of the American Statistical Association, June.

Hickman, B. G., 1965, Investment demand and U.S. economic growth (Brookings Institution, Washington, D.C.).

Hickman, B. G., ed., 1972, Econometric models of cyclical behavior, Studies in income and wealth no. 36 (Columbia University Press, New York).

Hickman, B. G., 1974, What became of the building cycle, in: P. A. David and M. W. Reder, eds., Nations and households in economic growth: Essays in honor of Moses Abramovitz (Academic Press, New York).

Hickman, B. G., M. Hinz and R. Willig, 1973, An economic–demographic model of the housing sector, Research Memorandum no. 147 (Center for Research in Economic Growth, Stanford University, Stanford, Calif.).

Hickman, B. G., R. M. Coen and M. D. Hurd, 1975, The Hickman–Coen annual growth model: Structural characteristics and policy responses, International Economic Review, Feb.

Hudson, E. A. and D. W. Jorgenson, 1974, U.S. energy policy and economic growth, Discussion Paper no. 372 (Harvard Institute of Econometric Research, Harvard University, Cambridge, Mass.).

Hurd, M. D., 1974, Wage changes, desired manhours and unemployment, Research Memorandum no. 155 (Center for Research in Economic Growth, Stanford University, Stanford, Calif.).

Jorgenson, D. W., 1963, Capital theory and investment behavior, American Economic Review, May.

Knowles, J. W., 1960, The potential economic growth in the United States, Study Paper no. 20, Joint Economic Committee, 86th Congress, 2nd Session, Jan. 30.

Kuh, E., 1966, Measurement of potential output, American Economic Review, Sept.

Lebergott, S., 1964, Manpower in economic growth: The American record since 1800 (McGraw-Hill, New York).

Lebergott, S., 1973, A new technique for time series? A comment, Review of Economics and Statistics, Nov.

Lipsey, R., 1960, The relation between unemployment and the rate of change of money wage rates in the United Kingdom, Economica, Feb.

Nadiri, M. I. and S. Rosen, 1969, Interrelated factor demand functions, American Economic Review, Sept.

Nelson, C. R., 1972, The term structure of interest rates (Basic Books, New York).

Okun, A. M., 1962, Potential GNP: Its measurement and significance, Proceedings of the Business and Economic Statistics Section of the American Statistical Association.

Osman, J., 1966, Dual impact of federal aid on state and local government expenditures, National Tax Journal, Dec.

Osman, J., 1968, The use of intergovernmental aid as an expenditure determinant, National Tax Journal, Dec.

Phelps, E. et al., 1970, The microeconomic foundations of employment and inflation theory (Norton, New York).

Phillips, A. W., 1958, The relation between unemployment and the rate of change of money wage rates in the United Kingdom, 1861–1957, Economica, Nov.

Preston, R. S., 1972, The Wharton annual and industry forecasting model (Economics Research Unit, University of Pennsylvania, Philadelphia, Penn.).

Preston, R. S., 1975, The Wharton long term model: Input–output within the context of a macro forecasting model, International Economic Review, Feb.

Scadding, J. L., 1974, An annual money demand and supply model for the U.S., Research Memorandum no. 177 (Center for Research in Economic Growth, Stanford University, Stanford, Calif.).

Solow, R. M., 1959, Investment and technical progress, in: K. Arrow et al., eds., Mathematical models in the social sciences (Stanford University Press, Stanford, Calif.).

Tella, A., 1965, Labor force sensitivity to employment by age and sex, Industrial Relations, Feb.

Witte, J. G., Jr., 1963, The microfoundations of the social investment function, Journal of Political Economy, Oct.

Index